PRO FASHION SKETCHPAD
PORTFOLIO BUILDER
FOR FASHION DESIGNERS & ILLUSTRATORS

K I D S   F I G U R E

All in one:
600 FEMALE
POSES & ACCESSORIES DESIGN
OUTLINE TEMPLATES

AEMILIANA MAGNUS

PRO FASHION SKETCHPAD
PORTFOLIO BUILDER
KIDS FIGURE

ISBN: 9781090487186

Designed and published in USA
by Aemiliana Magnus
Printed in USA

If you have any feedback, please send it to
aemiliana.art@gmail.com

www.aemilianamagnus.com

f @AemilianaArt
🐦 @AemilianaMagnus
📷 @aemiliana_magnus
📌 @AemilianaMagnus
──────────────
f @ProFashionSketchpad
📷 @pro.fashionsketchpad

Aemiliana Magnus
March 2019

CONTENTS

CONTENTS

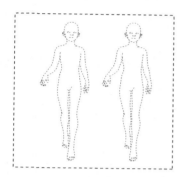

KIDS FIGURE POSE OUTLINE
Page 31

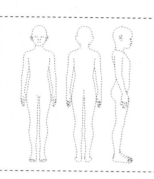

KIDS FRONT/BACK/SIDE POSE OUTLINE
Page 103

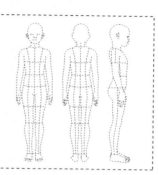

FLAT FIGURE OUTLINE
Page 175

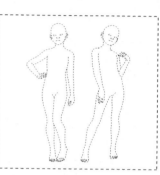

KIDS POSES OUTLINE
Page 247

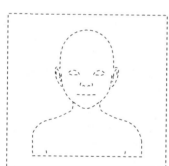

HEAD & SHOULDERS ACCESSORIES DESIGN
Page 309

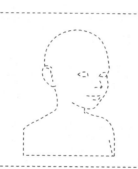

HEAD DISPLAY JEWELRY DESIGN
Page 335

HAND DISPLAY JEWELRY DESIGN
Page 359

SHOE LAST SHOE DESIGN
Page 383

BONUS KIDS POSE OUTLINES
Page 427

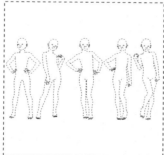

CROQUIS OUTLINE

Page 513

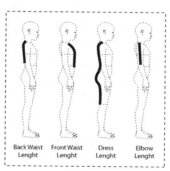

MEASUREMENTS

Page 557

TOP LUXURY BRANDS

LUXURY BRANDS DESCRIPTION LIST
Page 565

PREFACE

As a creative professional and a designer, I was constantly searching for a perfect and efficient solution in personal design workflow to help me achieve the best professional results when I am on a tight time schedule. Each new collection starts with new inspiration from colors, shapes, textures, cultures, locations, nature, and all around us. Everything needs to be organized for each collection.

Often I'd like to incorporate in my collection different designs varying from dresses, lingerie, accessories, jewelry, shoes etc. there is no other sketchpad that can combine all parts together so that all my design ideas stay together organized and accessible any time I need it.

This is why I have designed PRO Fashion Sketchpad, elegant, portable and all in one: Kids figure - 600 female poses & accessories designs templates.

When you have a new idea for a dress design, lingerie, jewelry or shoes you can quickly grab the PRO Fashion Sketchpad and start drawing your ideas immediately, without wasting your time to build the female figure first and only afterward start focusing on your design itself. Important: all your designs stay together and nothing gets lost.

PRO Fashion Sketchpad - All in one: Kids figure - 600 Female Poses & Accessories Design Outline Templates will help you to save time and deliver professional looking design sketches, all organized together. All you need is to be focused on your design ideas, and enjoy your new elegant and portable PRO Fashion Sketchpad.

I'd love to see your beautiful designs with this new PRO Fashion Sketchpad! Be sure to snap a pic on Instagram or Facebook and to tag me in it — #aemilianamagnus #profashionsketchpad #profashionsketchpadkids

Whether you are a student or professional individual I hope with this new PRO Fashion Sketchpad your design workflow will get more creative and efficient, saving you more time to focus on what is truly important for you.

Aemiliana Magnus

FASHION DICTIONARY

BONUS: MINI FASHION DICTIONARY

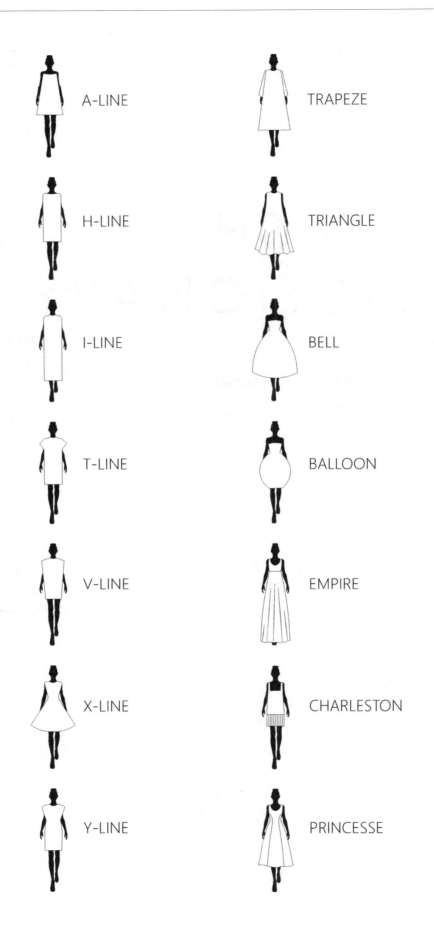

A-LINE

TRAPEZE

H-LINE

TRIANGLE

I-LINE

BELL

T-LINE

BALLOON

V-LINE

EMPIRE

X-LINE

CHARLESTON

Y-LINE

PRINCESSE

DRESS LENGHTS

     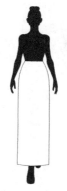 

| Mini Lenght | Above the Knee | Knee Lenght | Below the Knee | Mid calf Lenght | Maxi / Ankle | Floor Lenght |

WAISTLINES

Natural Waistline   Empire Waistline   Dropped Waistline   Basque Waistline

NECKLACE

1. Collar 36.5 cm
2. Choker 40.6 cm
3. Princess 45.7 cm
4. Matinee 50.8 cm
5. Matinee 61 cm
6. Opera 76.2 cm
7. Rope 83.8 cm

DARTS

| Stabdard 4 Dart | Armseye Darts | Waist Dart | Princess Style Line | Armseye Princess | H Dart Princess | Princess Seams |

PLEATS

| Pleated | Kick | Knife | Box | Inverted | Accordion |

A-Line Circle Accordion Knife Pleated Draped Gypsy

Layered Mermaid Ruffled Tube Pencil Mini

Wrap Asymmetrical Bubble Godet Tulip Paneled

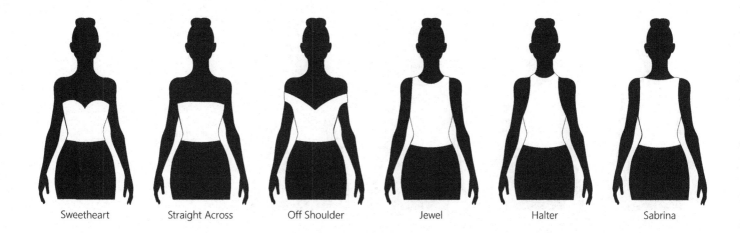

Sweetheart   Straight Across   Off Shoulder   Jewel   Halter   Sabrina

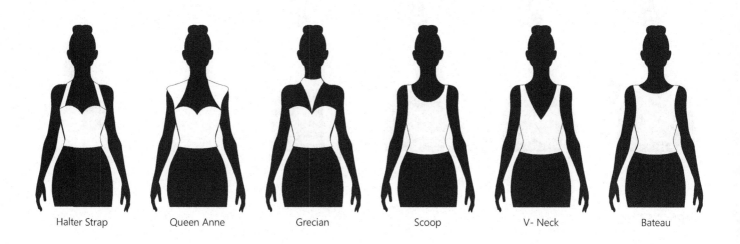

Halter Strap   Queen Anne   Grecian   Scoop   V- Neck   Bateau

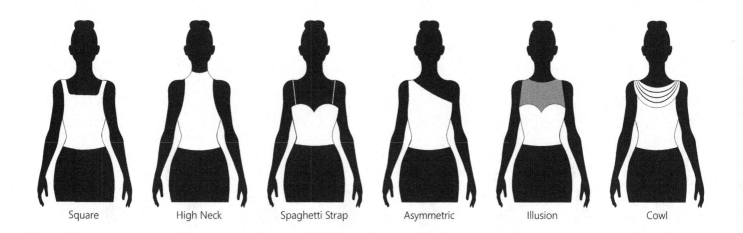

Square   High Neck   Spaghetti Strap   Asymmetric   Illusion   Cowl

SHIRT AND PENT LENGHTS & STYLES

SLEEVE LENGHTS

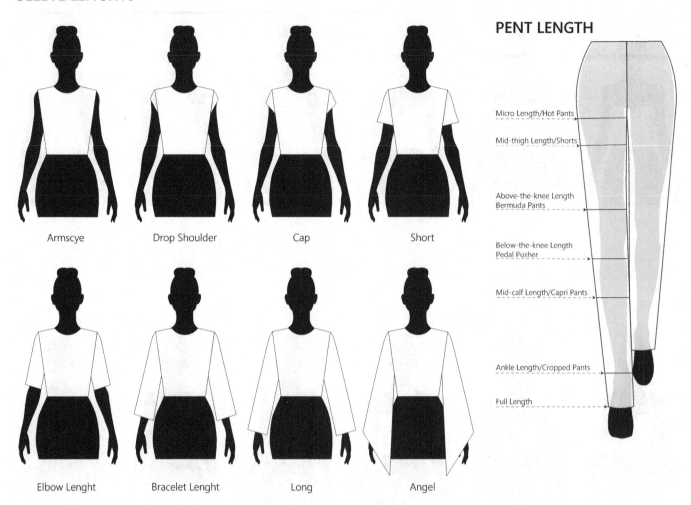

Armscye

Drop Shoulder

Cap

Short

Elbow Lenght

Bracelet Lenght

Long

Angel

PENT LENGTH

Micro Length/Hot Pants

Mid-thigh Length/Shorts

Above-the-knee Length
Bermuda Pants

Below-the-knee Length
Pedal Pusher

Mid-calf Length/Capri Pants

Ankle Length/Cropped Pants

Full Length

PENT STYLES

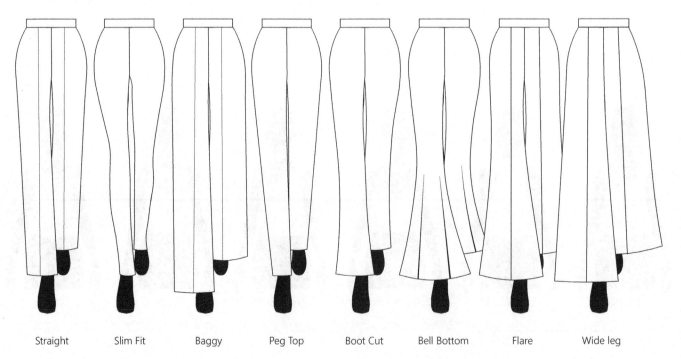

Straight

Slim Fit

Baggy

Peg Top

Boot Cut

Bell Bottom

Flare

Wide leg

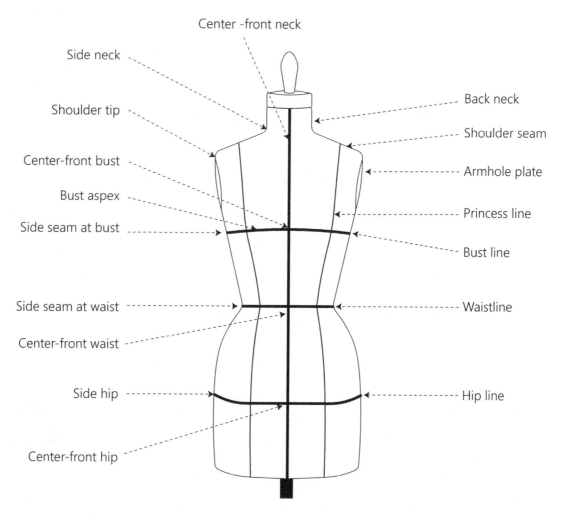

Center -front neck

Side neck

Shoulder tip

Center-front bust

Bust aspex

Side seam at bust

Side seam at waist

Center-front waist

Side hip

Center-front hip

Back neck

Shoulder seam

Armhole plate

Princess line

Bust line

Waistline

Hip line

Dress form are helpful for fitting a garment & draping a pattern. They are available in most standard sizes and can also be custom ordered for special clients.

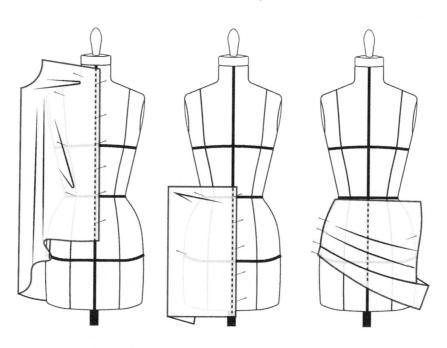

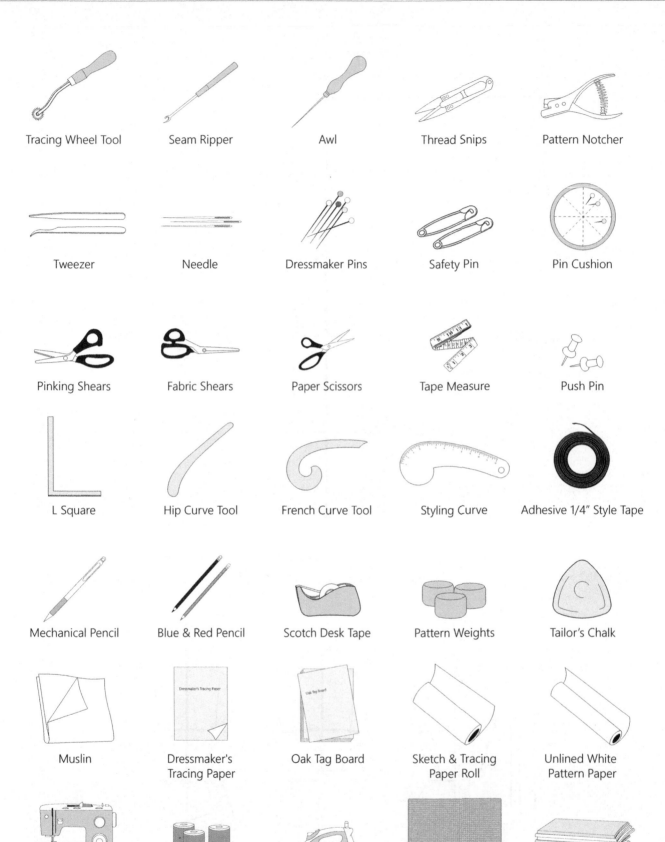

Tracing Wheel Tool	Seam Ripper	Awl	Thread Snips	Pattern Notcher
Tweezer	Needle	Dressmaker Pins	Safety Pin	Pin Cushion
Pinking Shears	Fabric Shears	Paper Scissors	Tape Measure	Push Pin
L Square	Hip Curve Tool	French Curve Tool	Styling Curve	Adhesive 1/4" Style Tape
Mechanical Pencil	Blue & Red Pencil	Scotch Desk Tape	Pattern Weights	Tailor's Chalk
Muslin	Dressmaker's Tracing Paper	Oak Tag Board	Sketch & Tracing Paper Roll	Unlined White Pattern Paper
Sewing Machine	Threads	Steam Iron	Cutting Mat	Fabrics

Draping	Pattern Making	Sewing Tools

WOMEN'S WEAR

As a designer, you must define your niche and the area of specialization. Afterward, you have to determine the age group, size range, and the price point. Also, you must decide which activity the garments serve to engage. As a designer, you must develop the service built around delivering the product, and the experience you wish your client to have.

SUBCATEGORIES OF WOMEN'S WEAR			
Daywear	**Eveningwear**	**Outerwear**	**Intimate Apparel**
Casual Separates	Dance, Club	Casual	Foundation Garments
Dresses	Special Occasion	Work	Practical Lingerie
Suiting	Dinner	Dress	Show Lingerie
Activewear	Cocktail	Weather	Sleepwear
Athletic Sportswear	Black Tie, Red Carpet	Athletic	Loungewear
Knits	Stage	Formal	
	Fantasy, Costume		

APPAREL PRICE POINT CATEGORIES

The price point category refers to where the product lies in the pricing spectrum ranging from discount to designer. The quality levels increase or decrease accordingly. The categories are:

Category	Price	Description
Haute Couture	**$10,000 or more**	Haute Couture is limited to syndicate members producing made to measure pieces. If you're not a syndicate member, you are not a couturier.
Designer	**$1,000 or more**	Superior fabrics, details, trims, and cuts
Bridge/Exchange	**Less than $1,000**	Bridge is the gap between contemporary and designer labels. Better known bridge labels are Lauren by Ralph Lauren and DKNY by Donna Karan.
Better	**Less than $500**	This is usually the lowest price point category for what consumers consider a "designer" line. Better fabric and styling than lower-priced clothing
Secondary Lines	**Less than $300**	Designers offer a line at a much lower price than their designer line
Private Label	**Less than $300**	Brand designed specifically for a store or retailer, costing less than name brands
Moderate	**Less than $100**	Nationally advertised, inexpensive
Discount/Off-price	**Less than $50**	Outlets selling clothes at discount prices

Cover

Originate the great first impression!

Jacket Flaps

Grab the interest of your target audience.

Contents

Determine a structure and a framework of your story.

Forward

Choose a spokeperson to endorse your product.

Act 1

Capture an audience's imagination.

Act 2

Define the challenges you might encounter on your journey and the solutions.

Act 3

Describe what the success means to you: (Success is the ability to do what you love every day.)

Summary

Engage and establish the emotional connection with your audience .

Bibliography

Educate, Engage and Excite Your Audience

THE SCIENCE OF STORYTELLING

A compelling story of your brand will help you to establish a strong tone of a voice that makes you stand out from others. You need to have a clear understanding of your target market, what you want to provide to your customers, and how your brand can evolve. As a designer you have to be able to describe your fashion brand in a few words. Exceptional branding provides a sense of comfort, acceptance, yet inspiration to keep your clients coming back for more each season. When creating your brand you must consider your brand future reputation status, the core values and visual appearance. It's not who makes it first, it's who make it better.

TOP CONTENT MARKETING TACTICS

88%
SOCIAL MEDIA

78%
OWNED ARTICLES

76%
EMAIL

72%
BLOGS

72%
VIDEOS

65%
IN-PERSON EVENTS

61%
3RD PARTY ARTICLES

46%
MOBILE CONTENT

43%
MICROSITES

41%
CASE STUDIES

USE IMAGES FOR MORE COMPELLING CONTENT

FABRIC SELECTION

I WANT TO DESIGN:

CASUAL WEAR ☐ TAILORED GARMENT ☐ EVENING WEAR ☐ BRIDAL WEAR ☐ SPORTSWEAR ☐ LINGERIE ☐

THE FABRICS I WANT TO USE IN THE COLLECTION:

CASUAL WEAR	TAILORED GARMENT	EVENING WEAR	BRIDAL WEAR
Jersey	Polyester	Velvet	Chiffon
Pique	Cotton	Chiffon	Crepe
Fleece	Wool	Georgette	Silk
Crepe	Tweed	Crepe	Organdy
Muslin	Flannel	Satin	English net
Velvet	Cashmere	Duchess Satin	Rayon
Tweed	Herringbone	100% Silk Organza	Charmeuse
Cashmere	Linen	Charmeuse	Taffeta
Brocade	Gabardine	Crushed Velvet	Lace fabrics
Damask	Velvet	Dupioni Silk	Batiste
Flannel	Cheviot	Jacquard	Satin
Doeskin	Mackintosh	Lace	Gabardine
Melange	Brocade	Linen	Netting / Tulle/ Crinoline
Twill	Damask	Matte	Knit
Poplin	Doeskin	Peau de soie	Organza
Pinpoint Oxford	Chino	Peau Satin	Georgette
Chambray	Coating	Shantung	Faille
Denim	Cheviot	Taffeta	Shantung

FIBER CODE & NAMES:

AC	Acetate	WS	Cashmere	PA	Nylon	RA	Ramie	WO	Wool
PC	Acrylic	CO	Cotton	PE	Polyester	VI	Rayon	
WA	Angora	LI	Linen	PU	Polyurethane	SE	Silk	

SPORTSWEAR	LINGERIE	INTERFACING	LINING FABRIC
Bamboo	SPANDEX	Polyester	Satin polyester
Cotton	Nylon	Rayon blend welt	Satin acetate
Nylon	Cotton	Tricot 100% nylon	Taffeta polyester
Polyester	Linen	100% polyester Tricot	Taffeta acetate
Polypropylene	Silk	100% woven cotton	Cotton
Spandex	Bamboo	Nonwoven all purpose polyester	Polyester blend lining
TENCEL	Rayon	Nonwoven all purpose nylon	Acetate lining
Wool	Nylon tricot		Rayon blend acetate
X-STATIC	Single jersey		Crepe lining
Lycra	Light double knit		Crepe -back satin
Mesh	Simplex		
Neoprene	Stretch Lace		
Waterproof	Mesh		
Micro fibre	Power Net		
Waddings	Nylon/spandex satin knit		
Sports fleece	Crepe de Chine		
Merino wool	Voile and lawn		
Stretch	Lace		

FASHION MOODBOARD

Mood boards are combination and mix of sketches, texts, color concepts, fabric swatches and photographs of cultural trends, icons, silhouettes and accessories, used to develop concepts and to communicate, they help to direct and explain style, mapping out the mental process involved in development of the collection.

A tactile display of all your sources of inspiration as three-dimensional components allows you to look for connections and contradictions stepping back and seeing how it reads as an overall message.

Fashion Mood Board creation tips

A compelling story of your brand will help you to establish a strong tone of a voice that makes you stand out from others. You need to have a clear understanding of your target market, what you want to provide to your customers, and how your brand can evolve. As a designer you have to be able to describe your fashion brand in a few words. Exceptional branding provides a sense of comfort, acceptance, yet inspiration to keep your clients coming back for more each season. When creating your brand you must consider your brand future reputation status, the core values and visual appearance. It's not who makes it first, it's who make it better.

At the start of every new season, you need to do a research and evaluation to create a visual diary of details and inspirations that will later serve as a guideline and constant source of further inspiration while finalizing the new collection. The fashion Mood board makes your mind focus on the aesthetic and style direction of the collection, considering color influences, producing as a summary of your findings and before any serious design development begins. Fashion Mood Board also serves as a tool to refresh your mind, enabling you to return to it throughout the designing process and to discover something new.

Fashion Mood Boards can be created in digital or physical format.
Physical format allows you to display your work on to boards, giving you an extra tactile element, while having physical objects mixed in with images, telling a richer story.

Digital format enables you to scan imagery, and with Photoshop and Illustrator programs you can easily manage and re-arrange them. Also it helps you testing out different layouts, manipulating them, resizing and recoloring, overlaying or adding different special effects.

While creating your fashion mood board try to keep things simple to deliver your message clearly to you and your audience. The mood board should contain a number of key elements:

Color Palette Story
Your color palette should tell a story about the overall atmosphere and be defined through the imagery you're using. You have to decide if you are using warm or cold colors, harmonious or contrasted, dark or light, or both... You can also include color cards, fabric swatches, or physical items that represent the colors.

Fabric and texture
You should include fabrics that represent texture, trimmings, prints and embellishments, helping to add depth to your research.

Theme
You need to choose the theme on which your collection will be based. Defining the theme on the mood board allows you be more focused during the design process.

Target Market
You need to decide also who you are designing for. Including the image references about your client or muse and their perceived lifestyle, helps you to refer to their taste and interests for more focused fashion mood board.

Typography
The inspiration for your fashion mood board can come from different sources, not only just from images and colors. If typography is a vital part of your styling, annotating your board with short paragraphs or descriptive words can sometimes be more powerful than images.

Styling
Including imagery or props of your client or muse lifestyle and hair and make-up suggestions, will contribute creating an ideal image for your collection.

Finalizing
Prior finalizing your Fashion Mood Board you should consider analyzing the chosen images, determining the mood and overall massage you want to convey and deciding on physical or digital approach. Also you should be exploring and refining your layout and images and undertake more research if required.

NOTES FOR SHORT DESCRIPTION OF FASHION MOOD BOARD

Color Palette Story:

Fabric and texture:

Theme:

Target Market:

Typography:

Styling:

MOODBOARD

Color Palette Story:

Color Palette Story:

Color Palette Story:

Fabric and texture: (you can make first draft sketches of the main fabrics and textures you want to use)

Theme:

Target Market:

Typography:

Now you can focus on the Styling and then on Finalizing your fashion moodboard.

FASHION FIGURE

KIDS FIGURE POSES OUTLINE

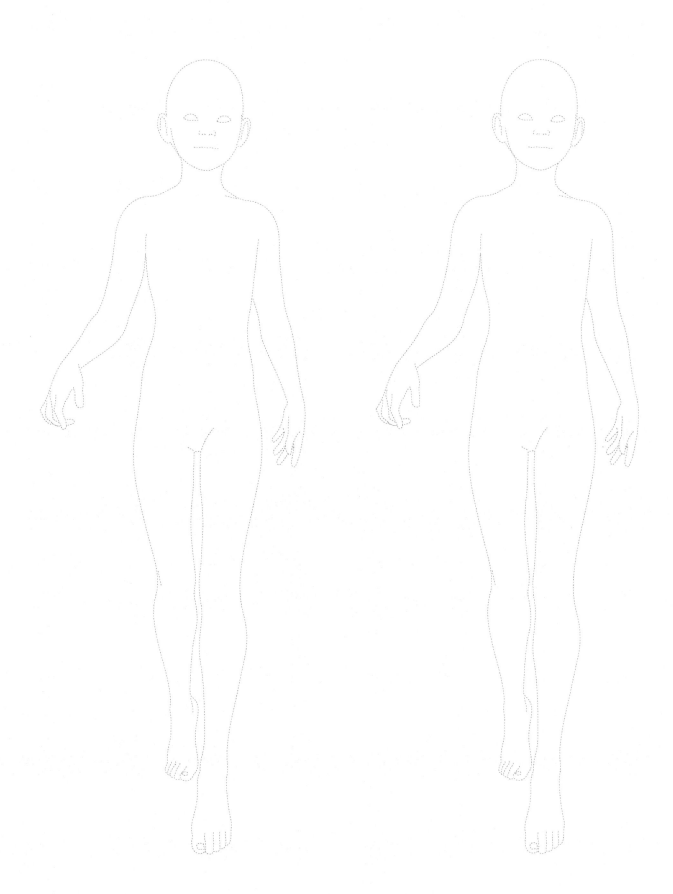

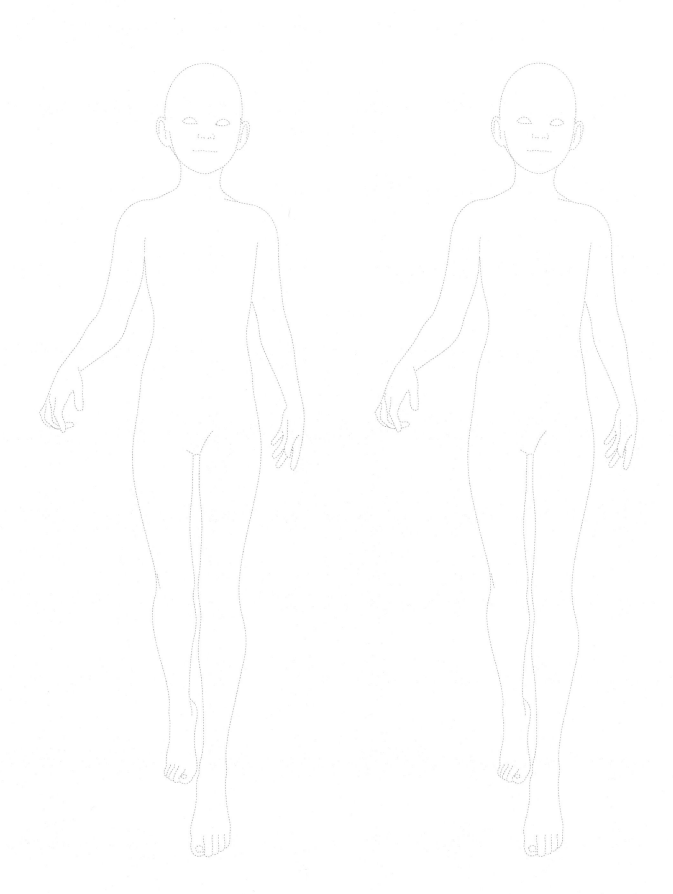

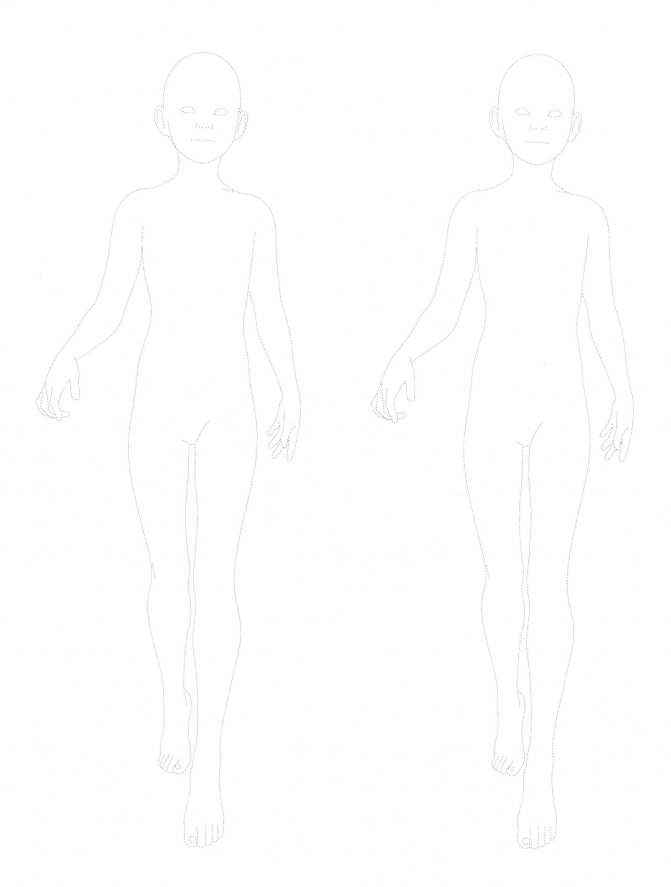

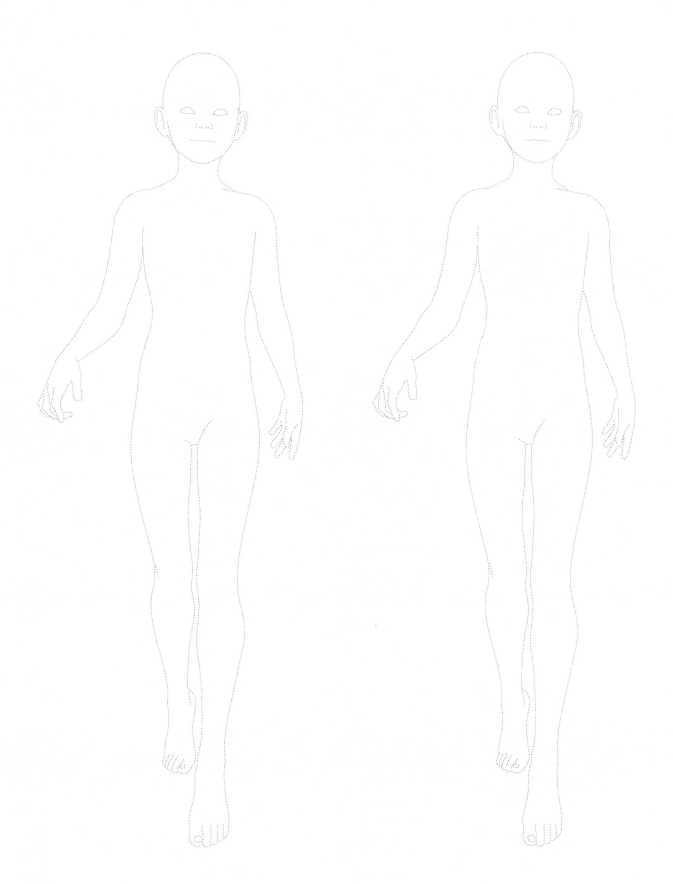

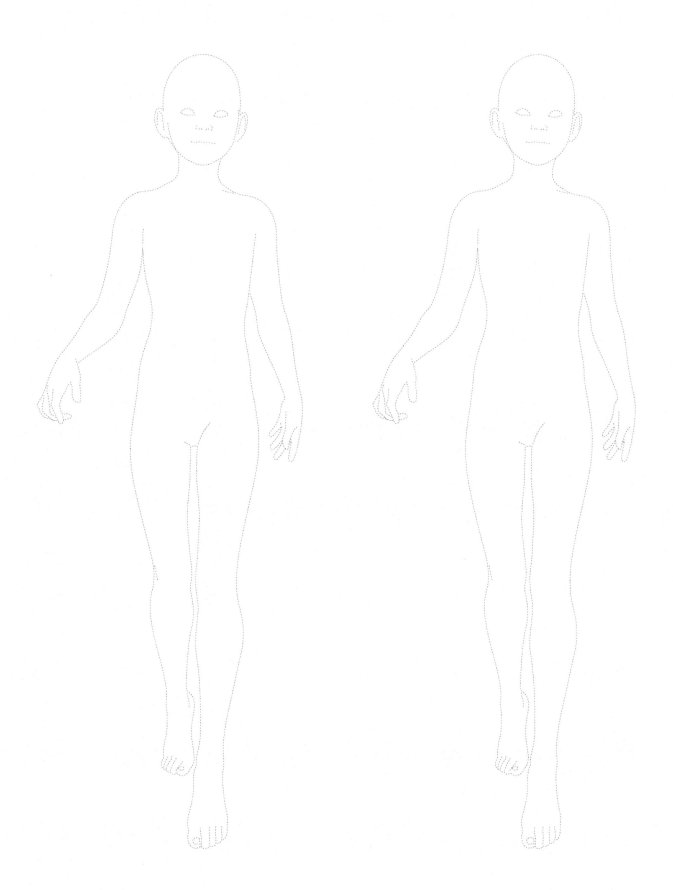

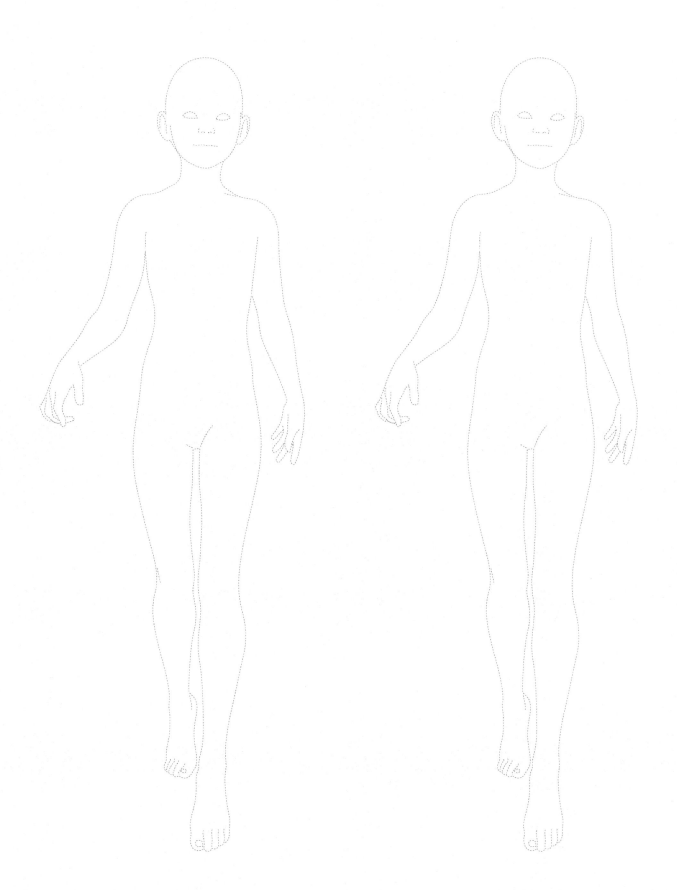

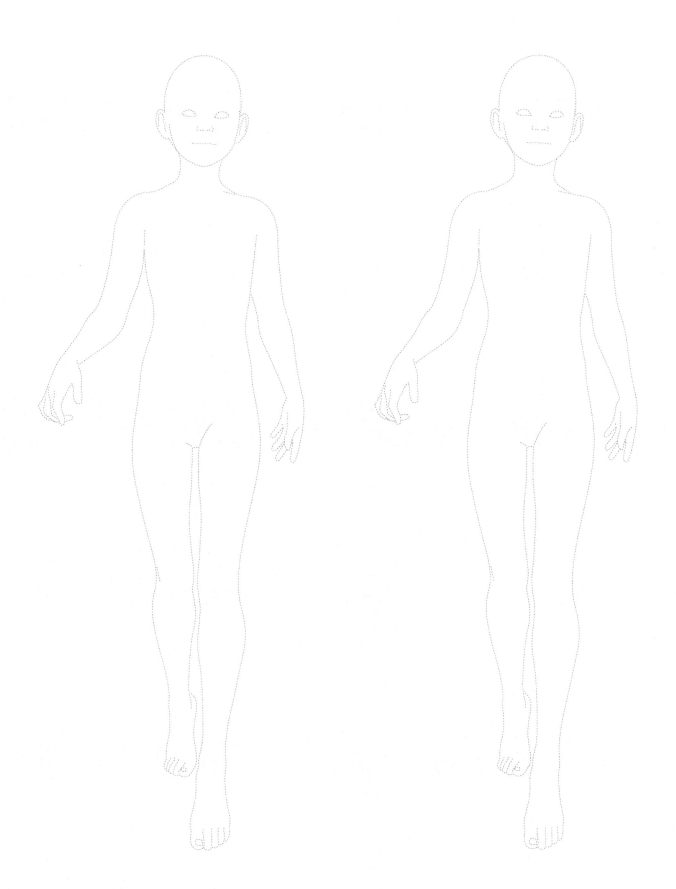

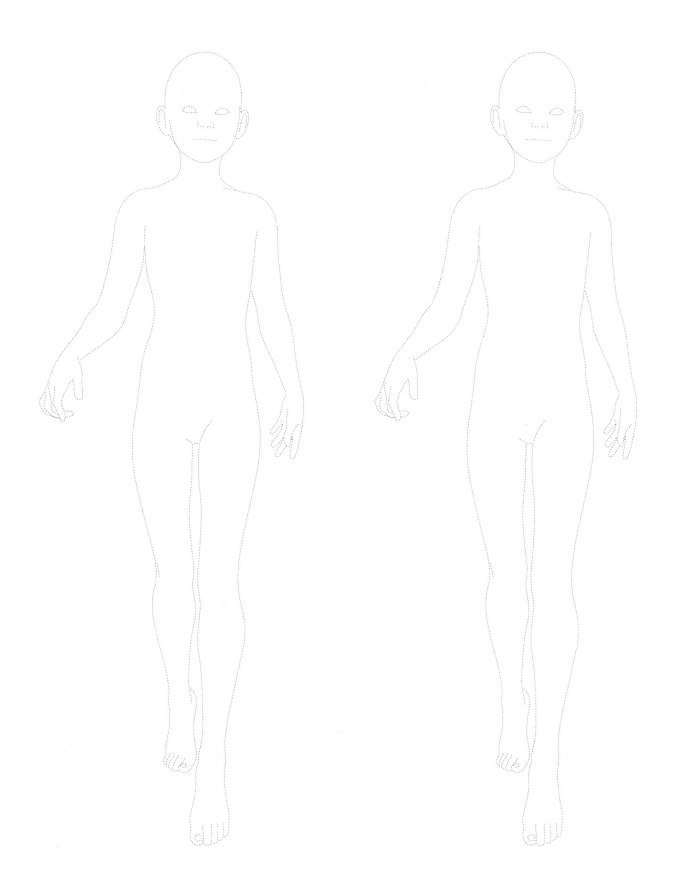

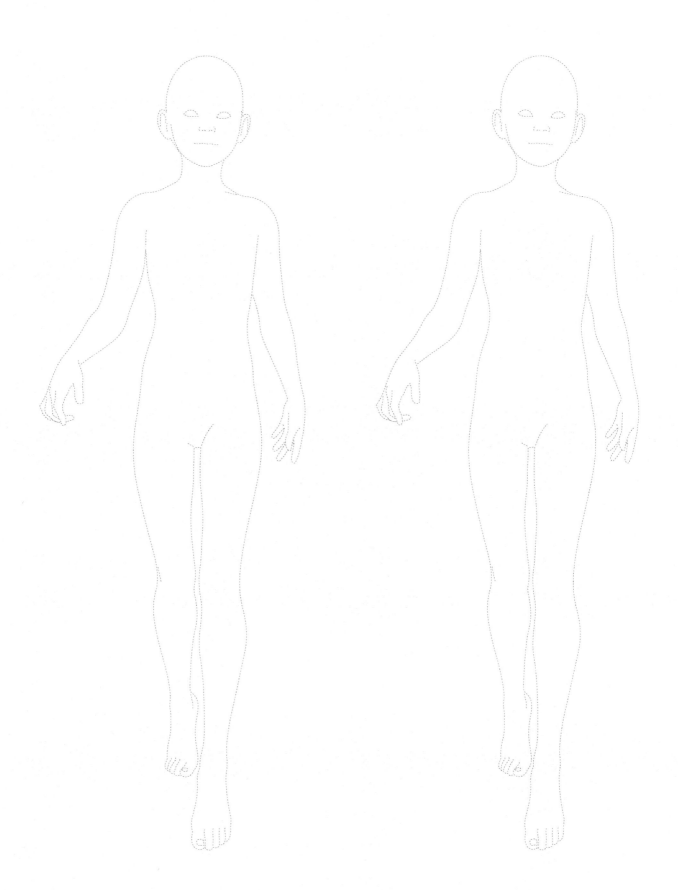

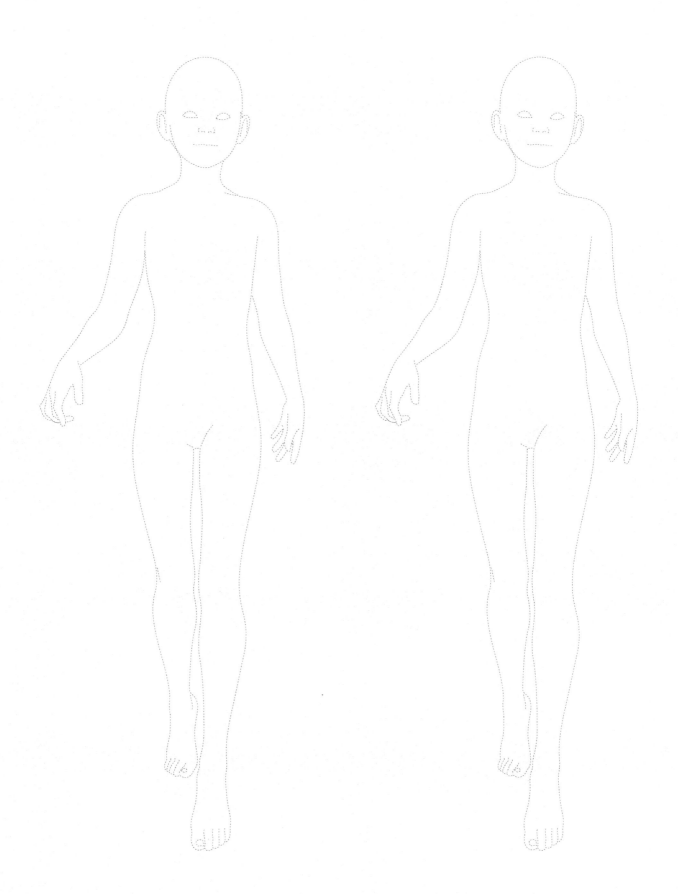

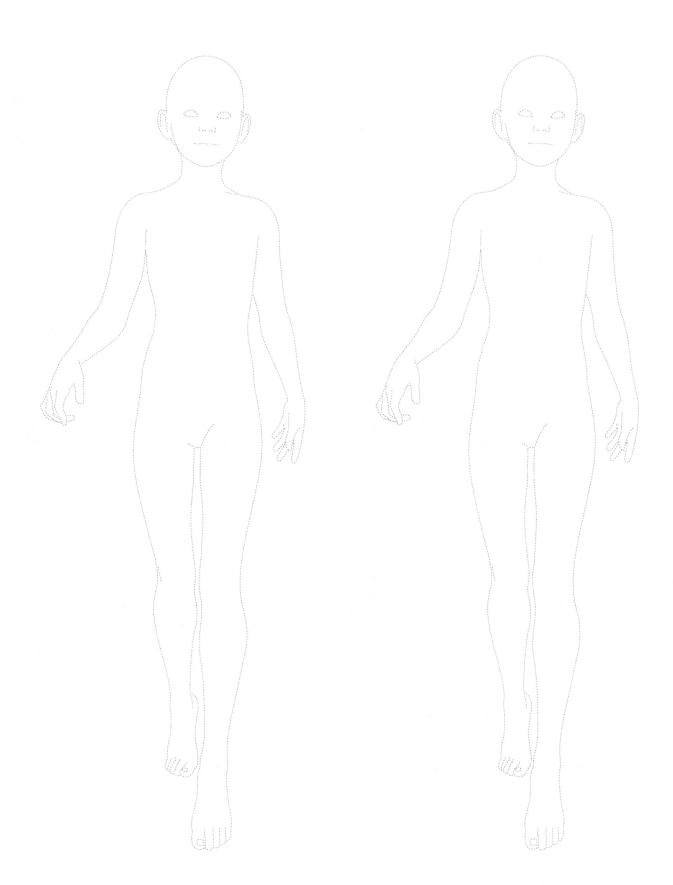

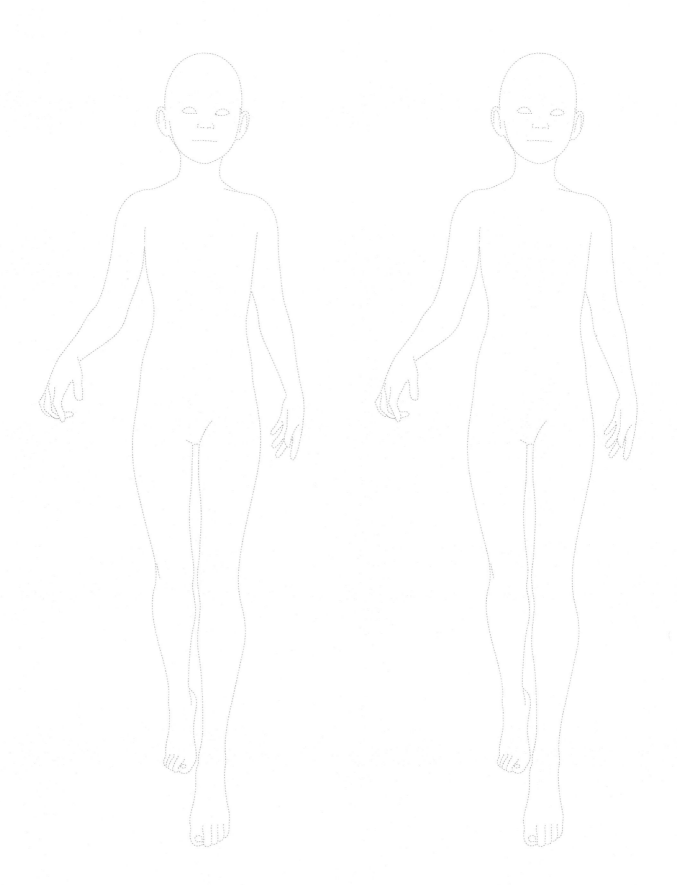

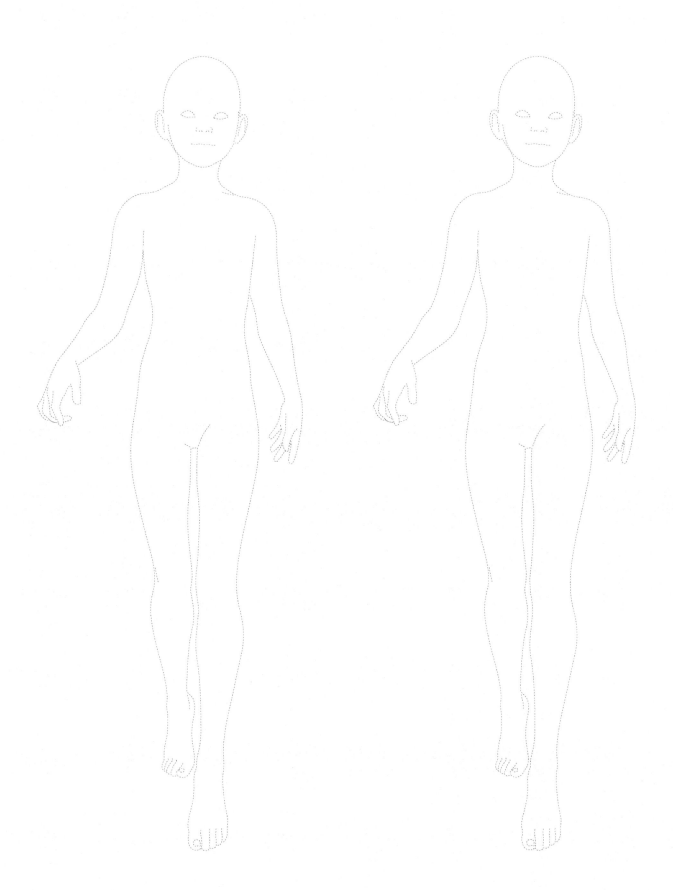

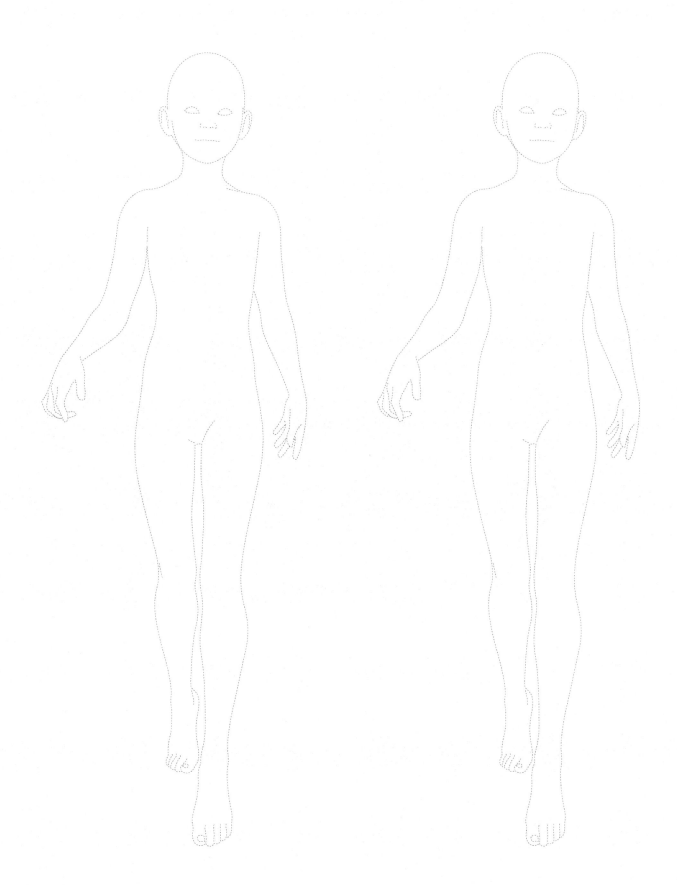

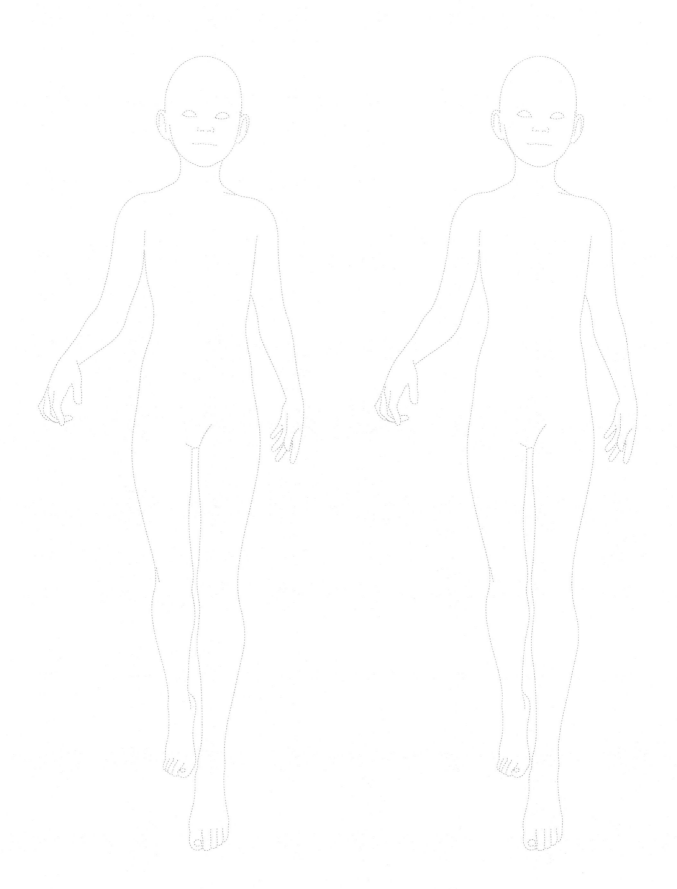

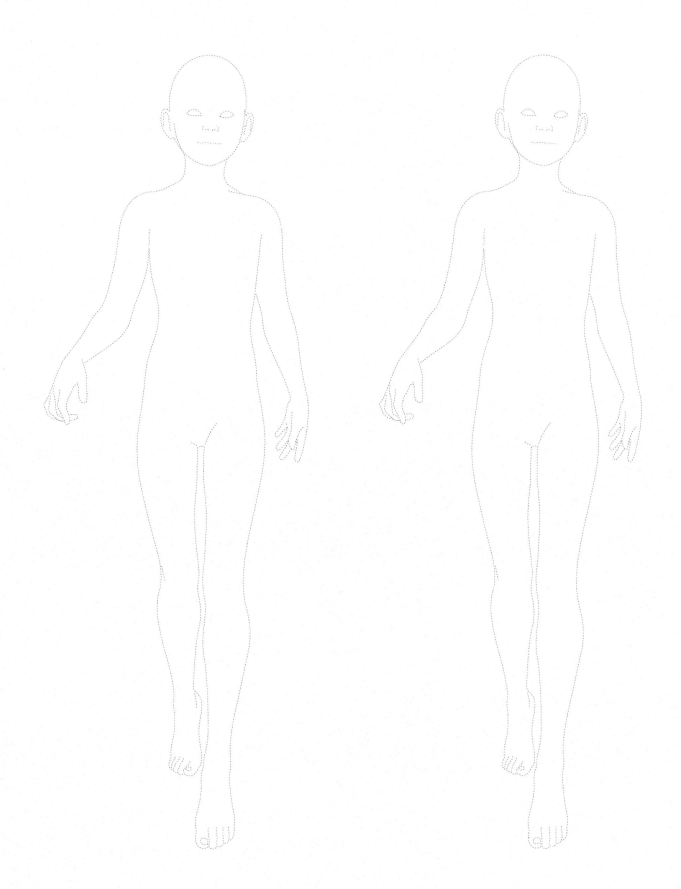

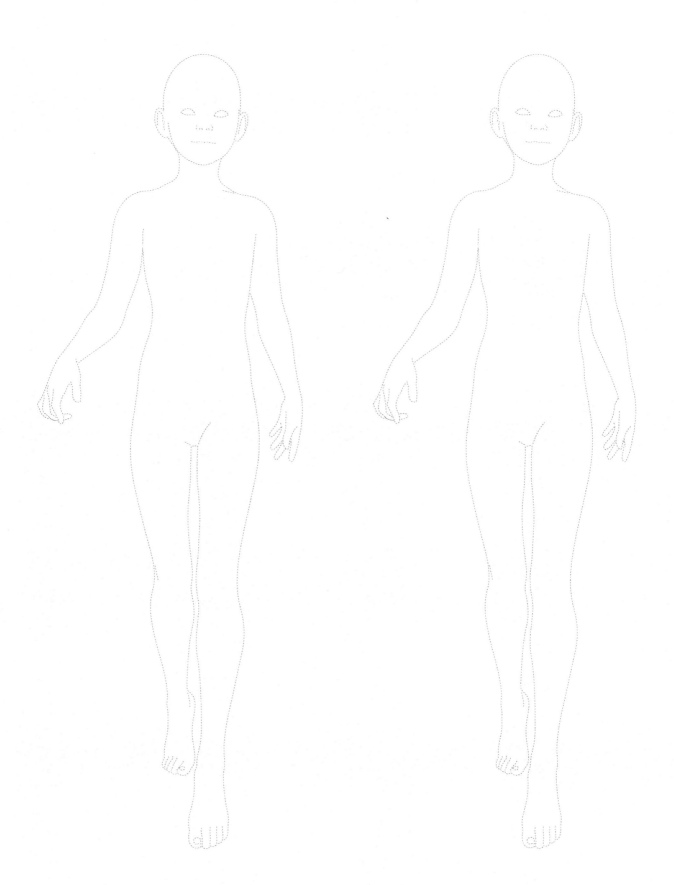

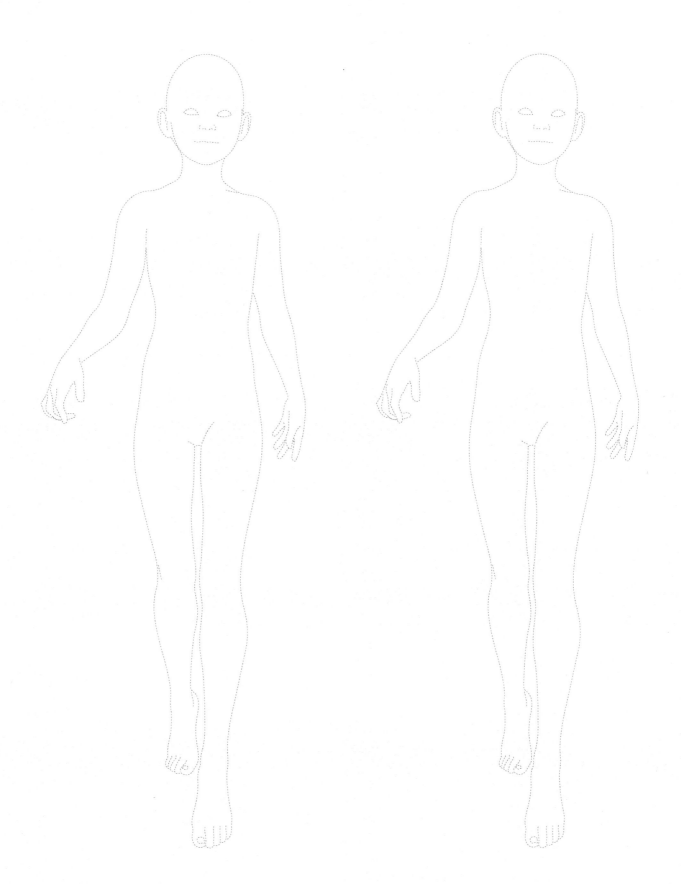

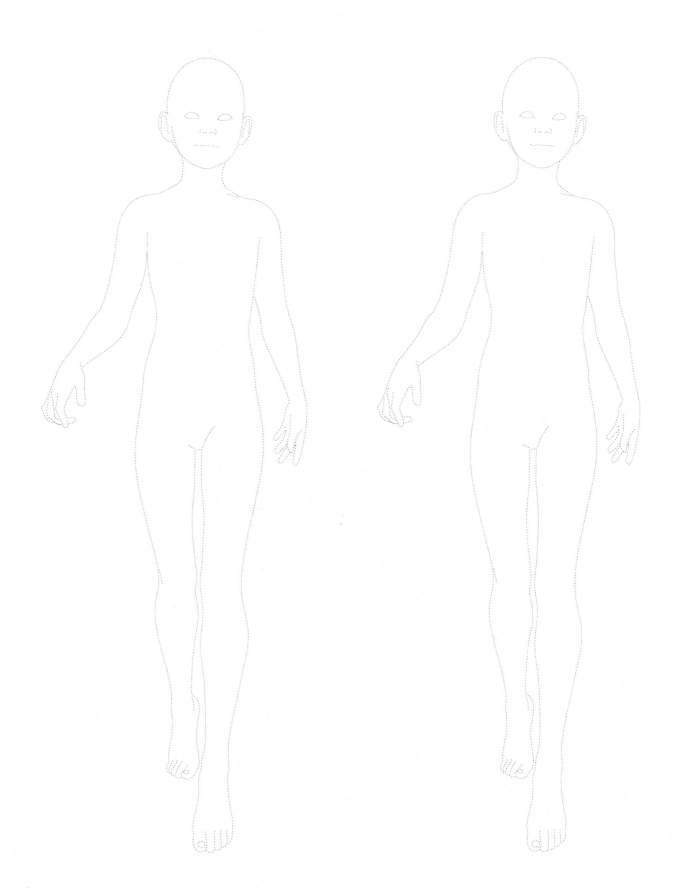

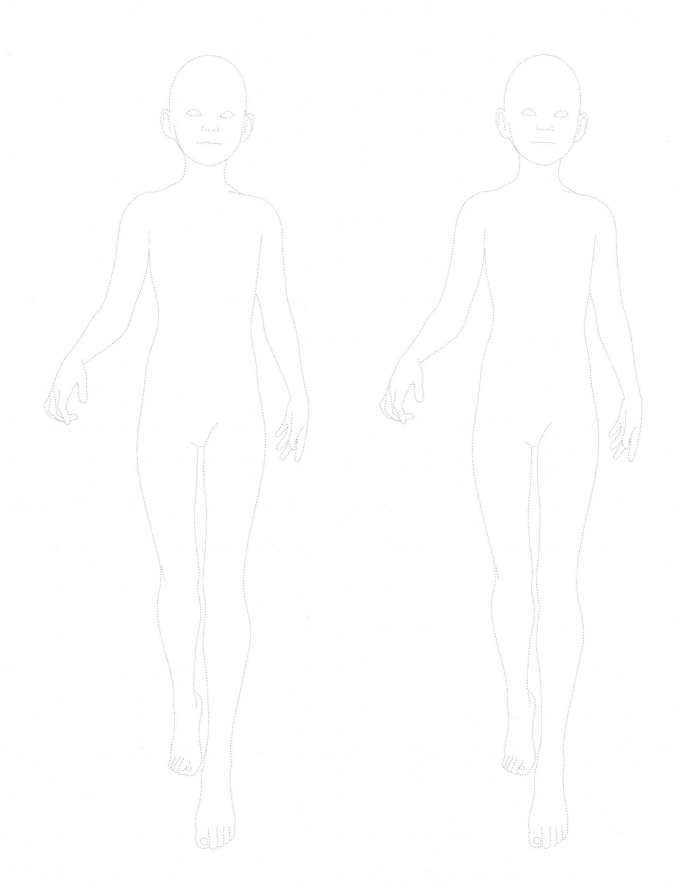

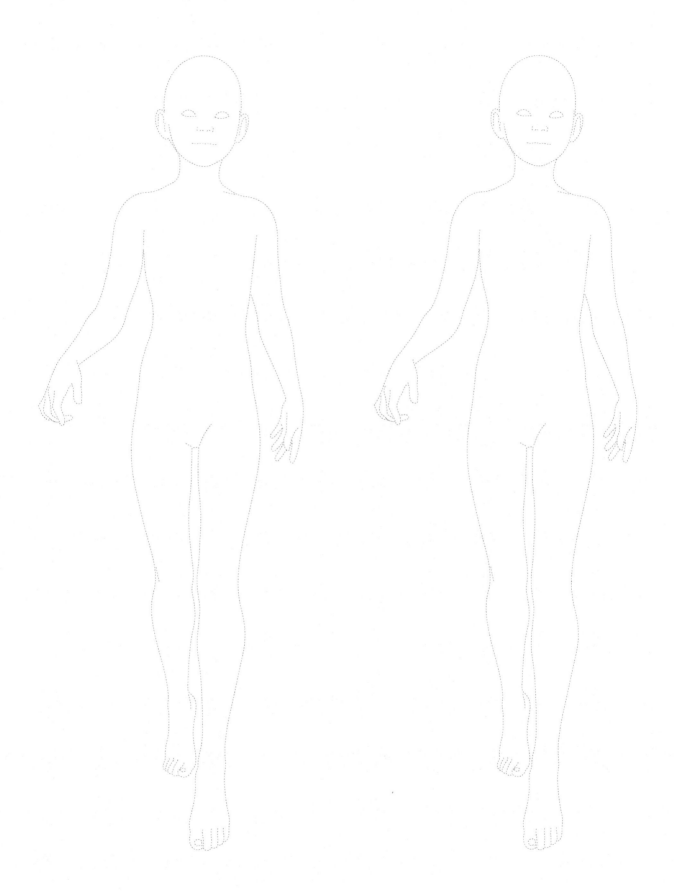

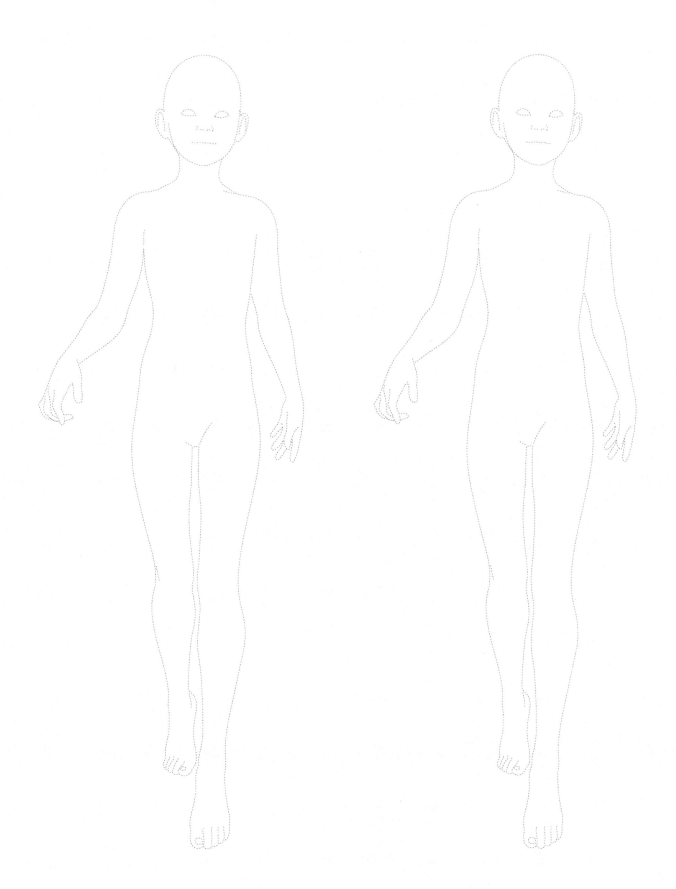

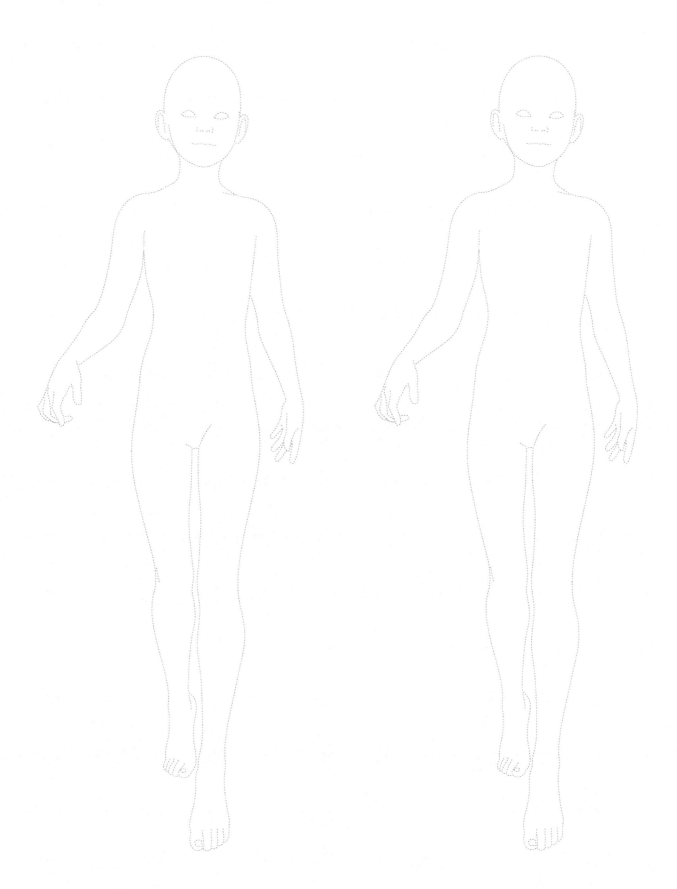

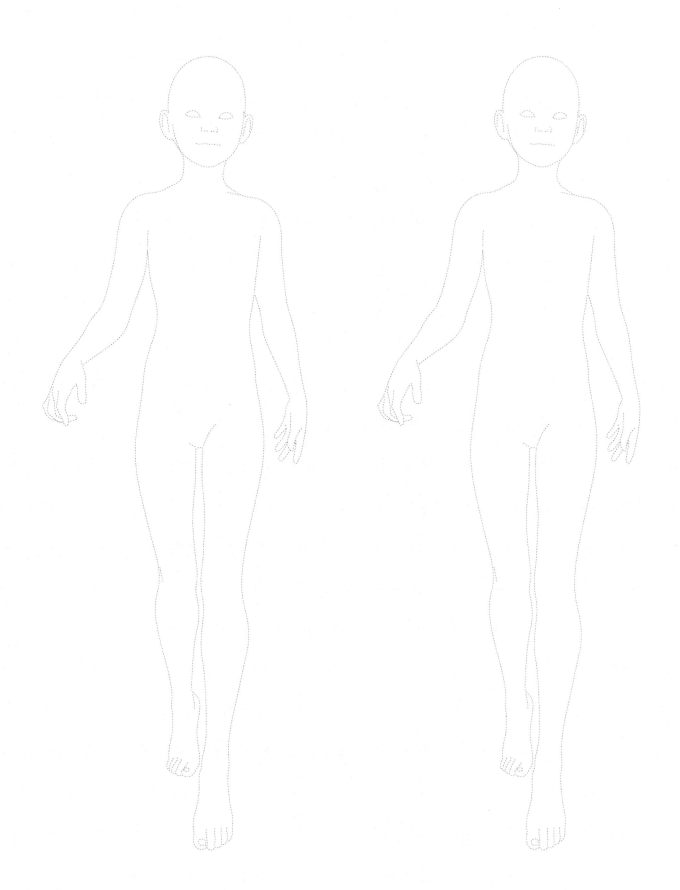

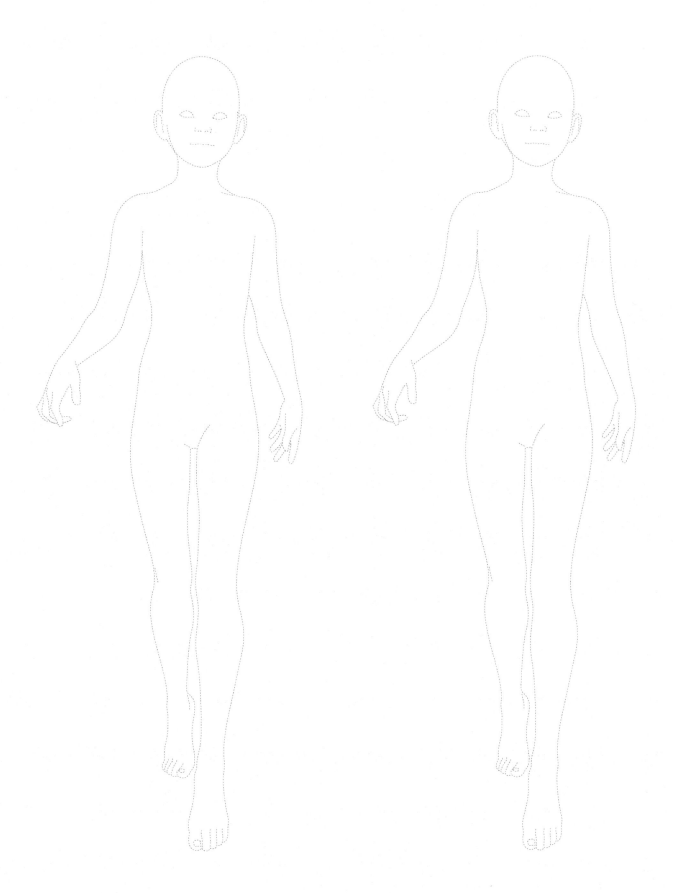

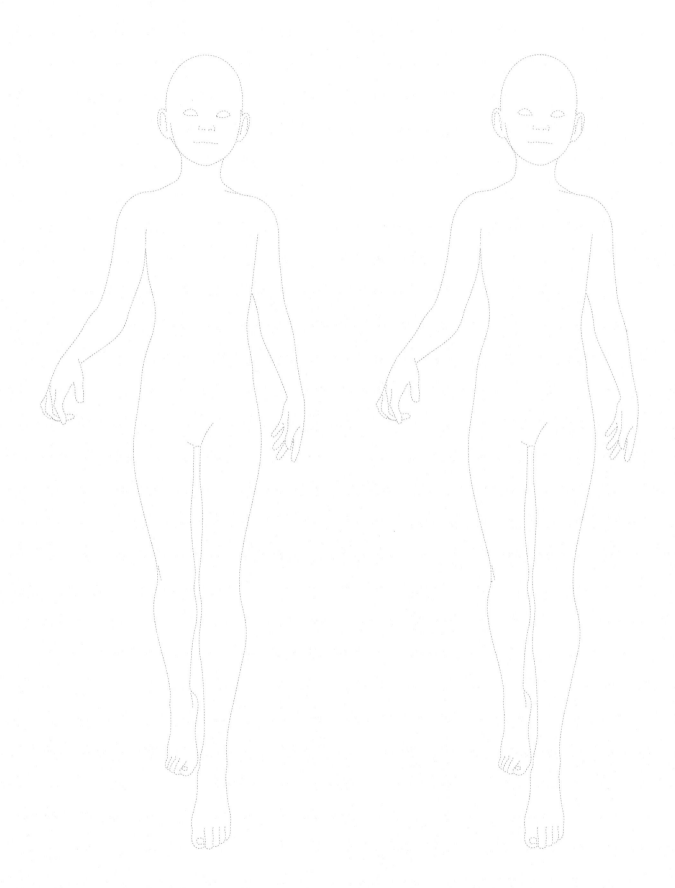

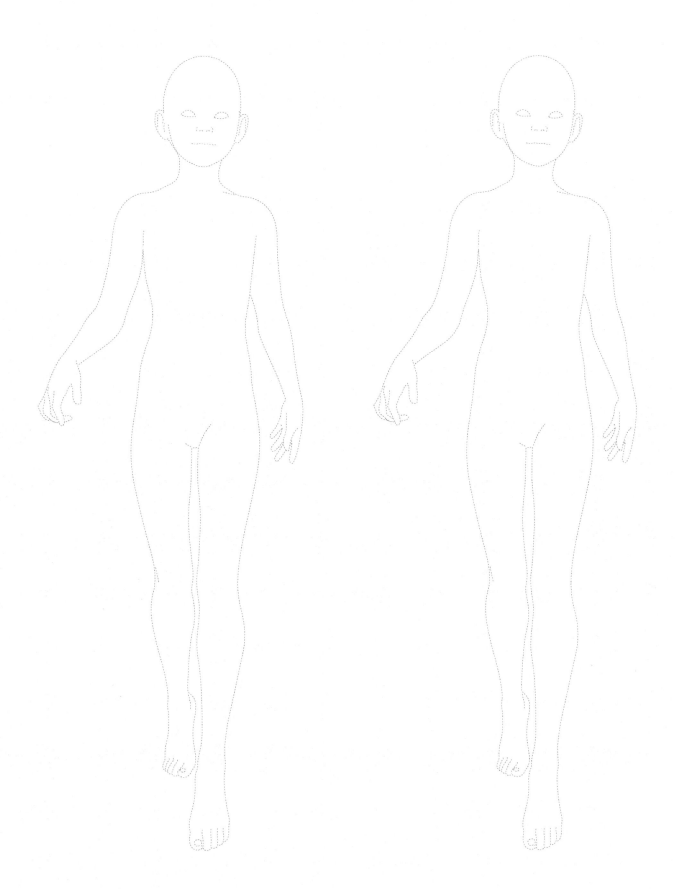

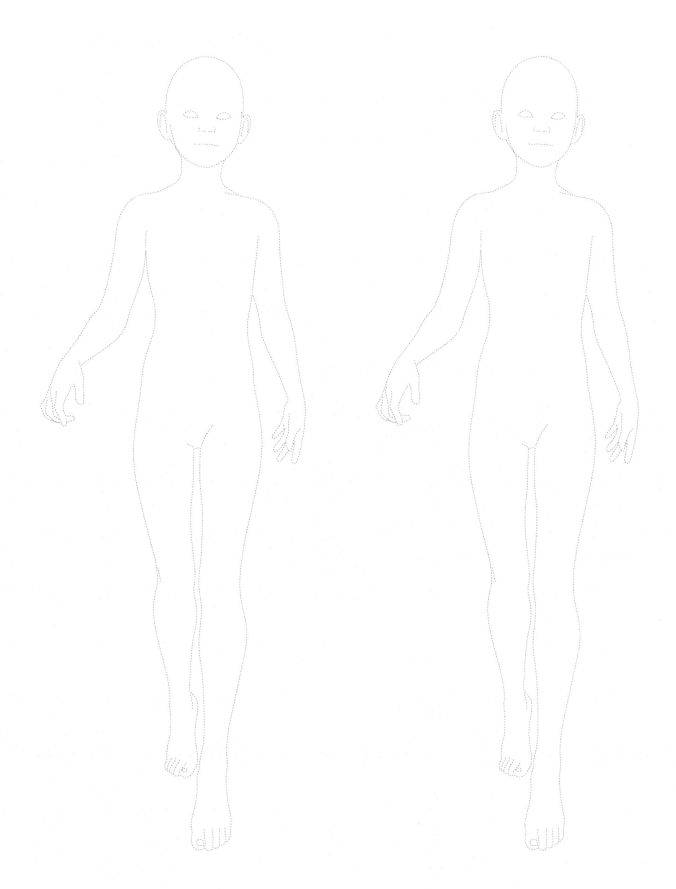

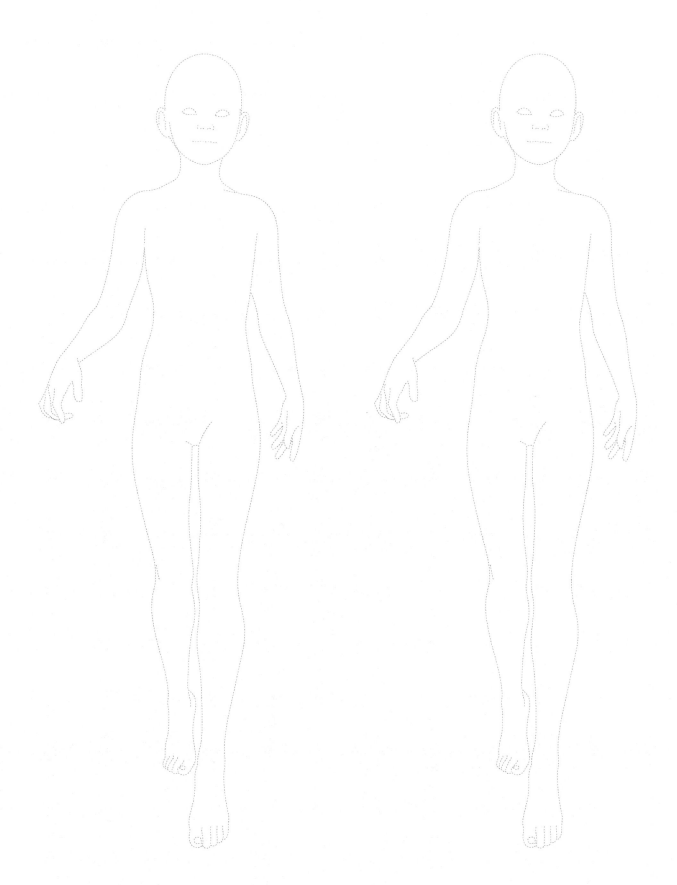

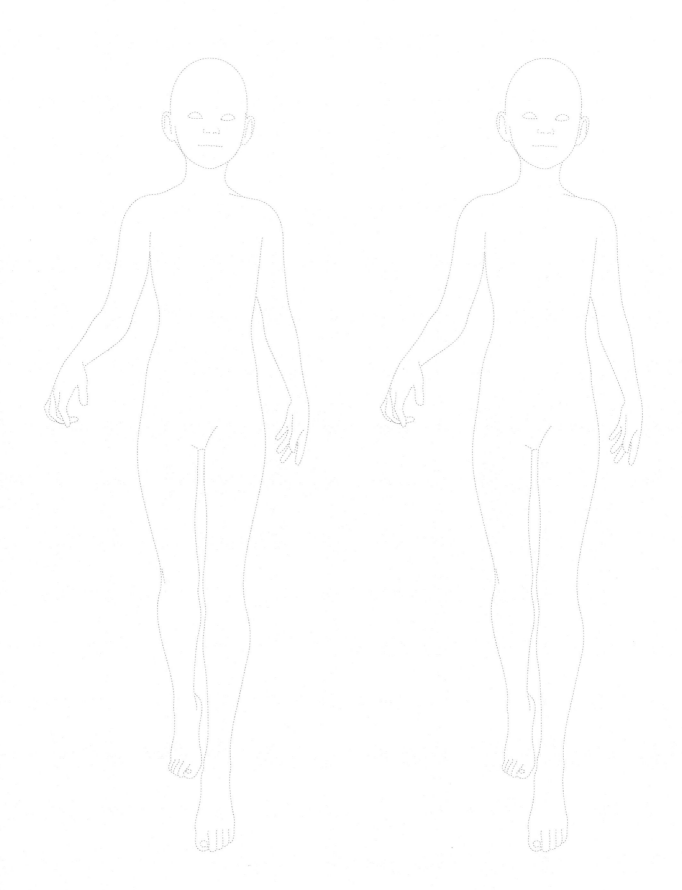

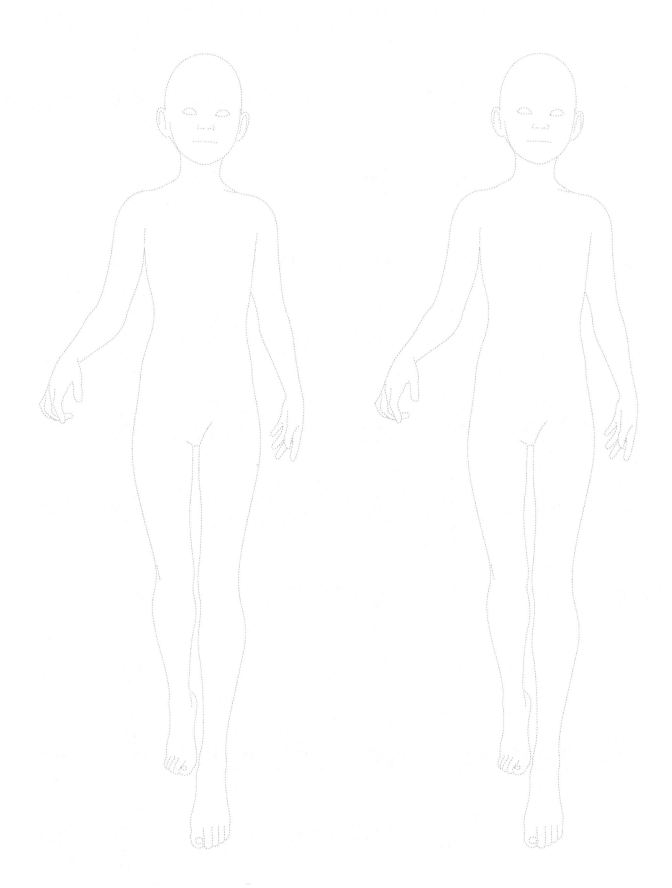

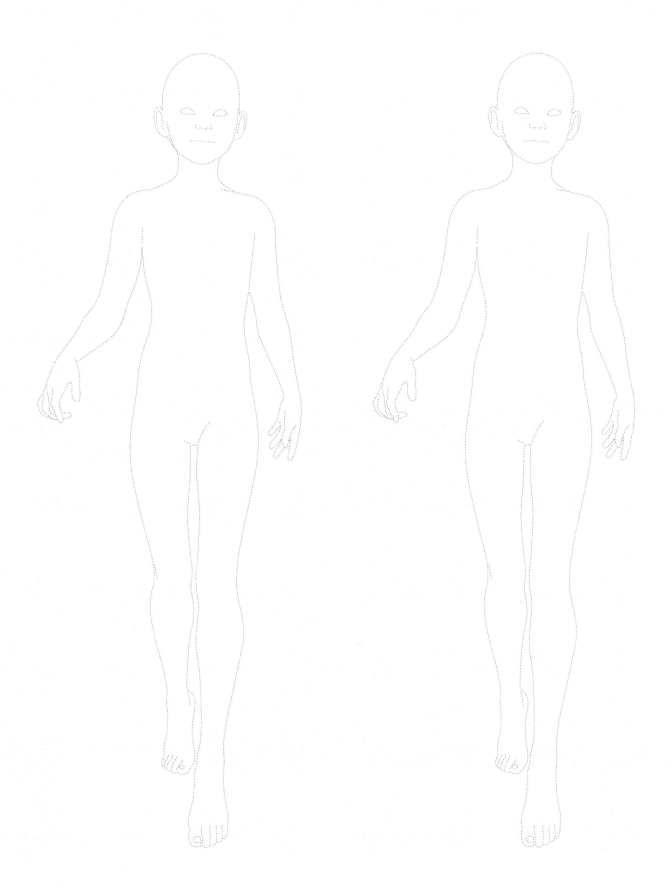

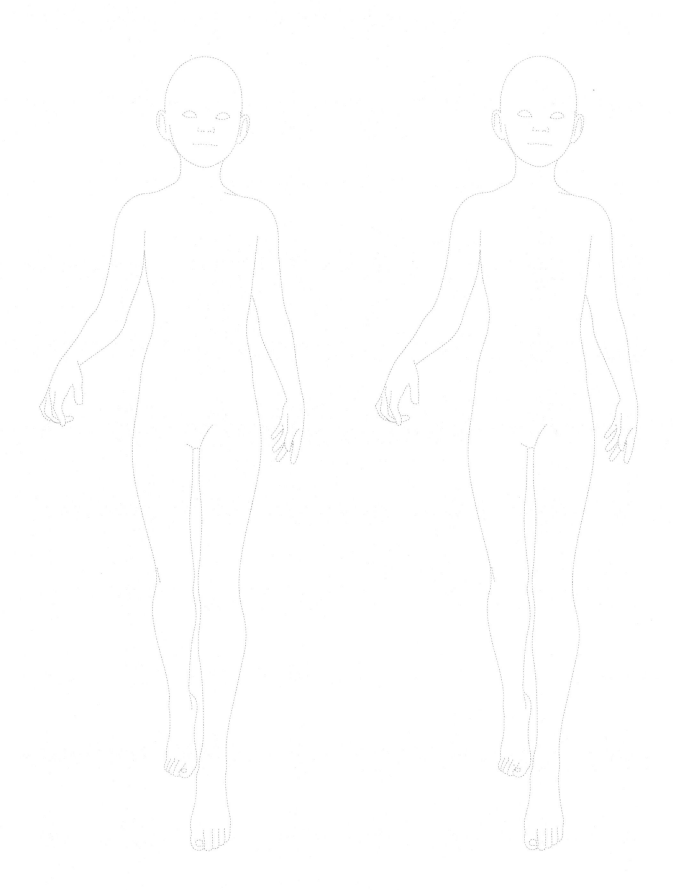

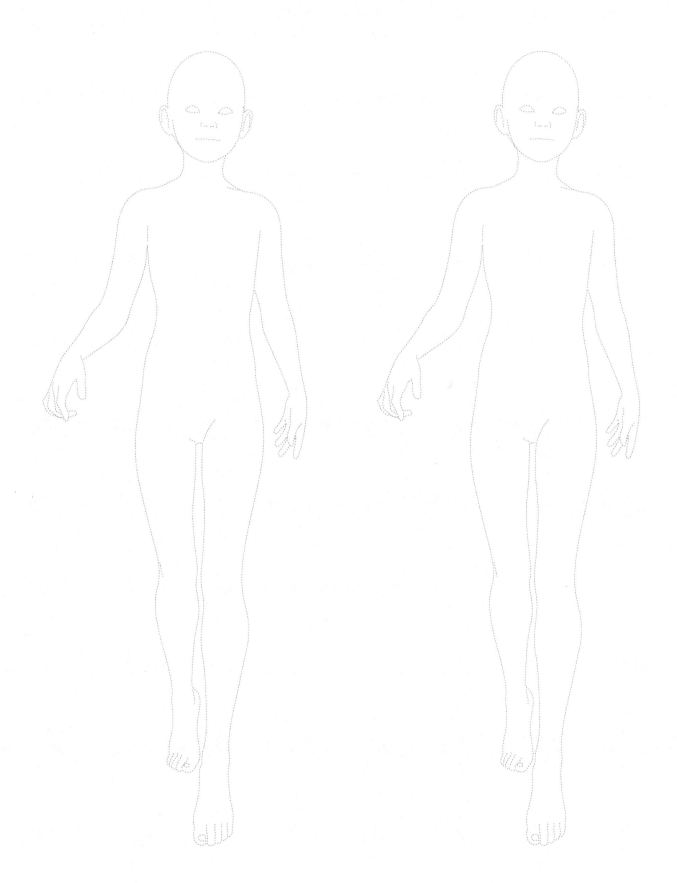

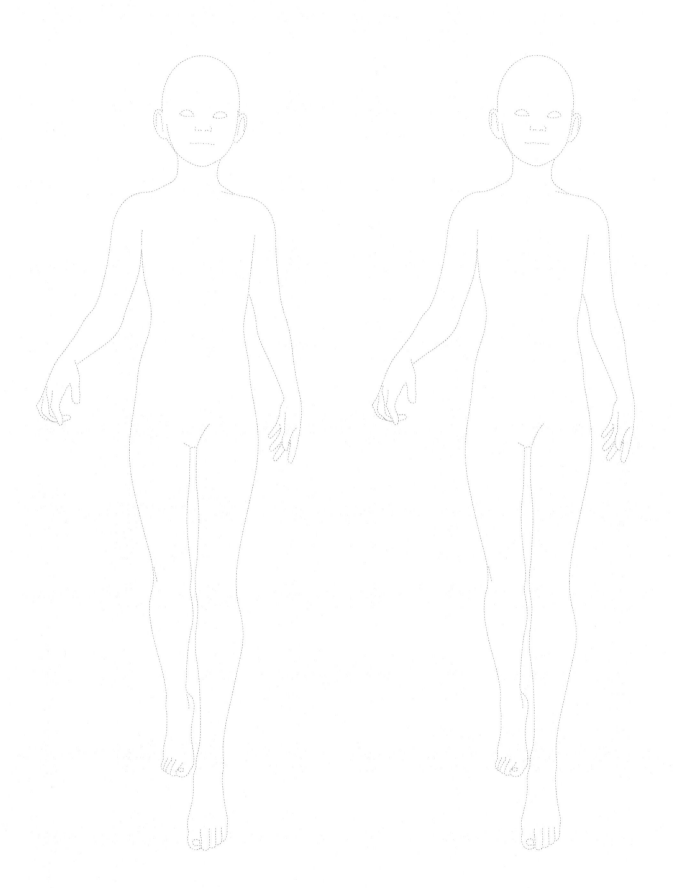

FASHION FIGURE

KIDS FRONT/BACK/SIDE POSE OUTLINE

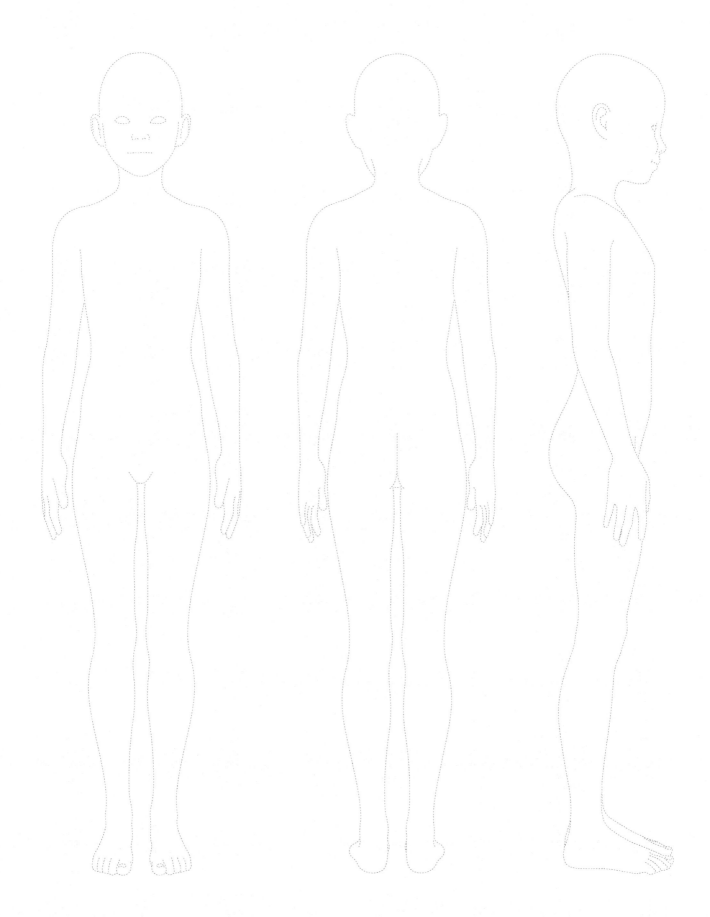

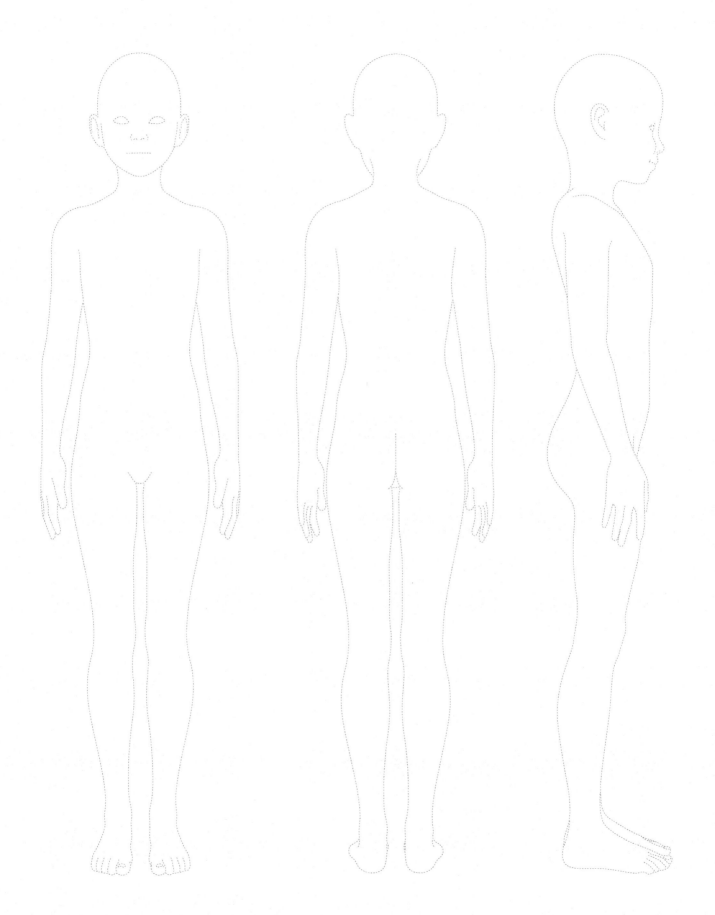

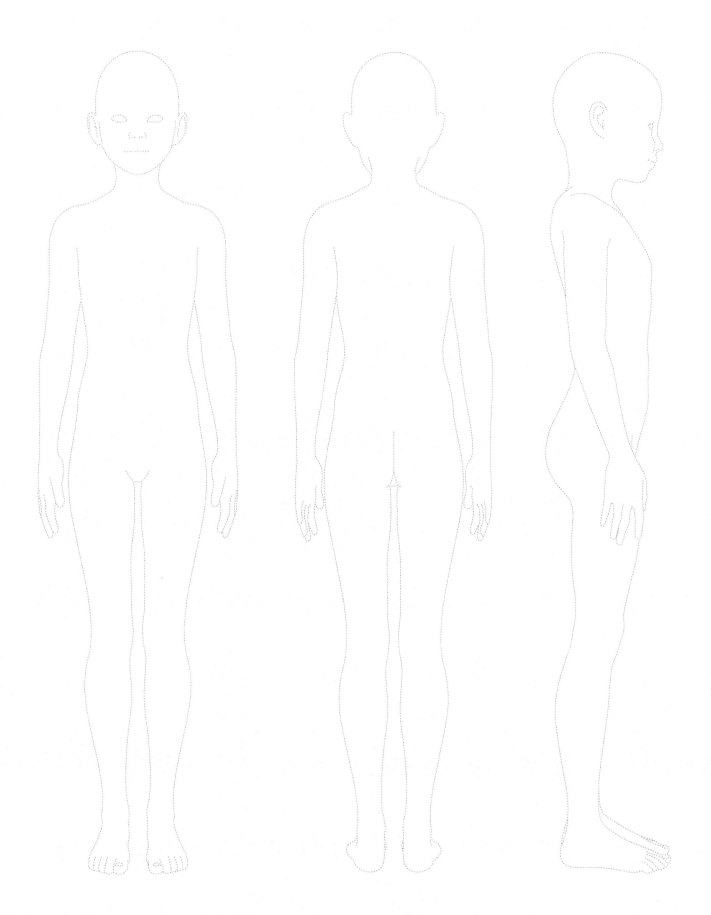

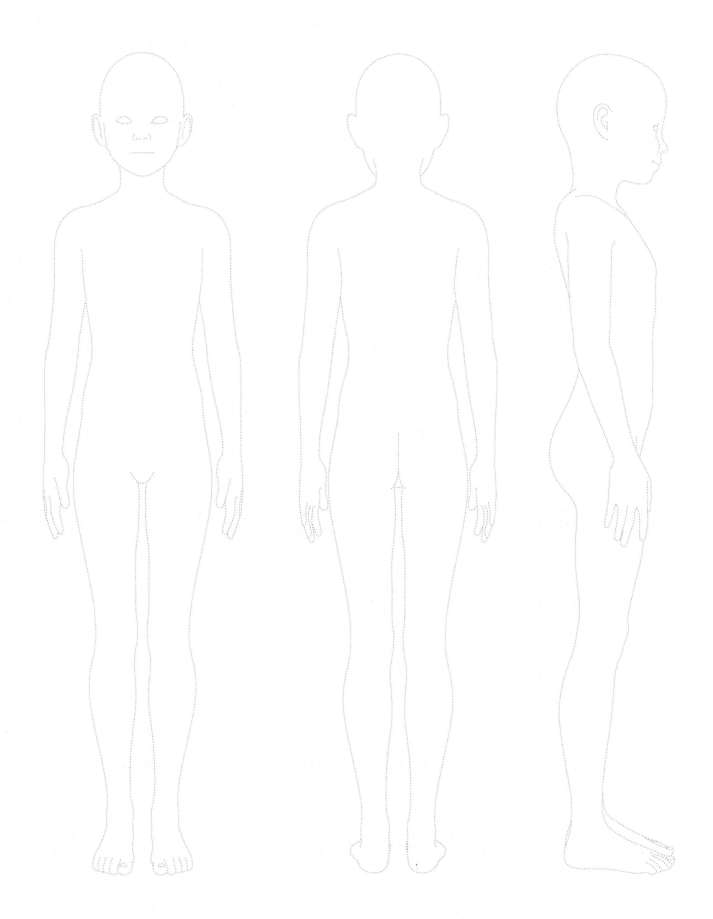

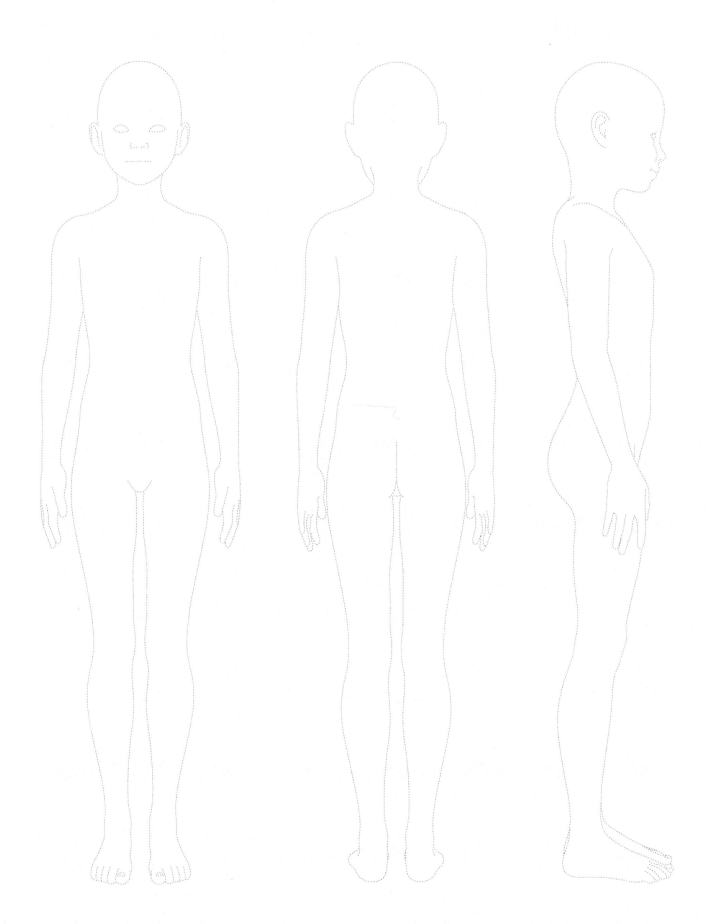

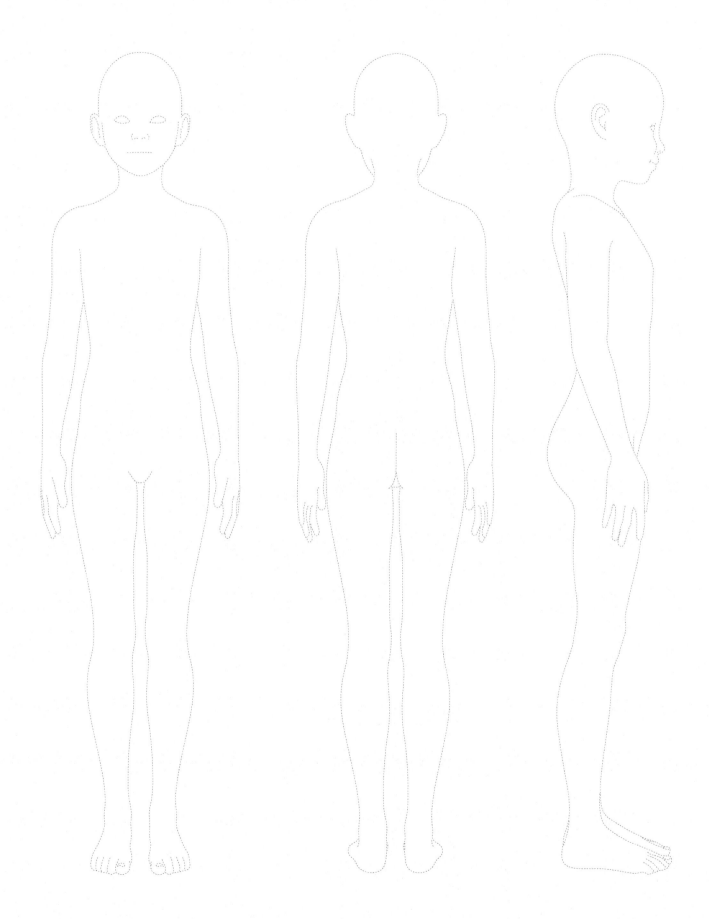

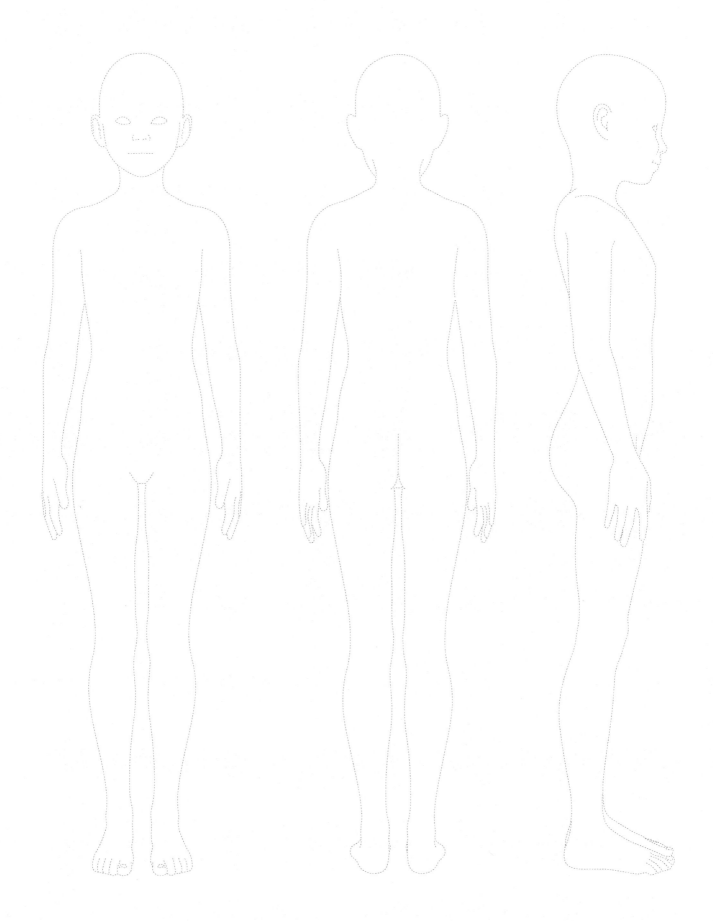

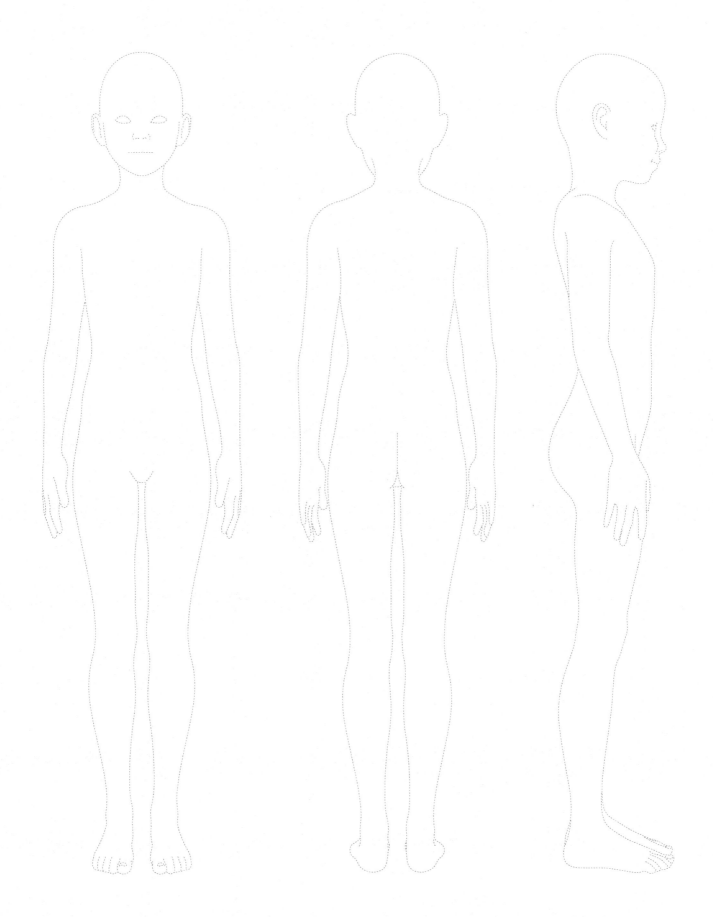

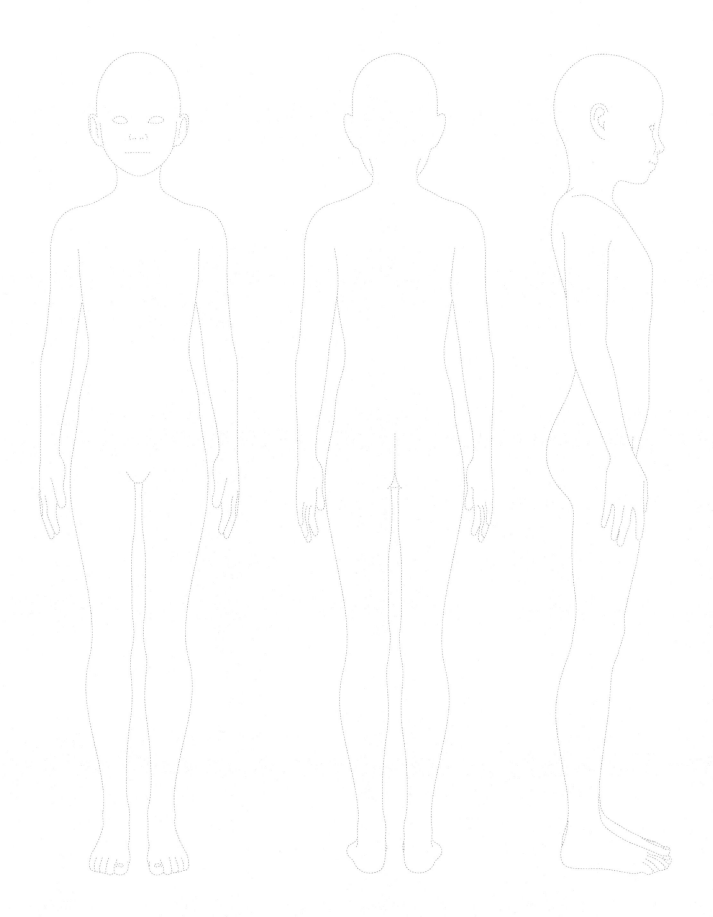

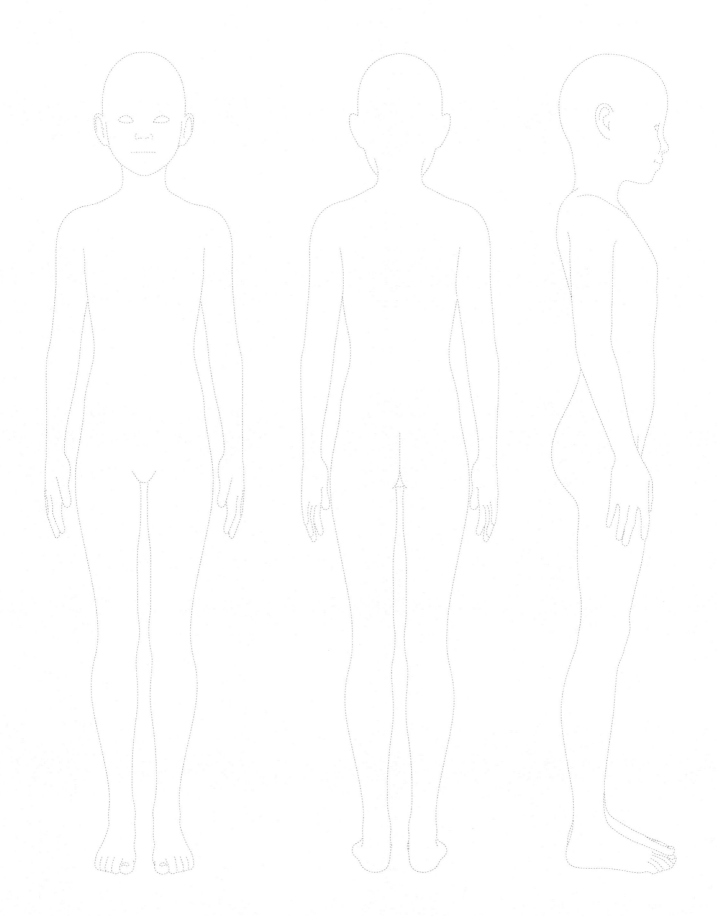

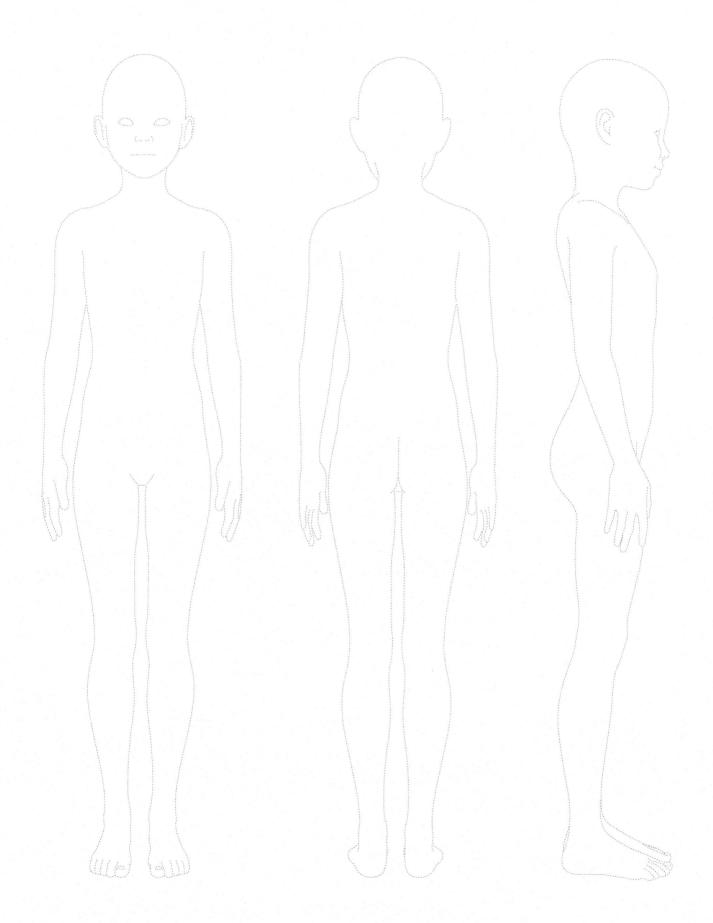

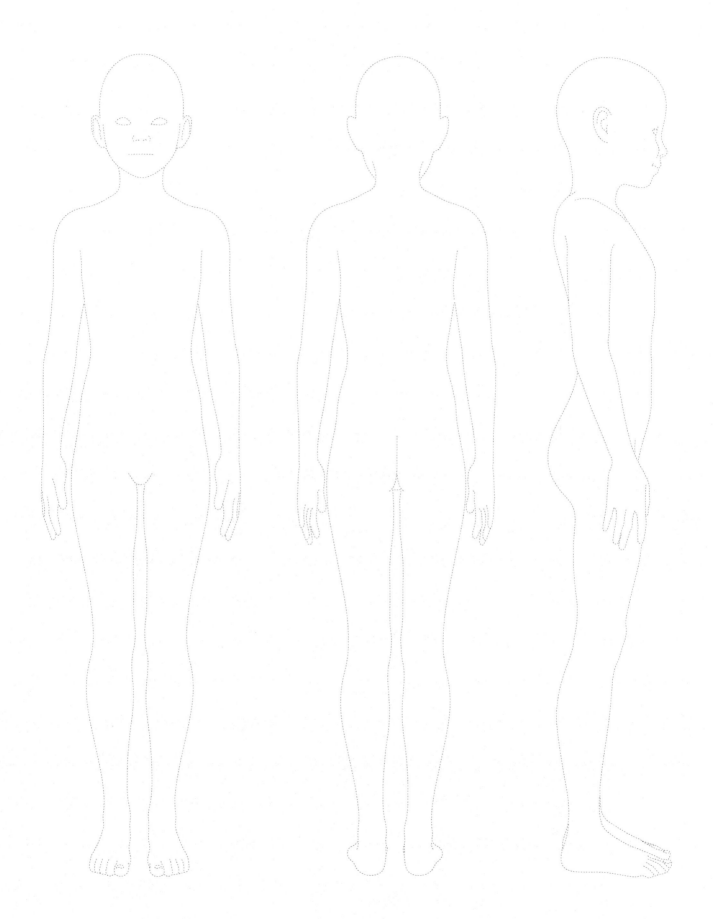

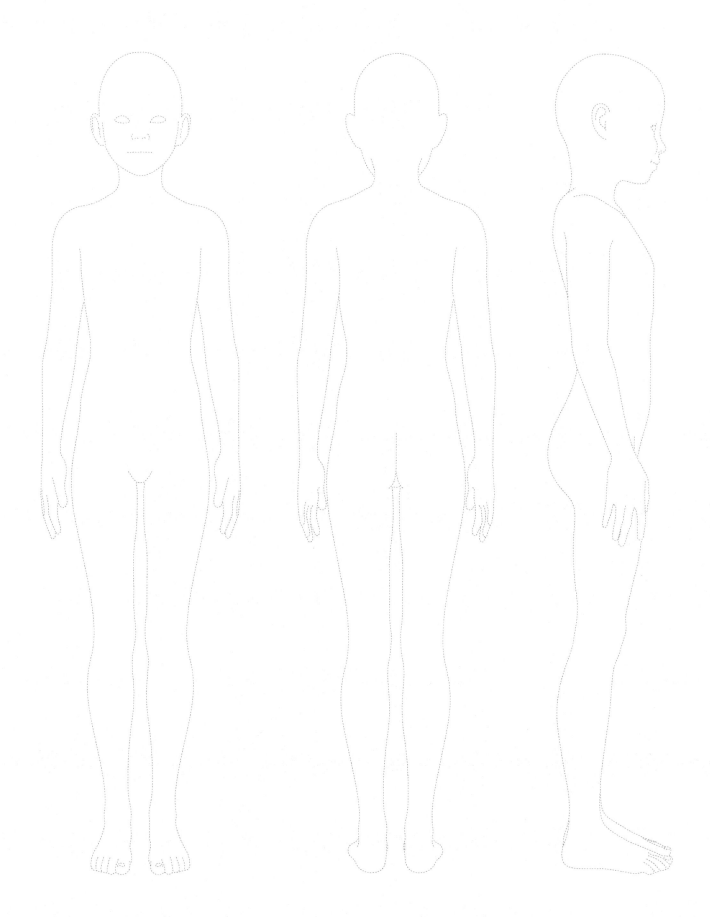

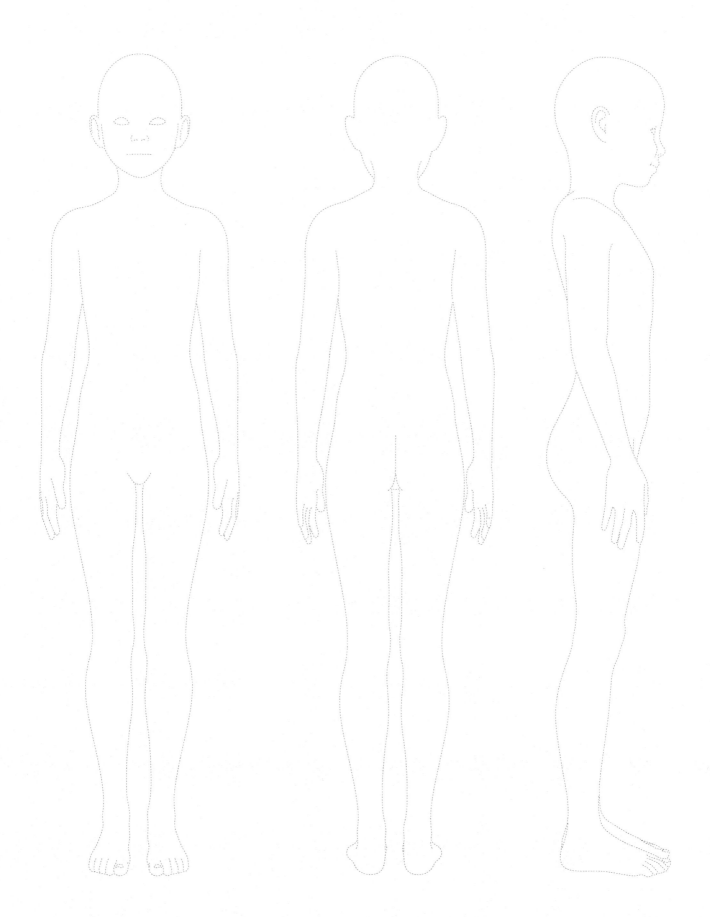

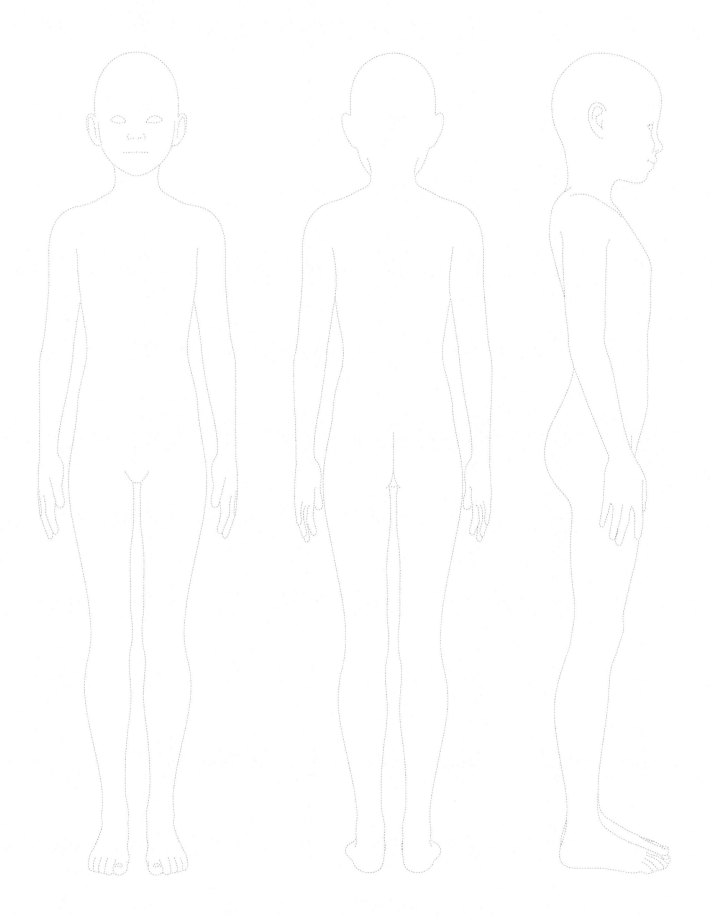

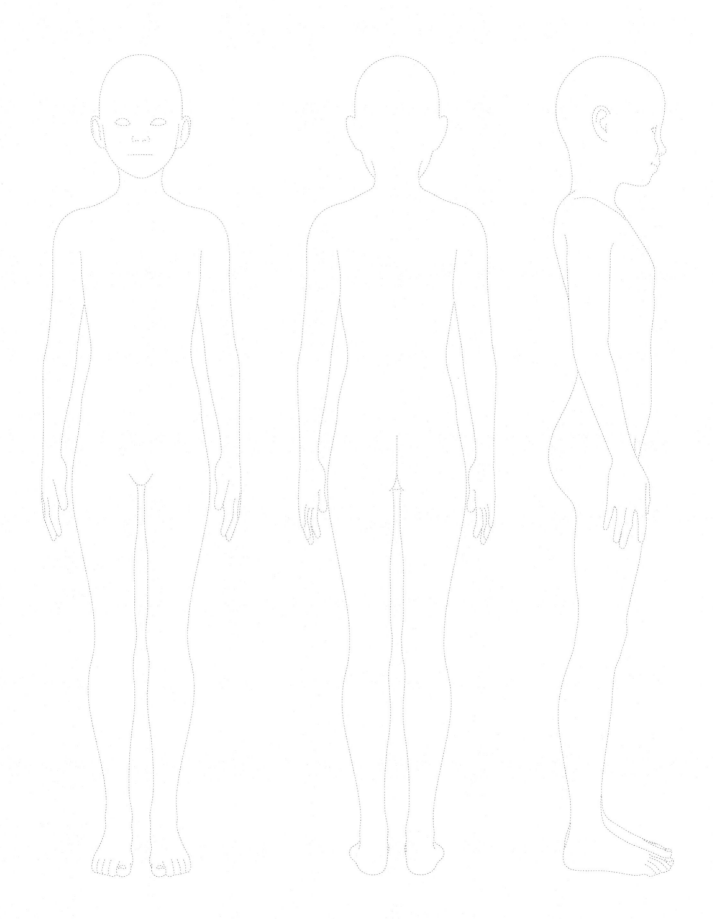

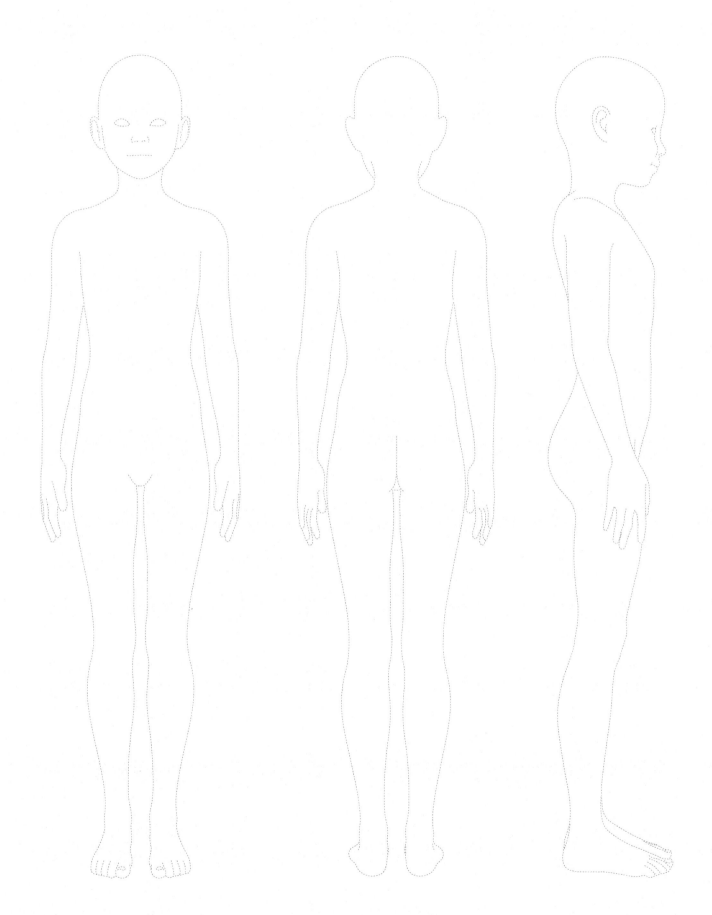

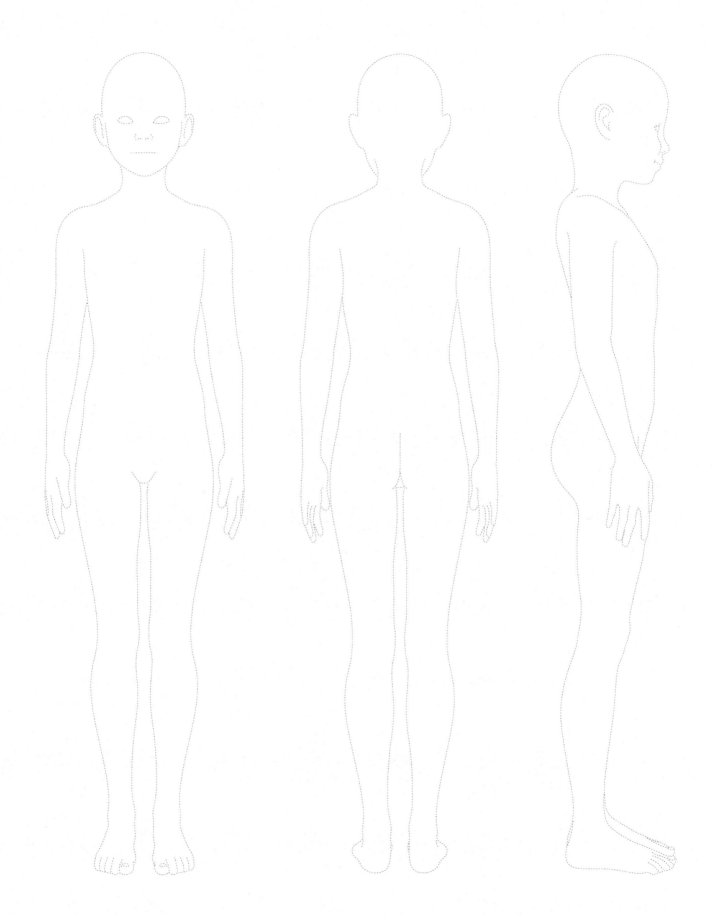

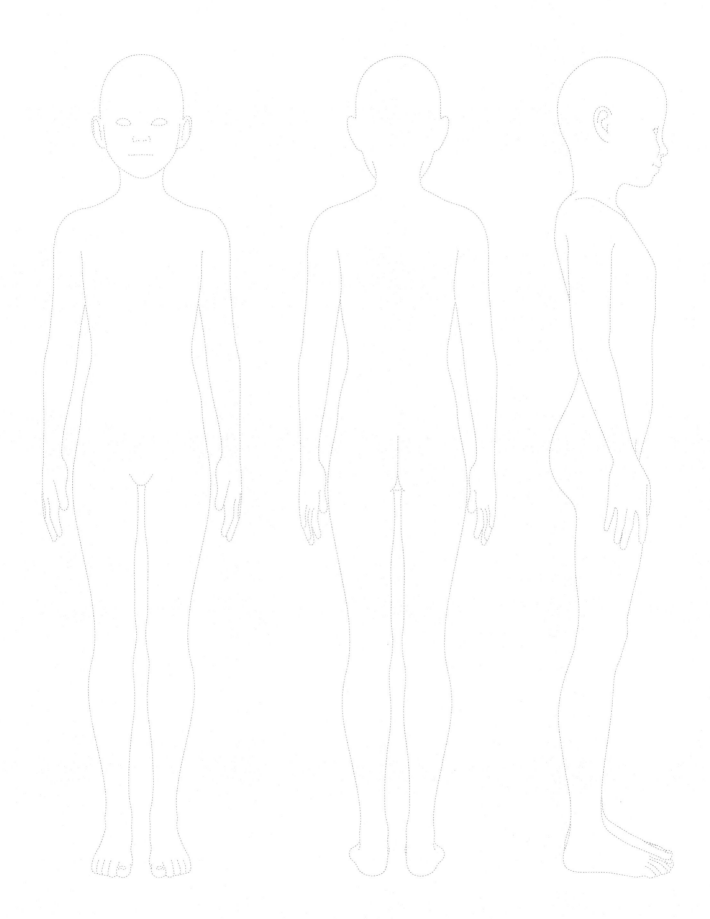

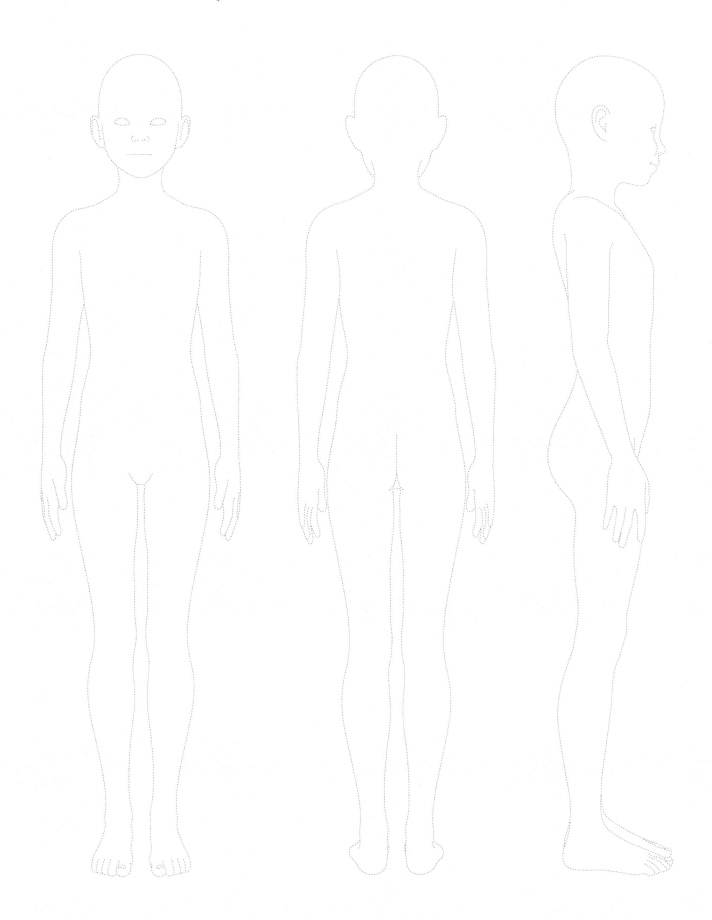

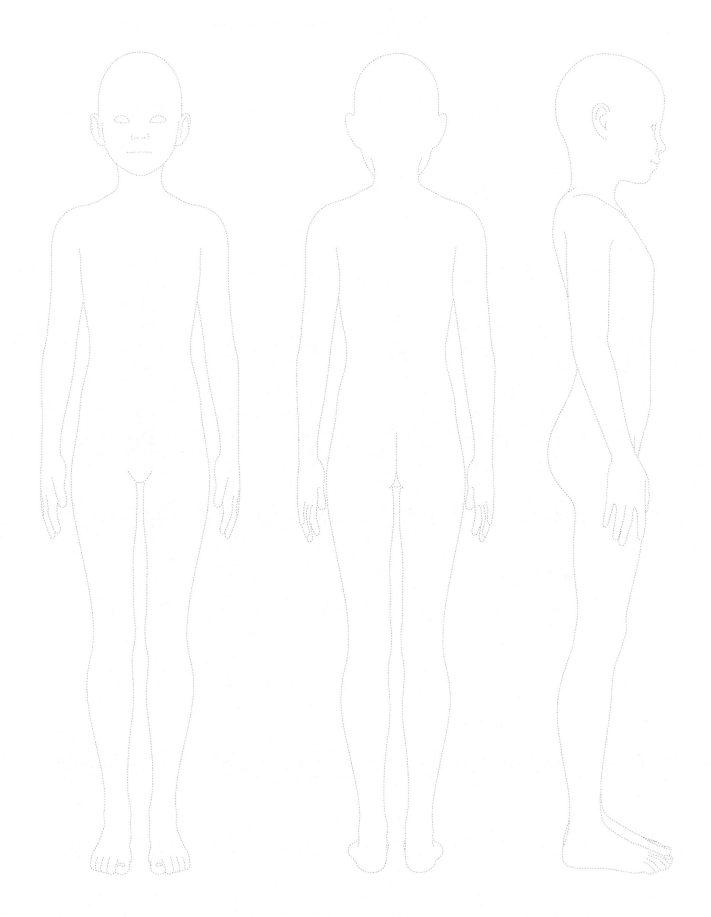

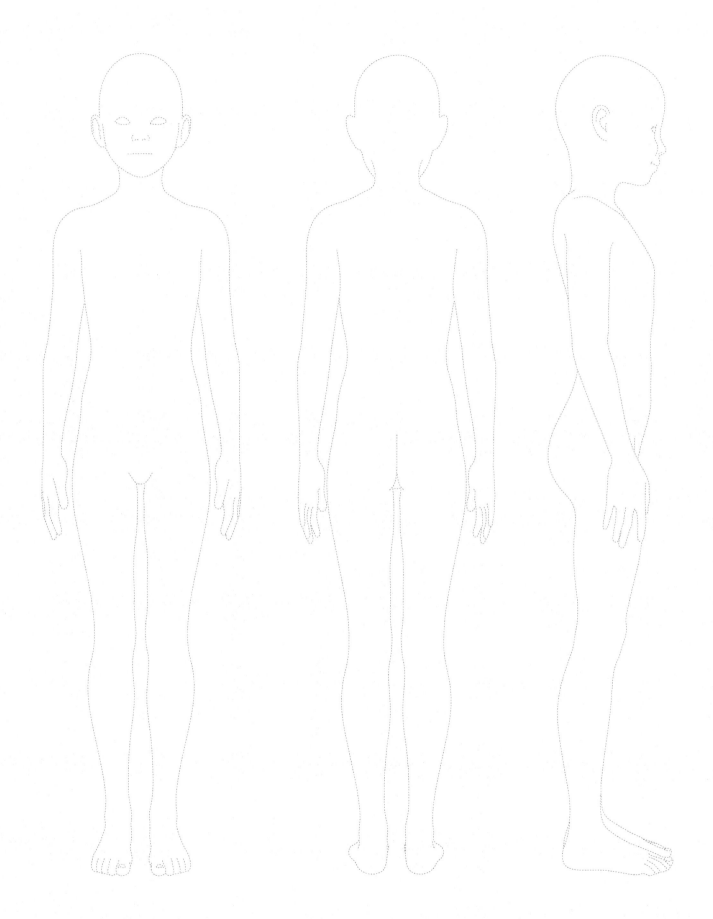

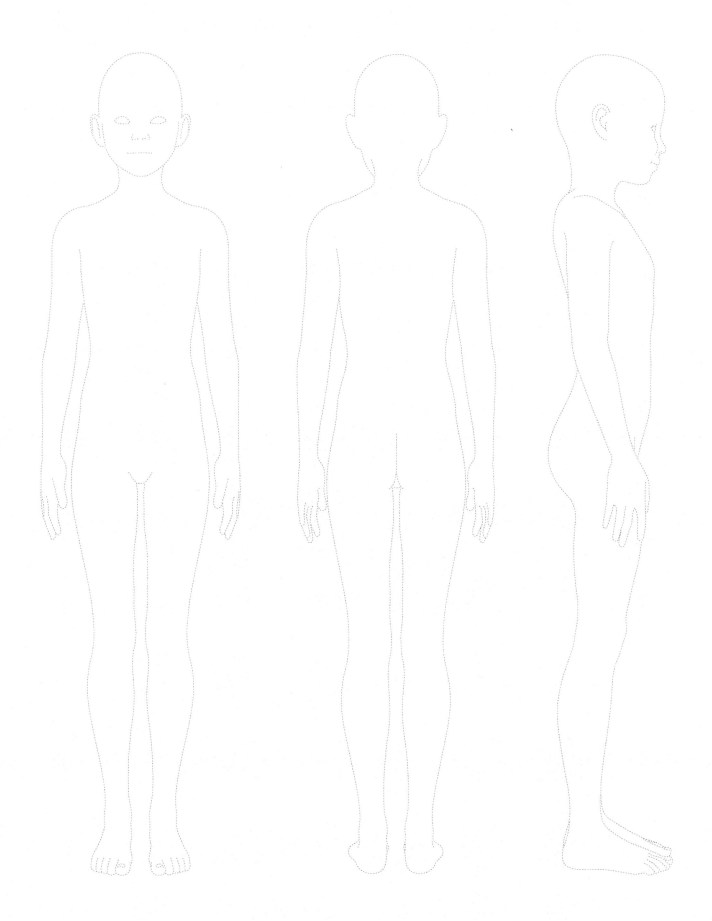

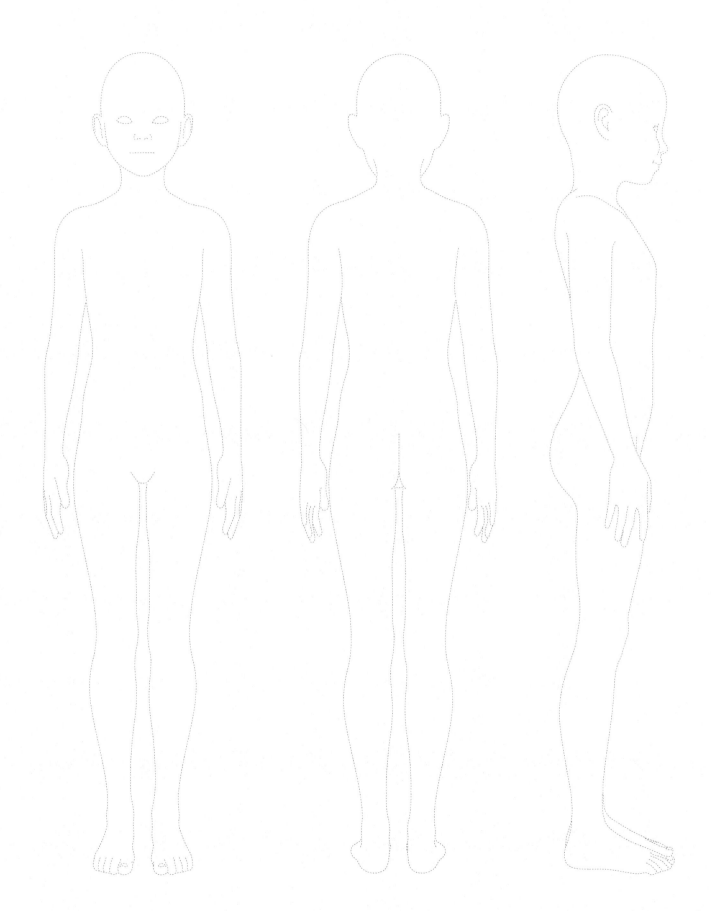

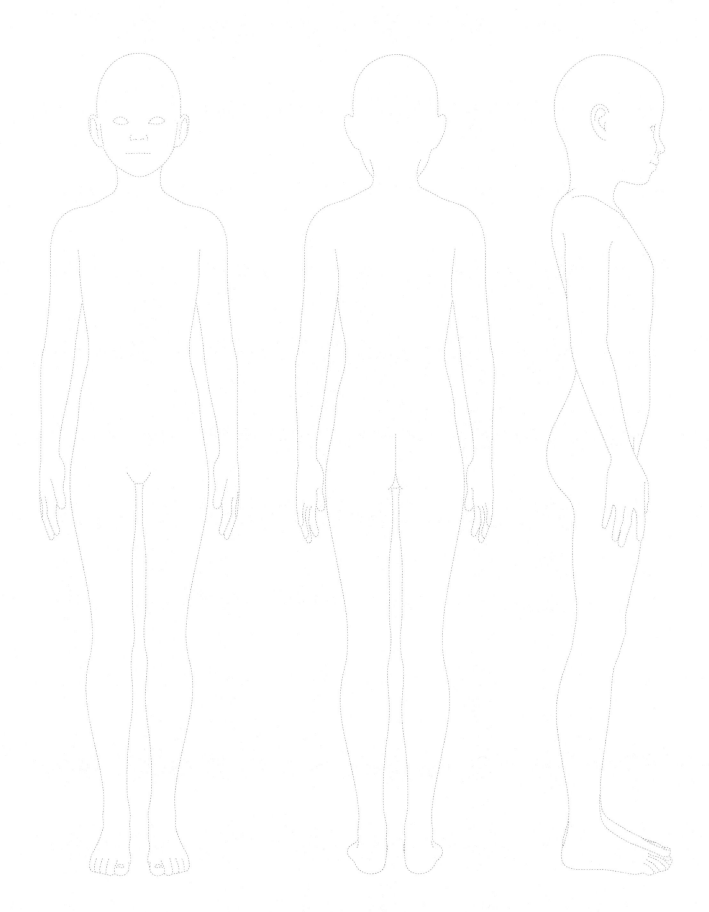

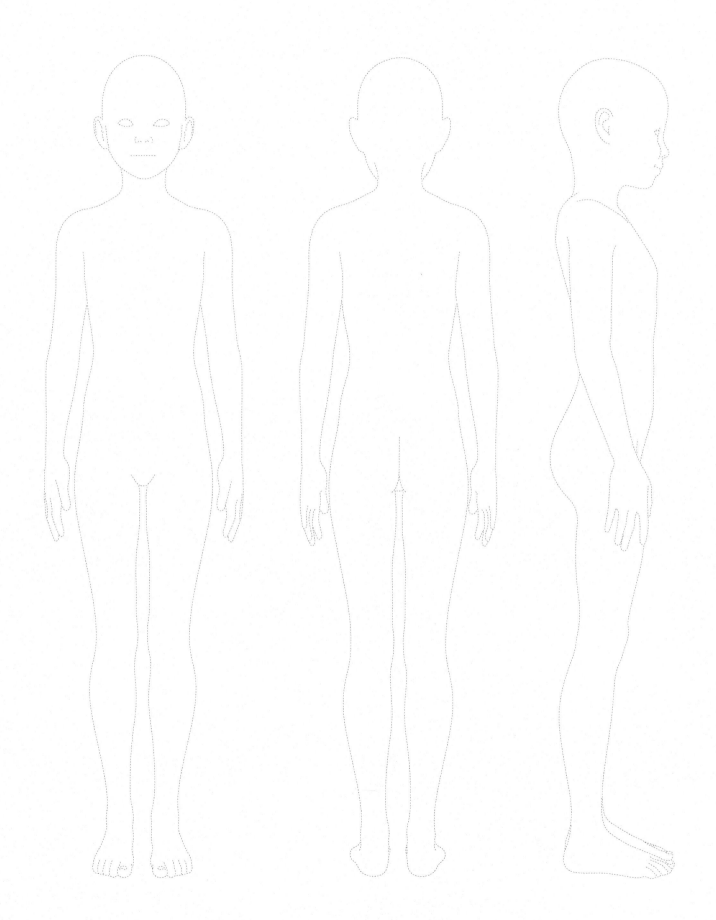

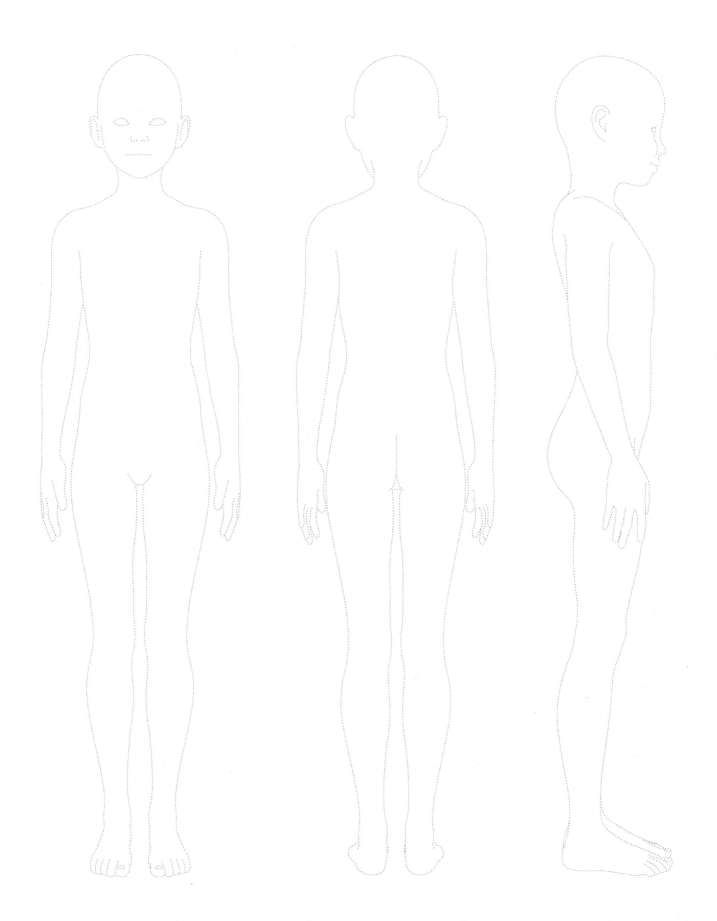

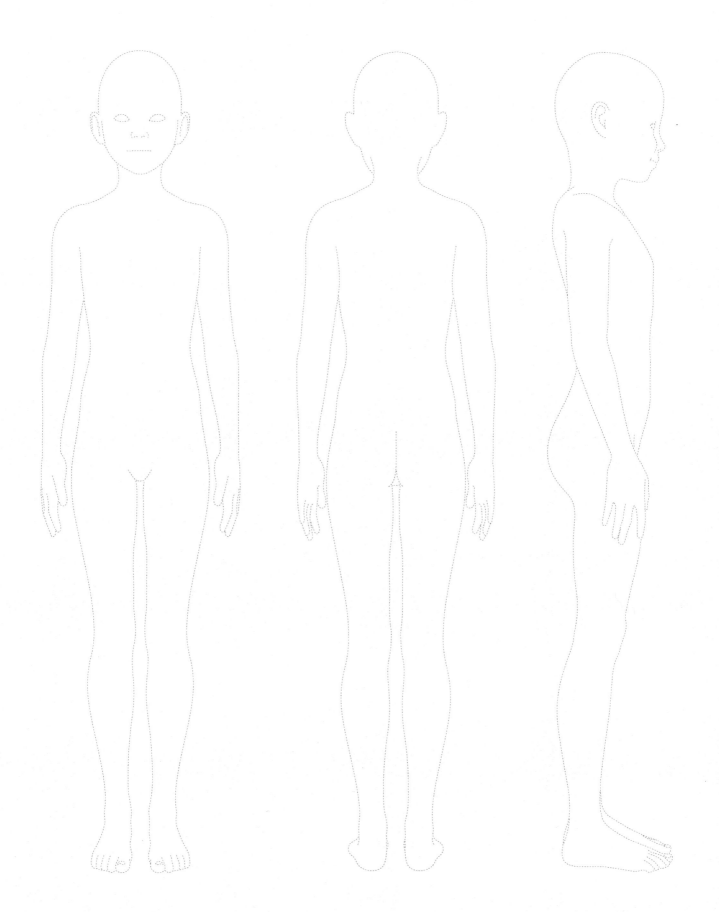

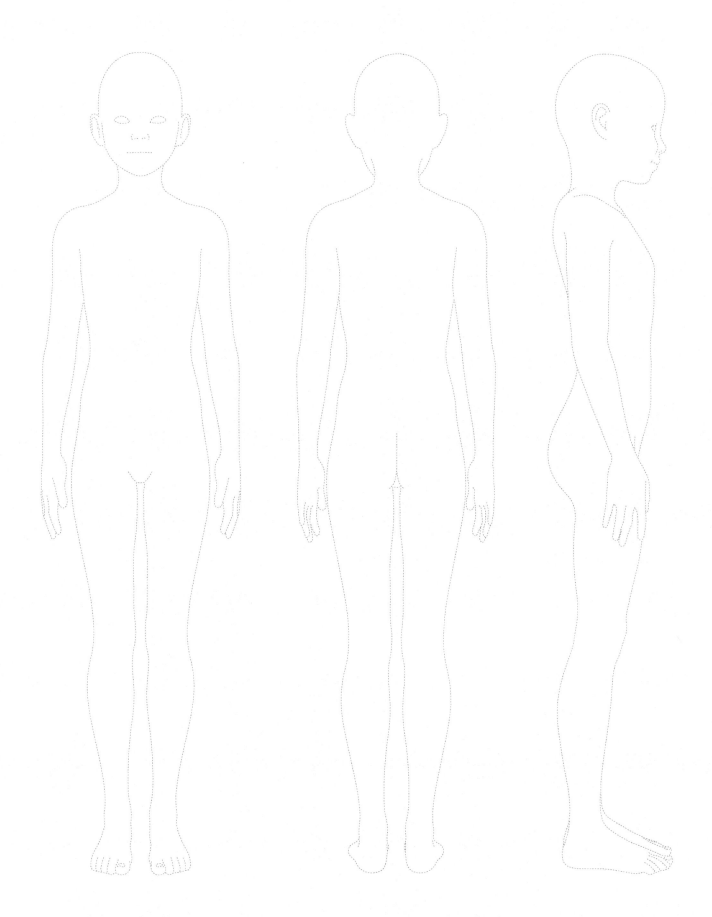

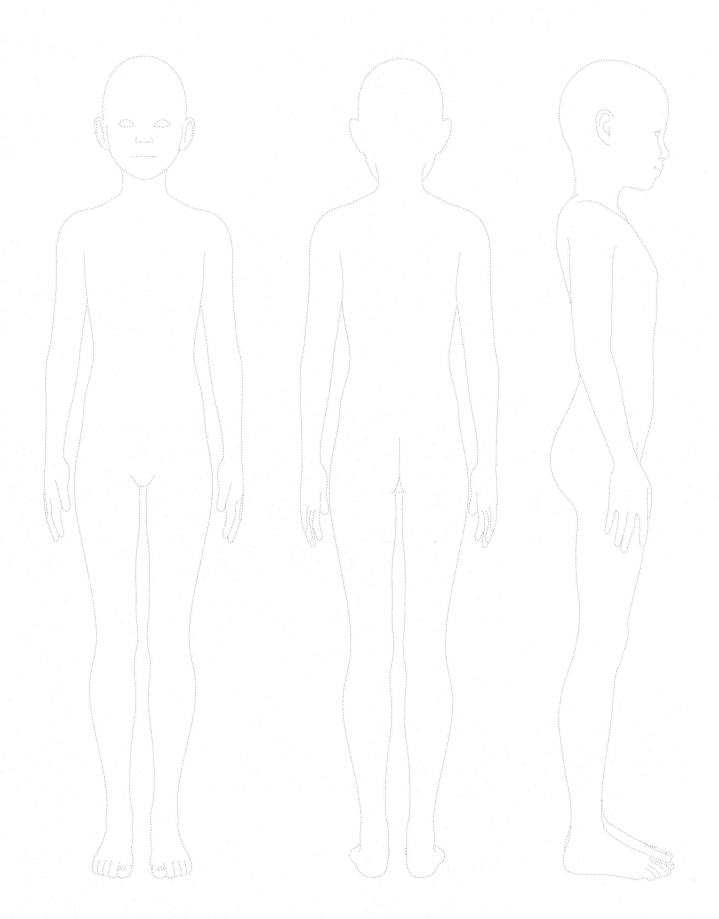

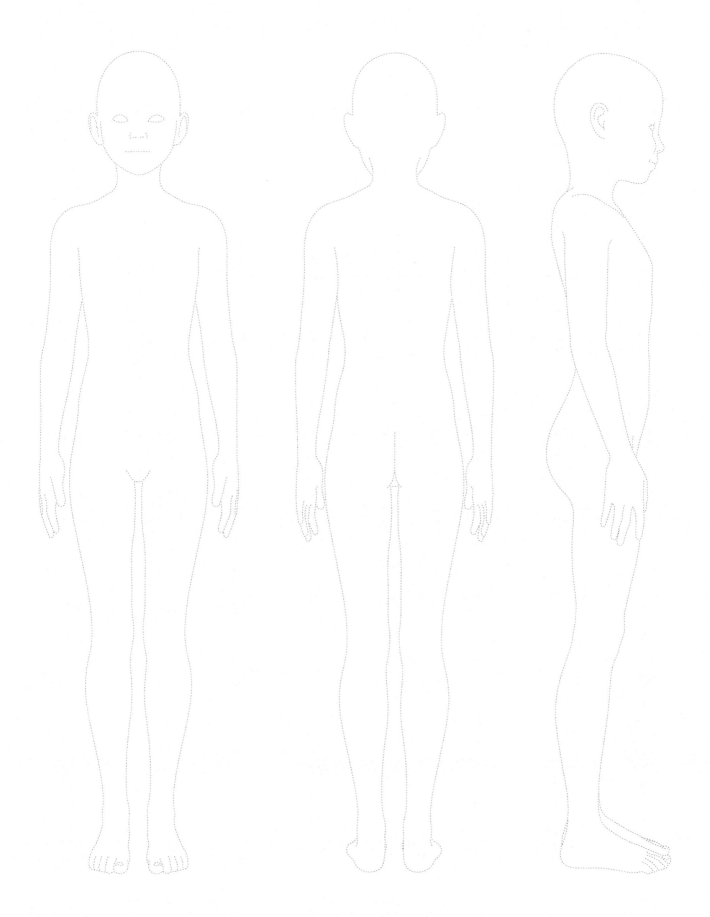

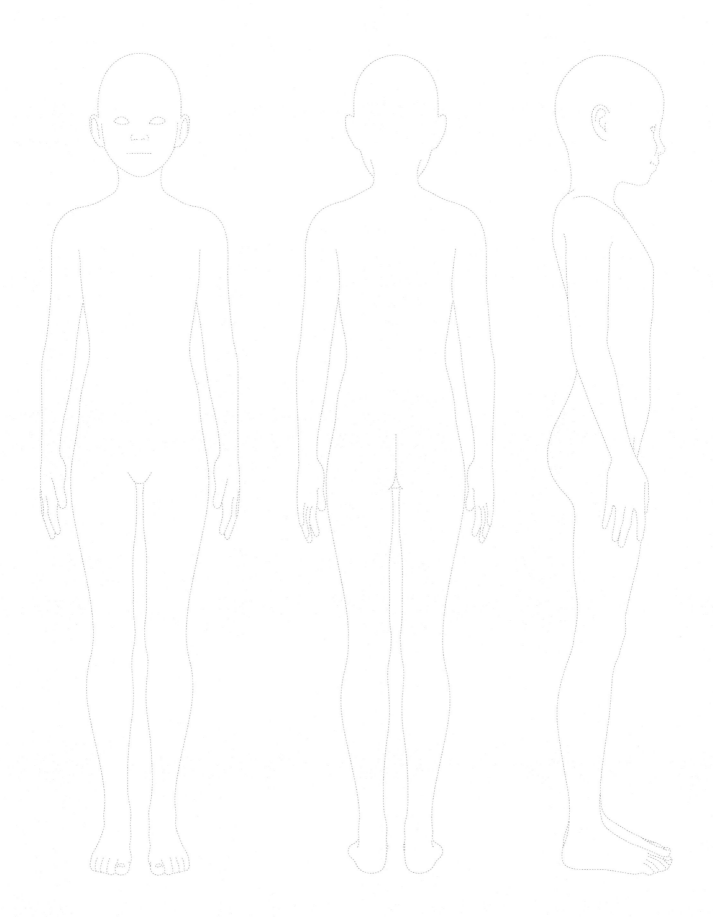

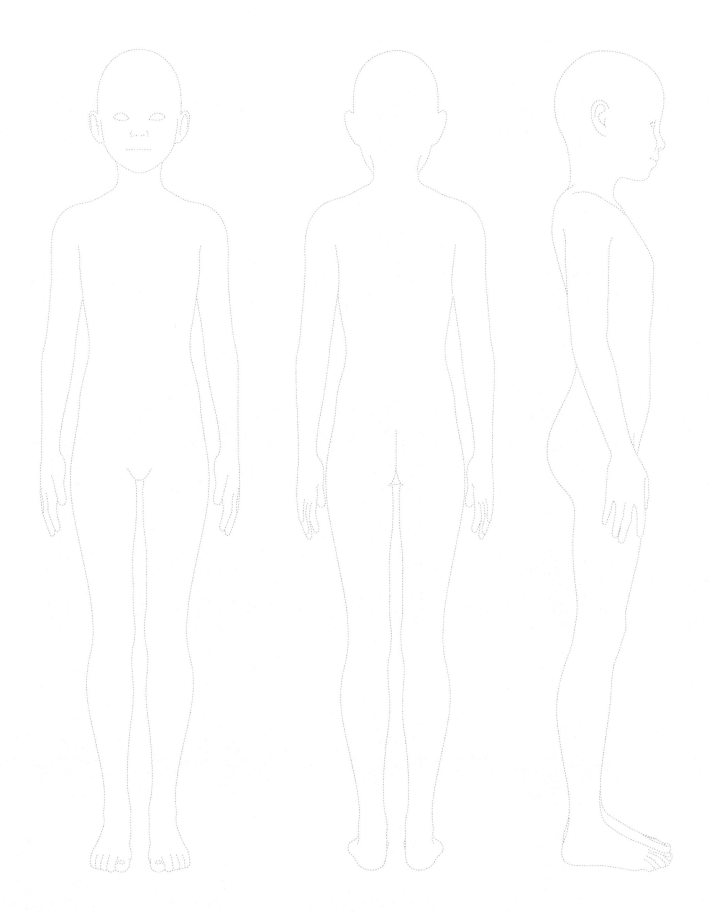

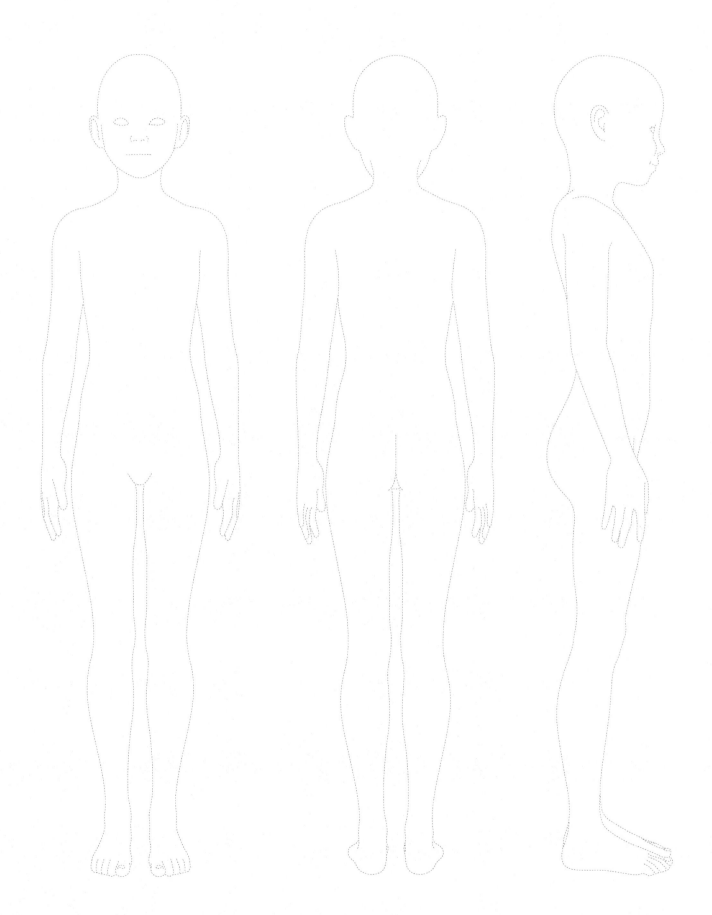

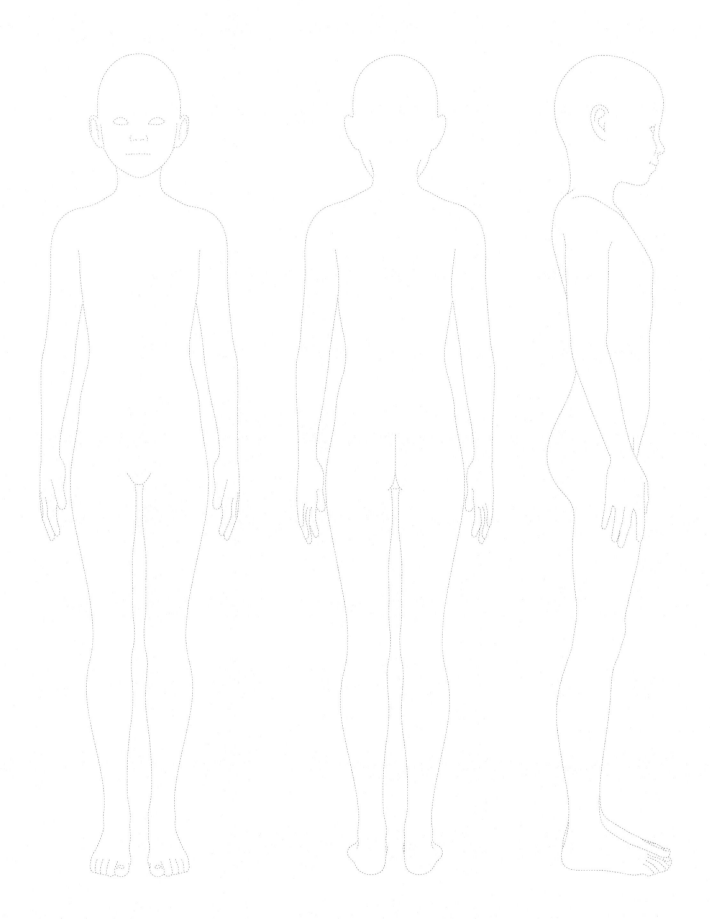

FLAT

FLAT FIGURE OUTLINE

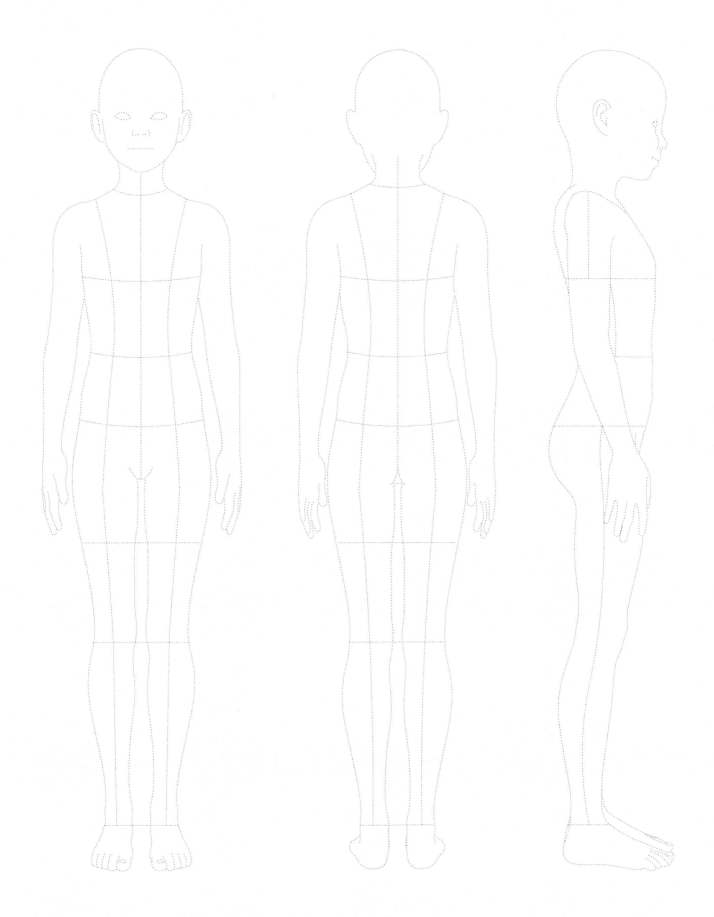

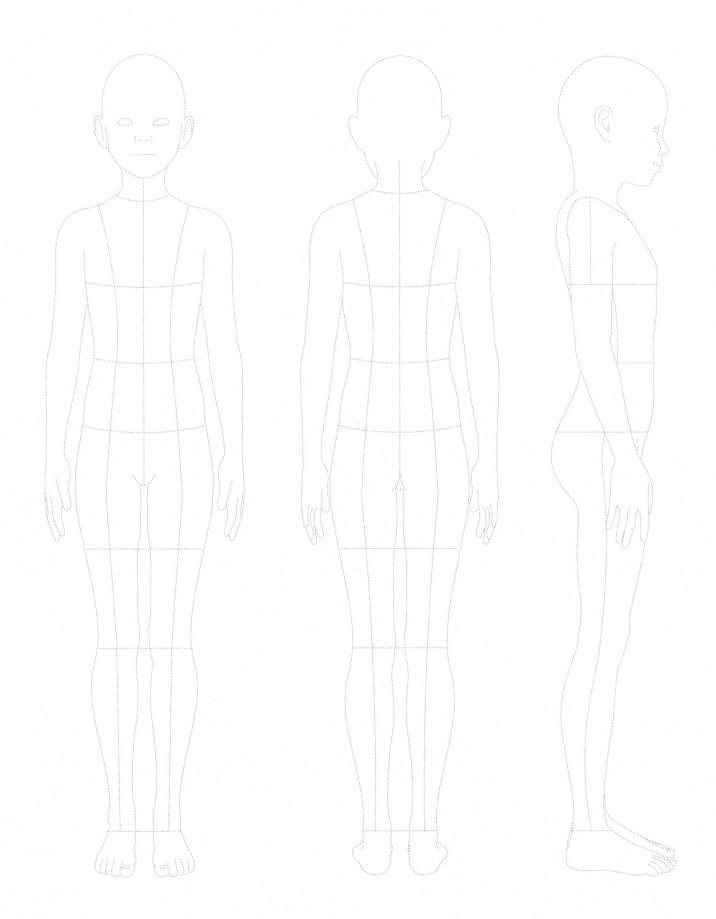

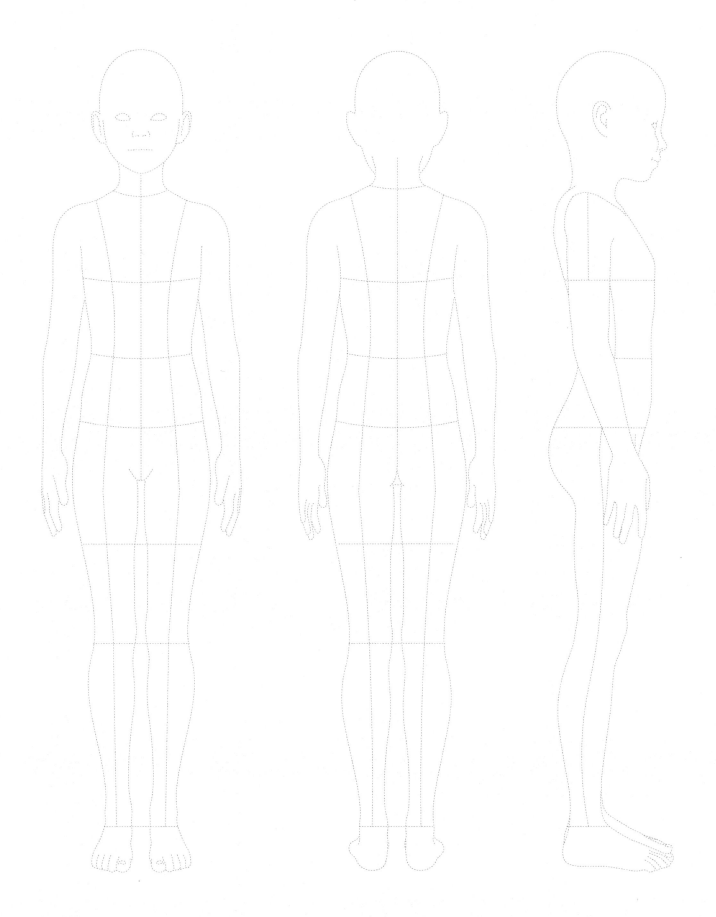

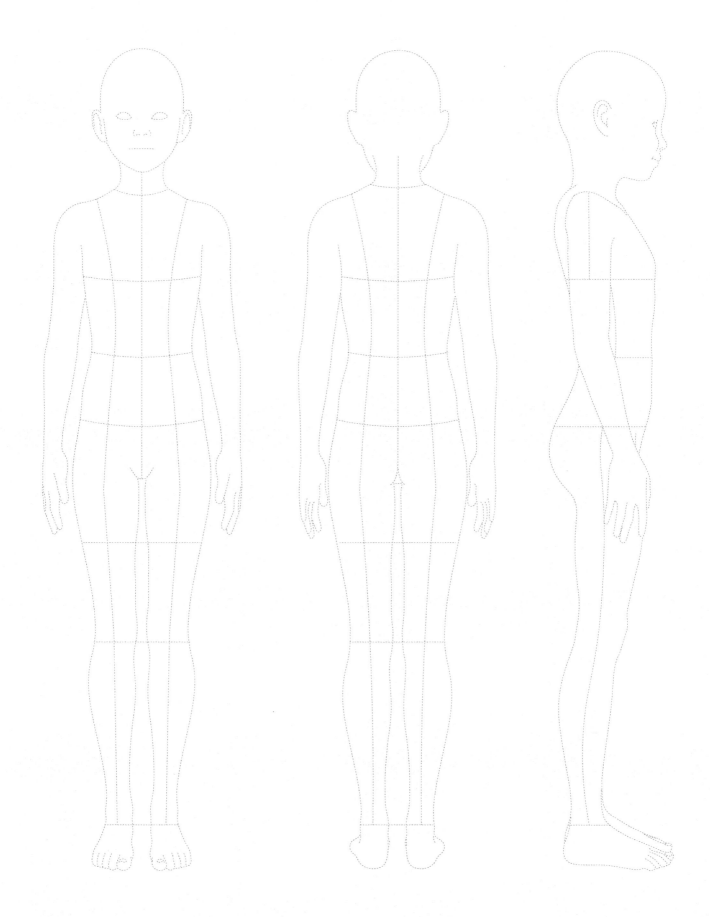

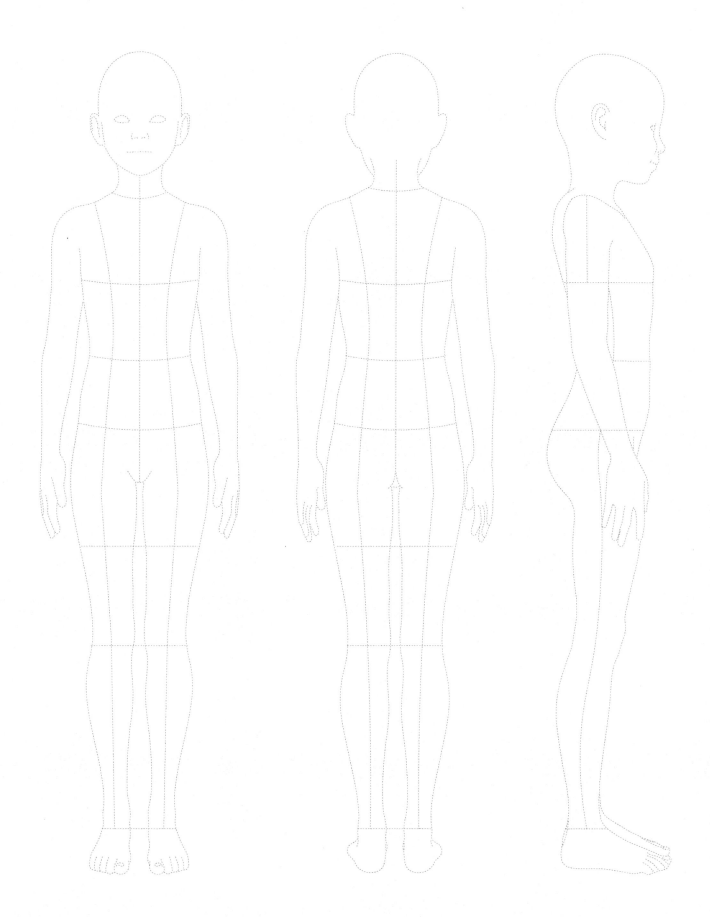

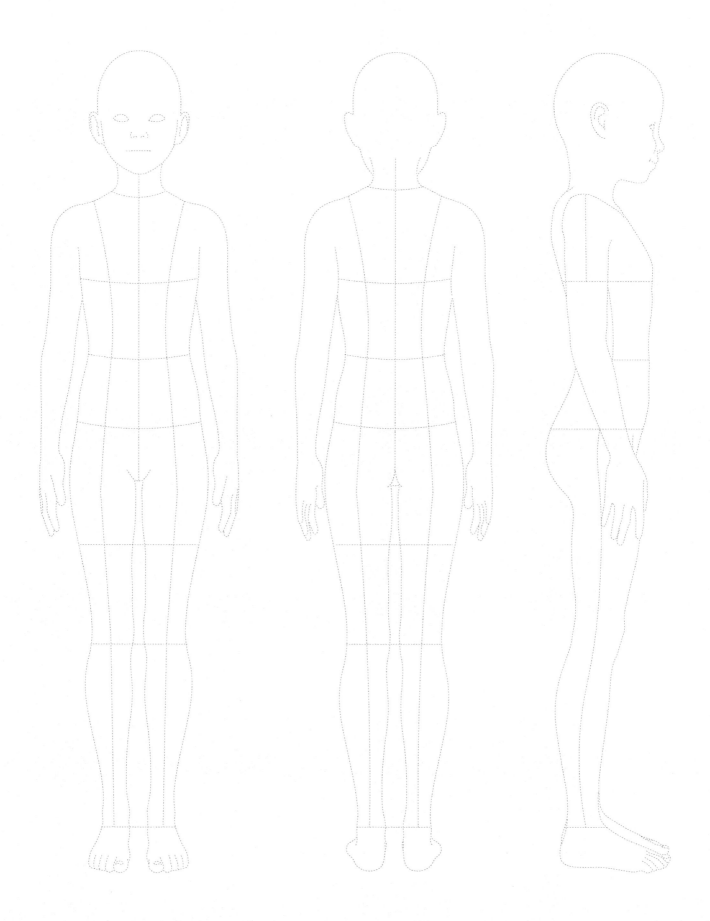

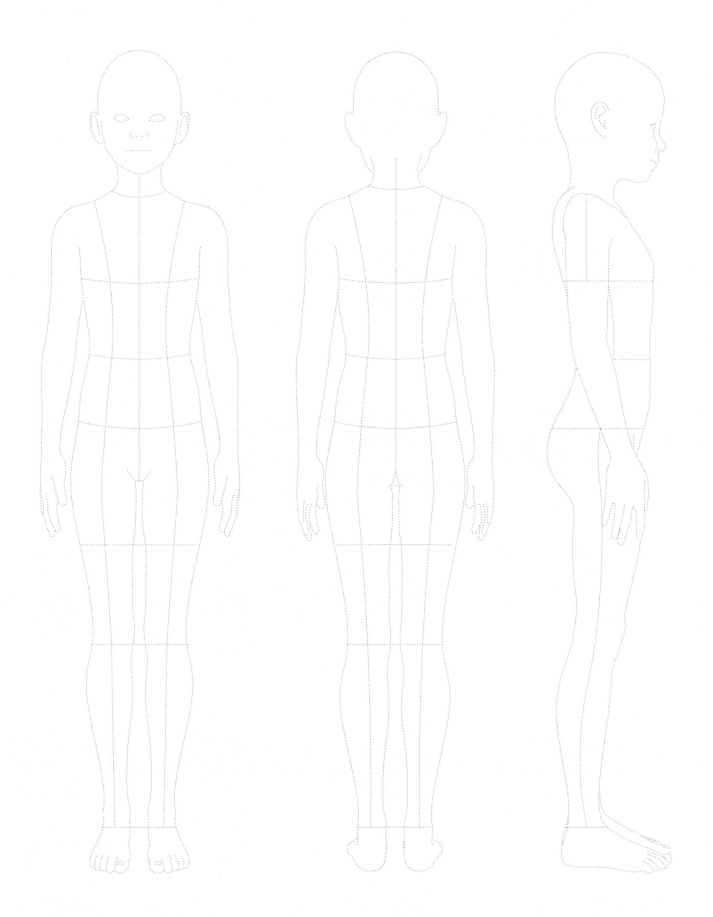

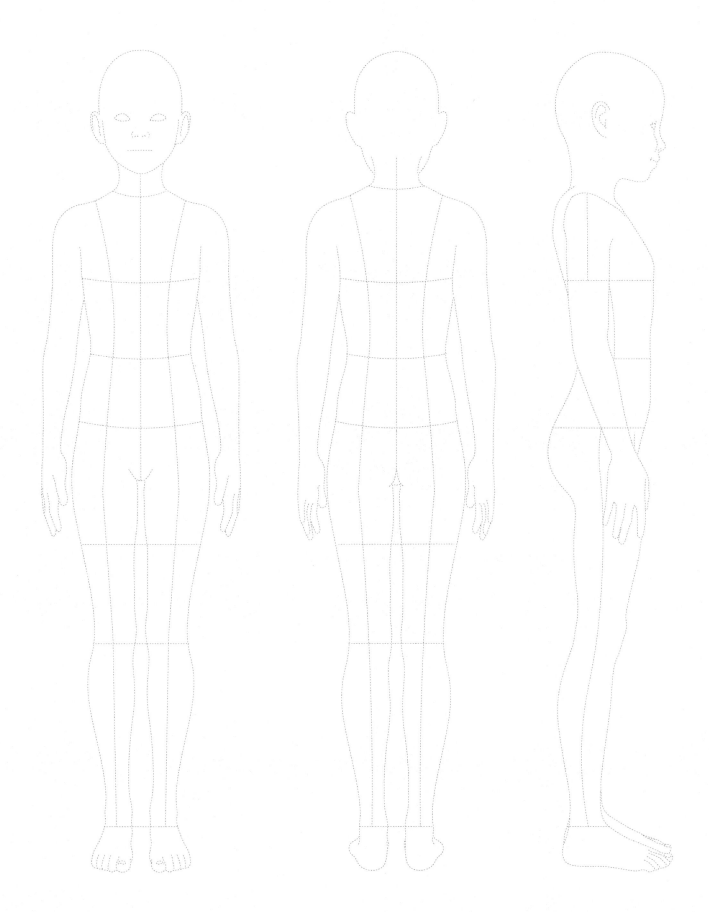

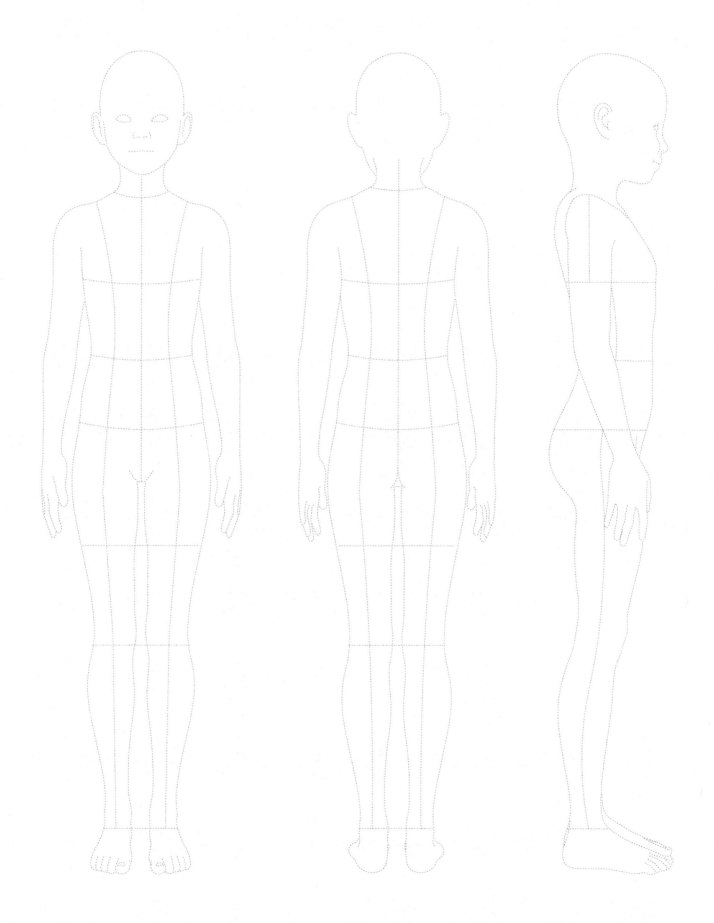

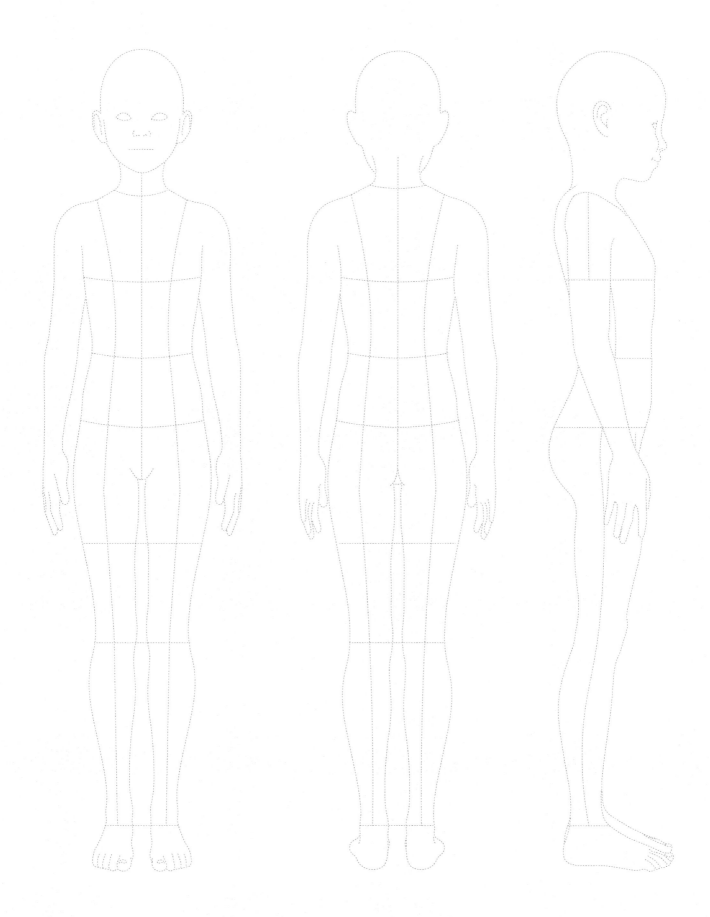

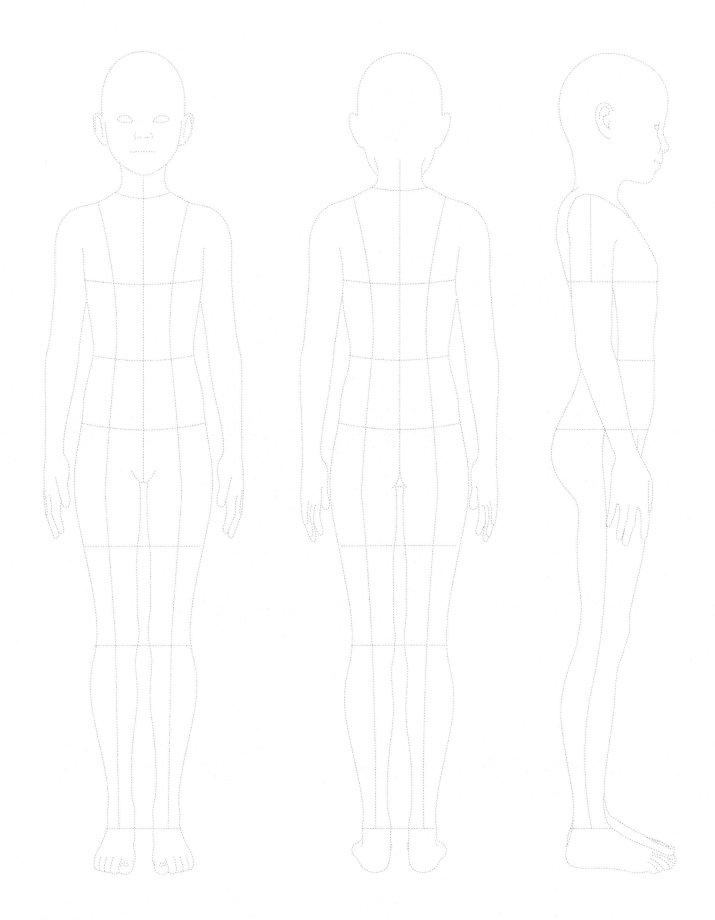

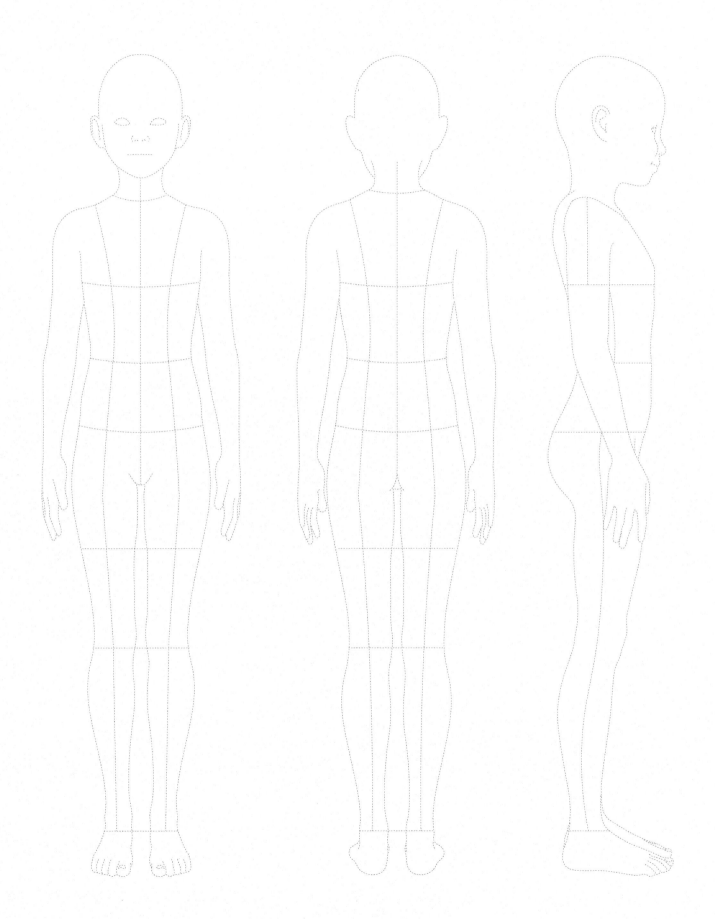

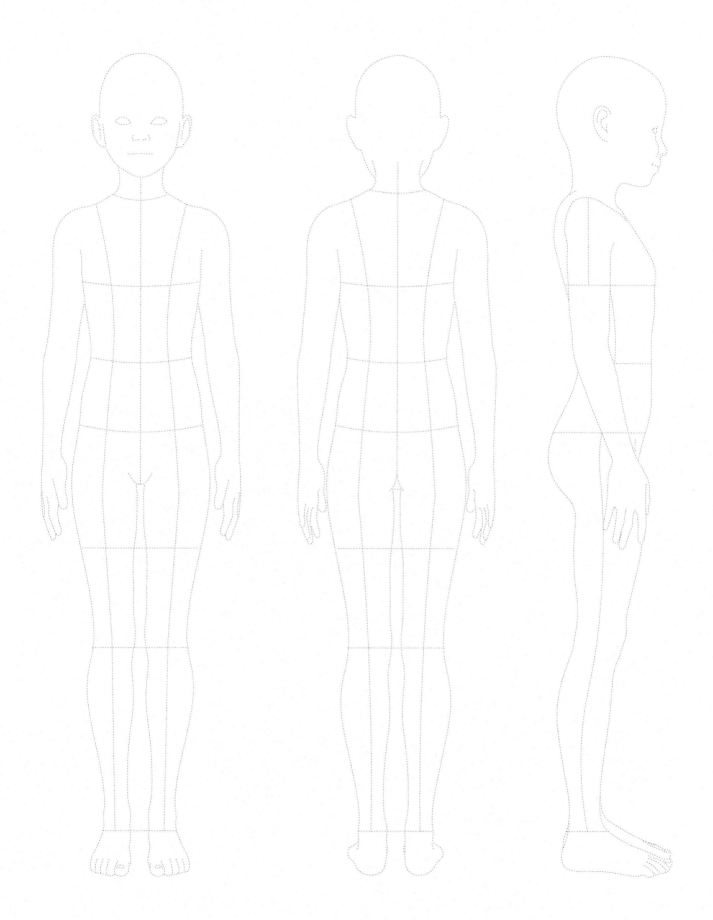

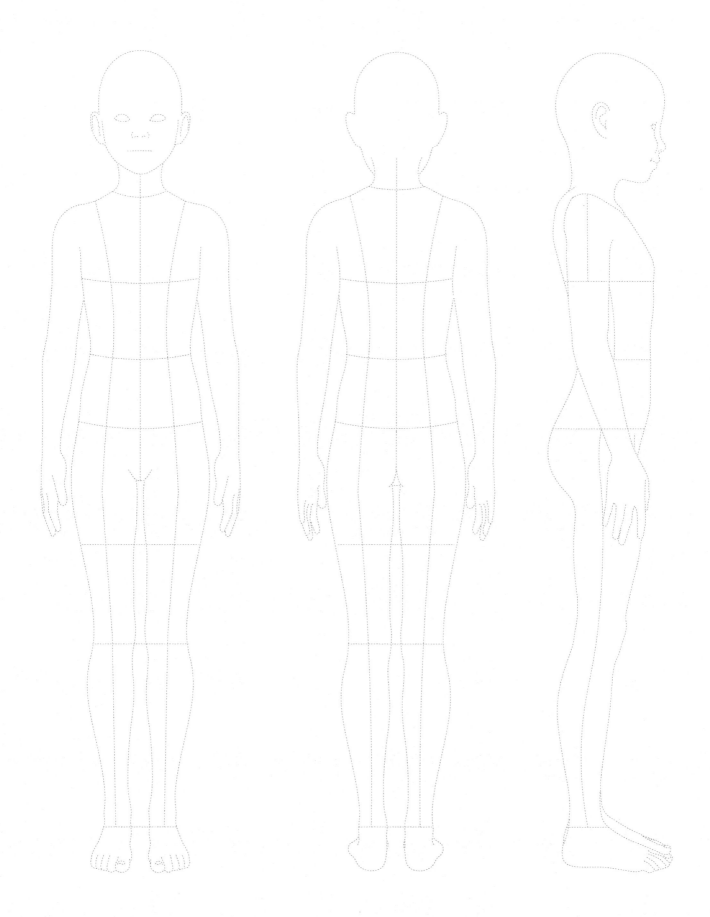

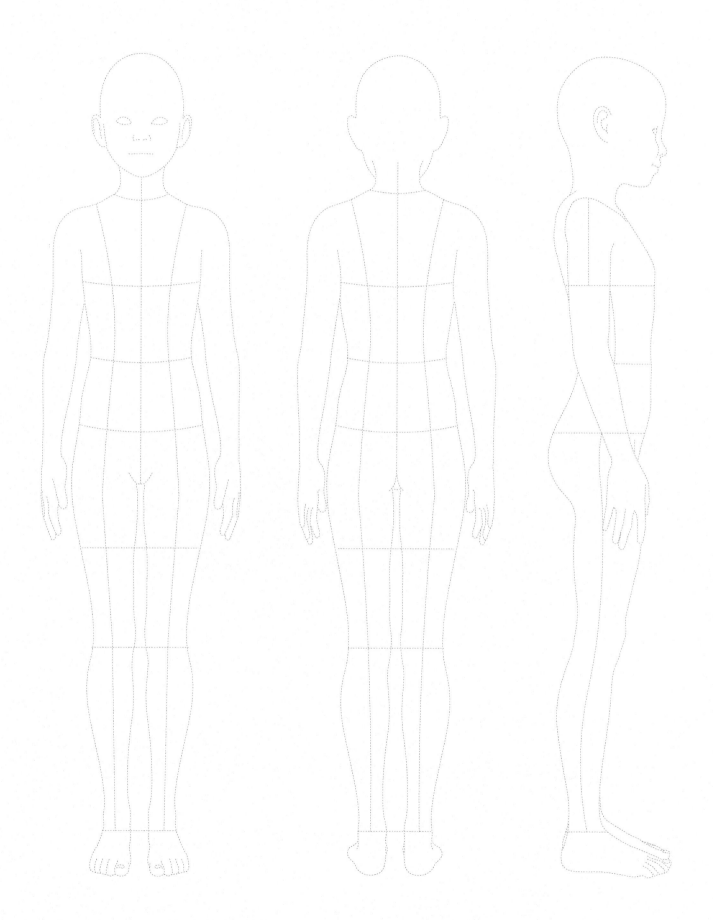

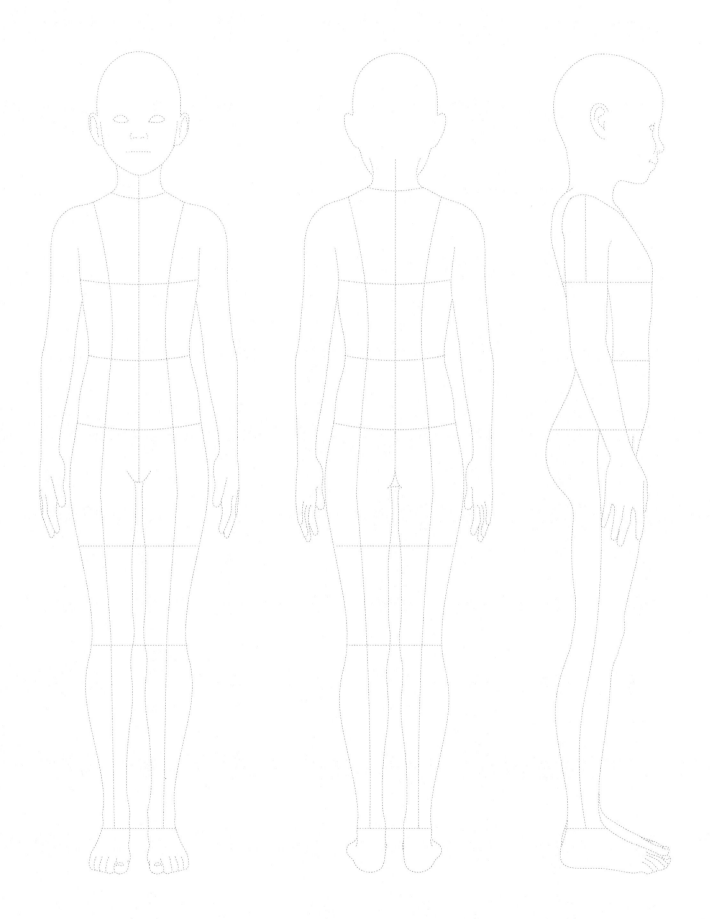

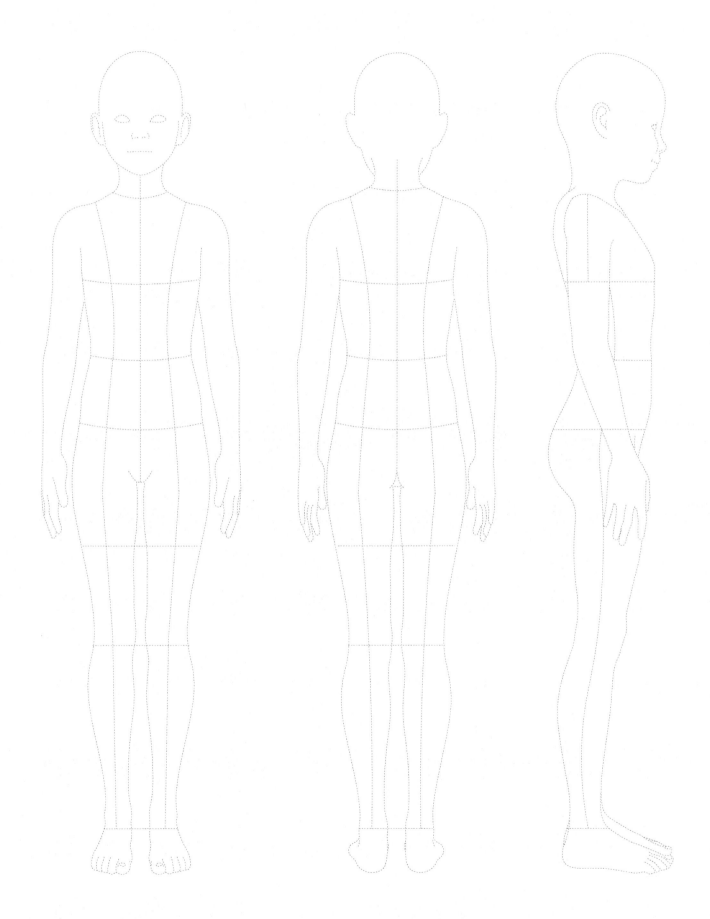

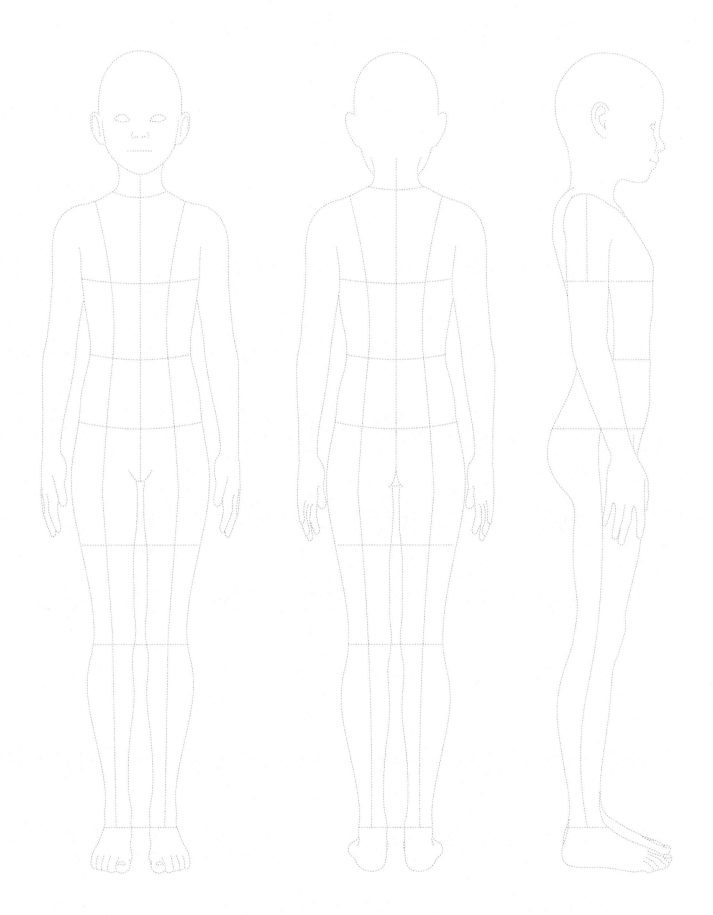

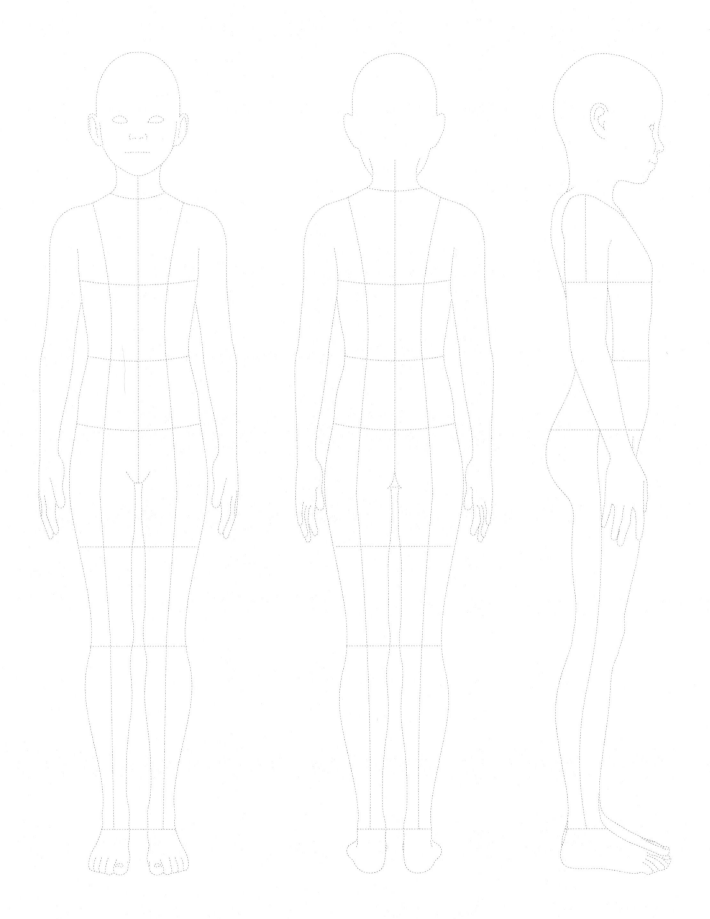

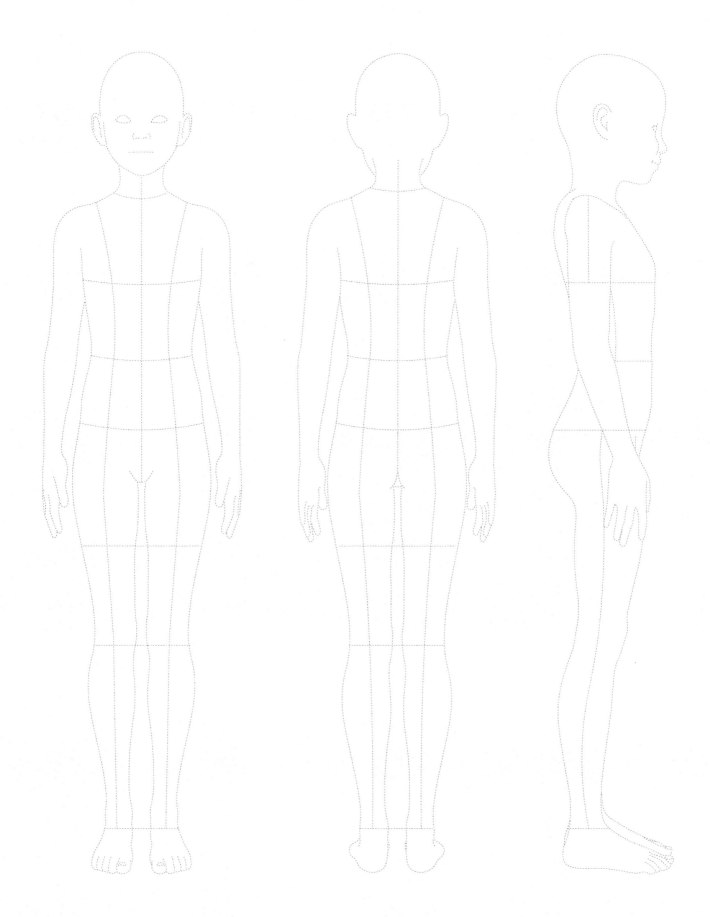

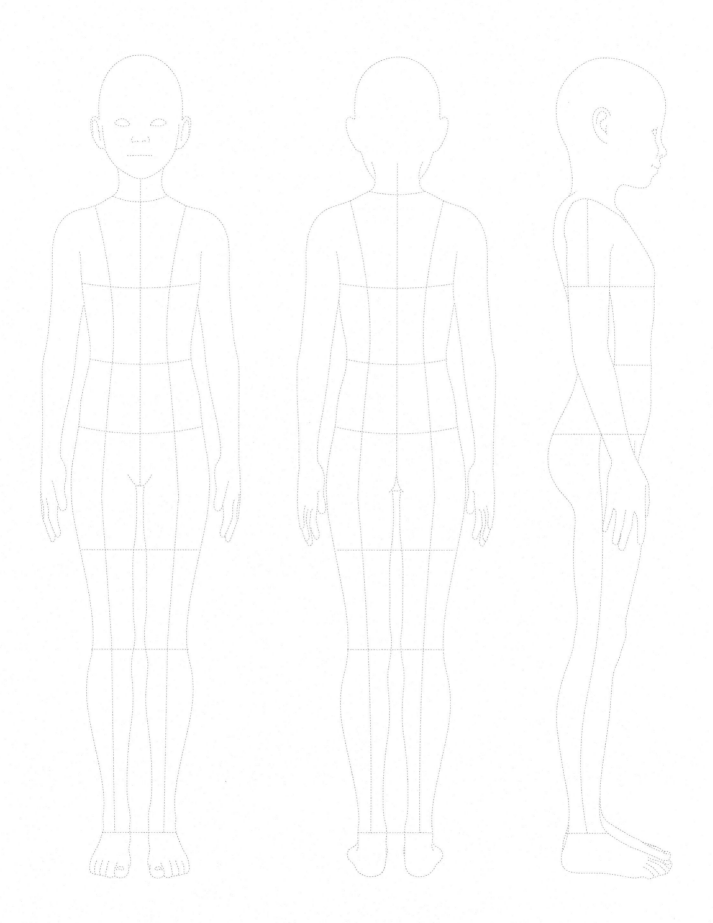

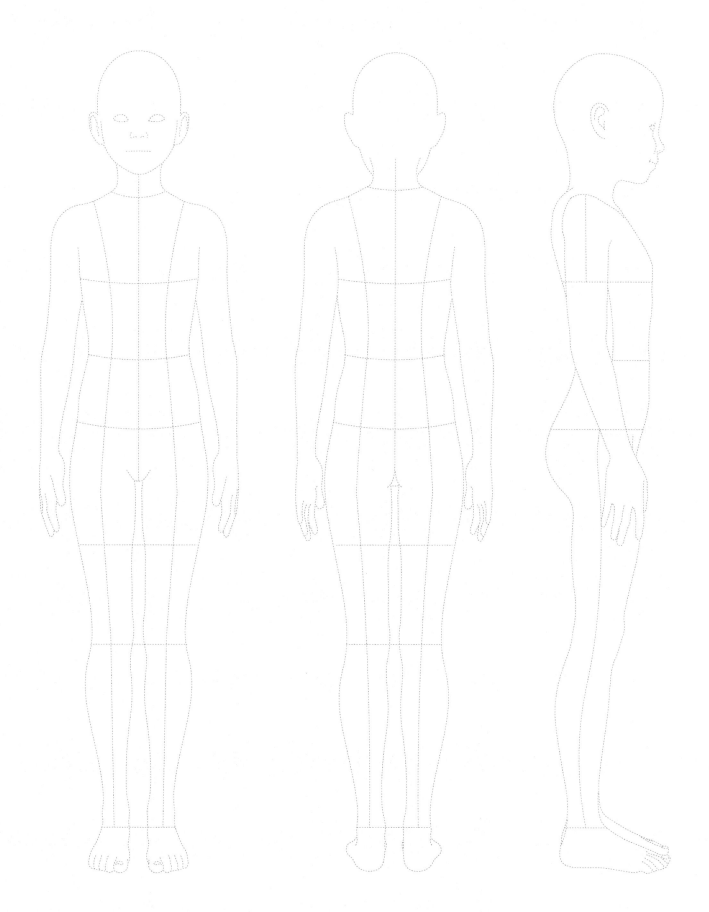

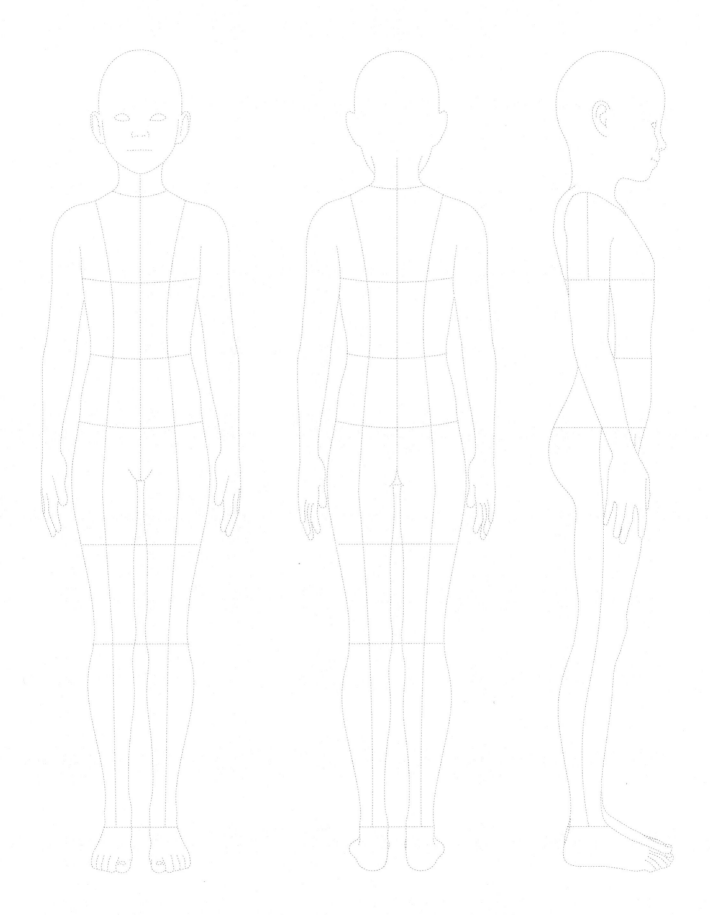

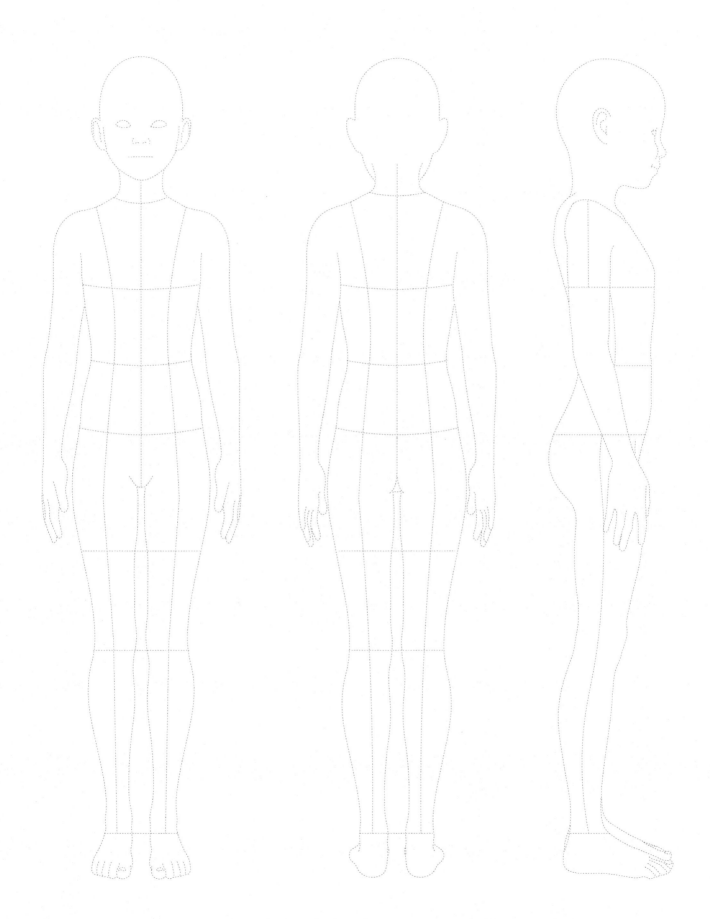

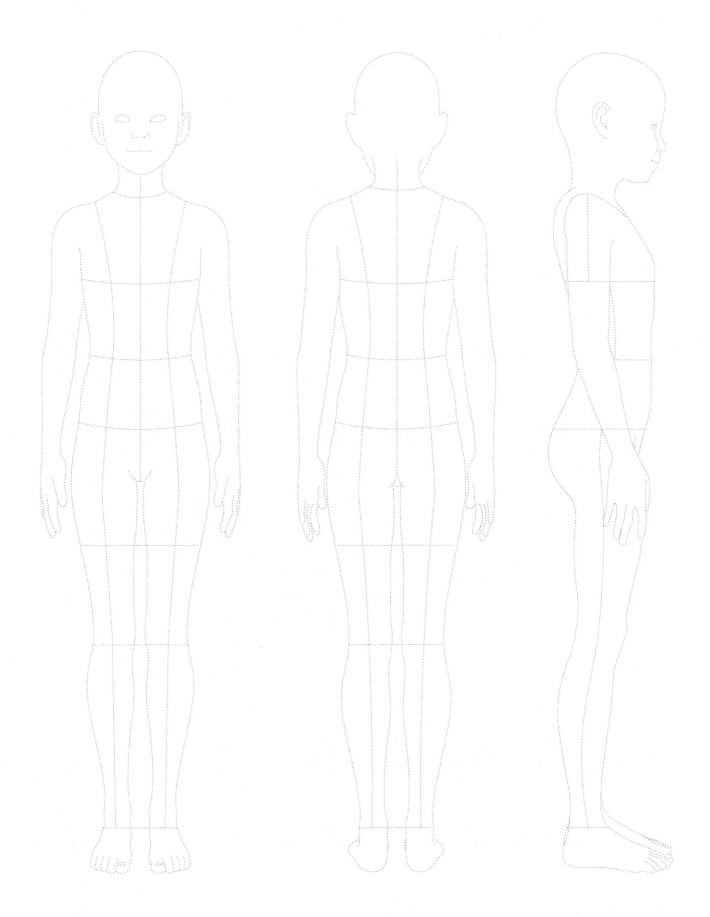

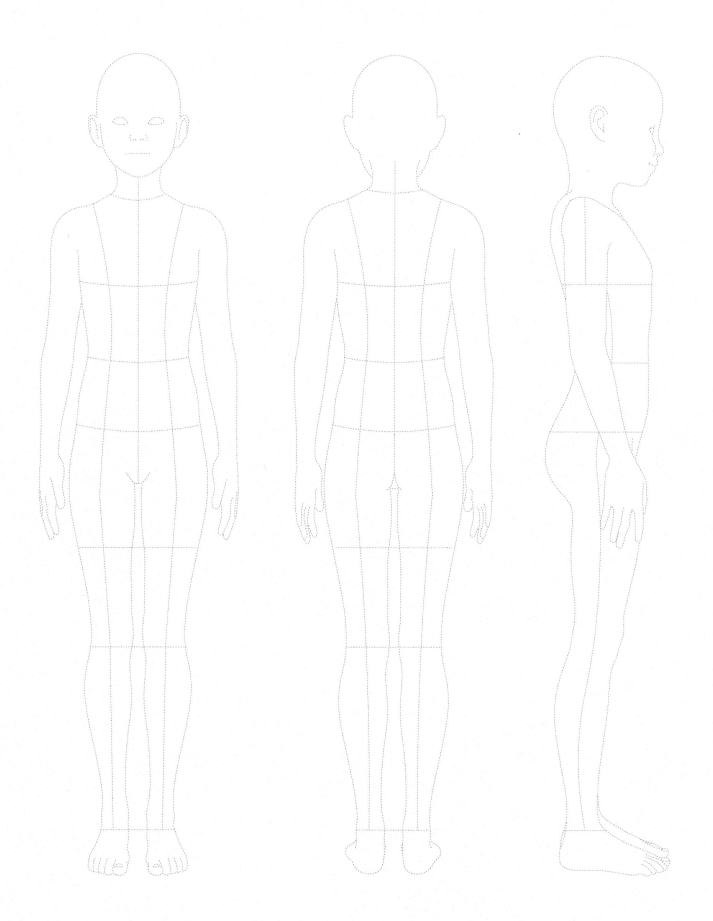

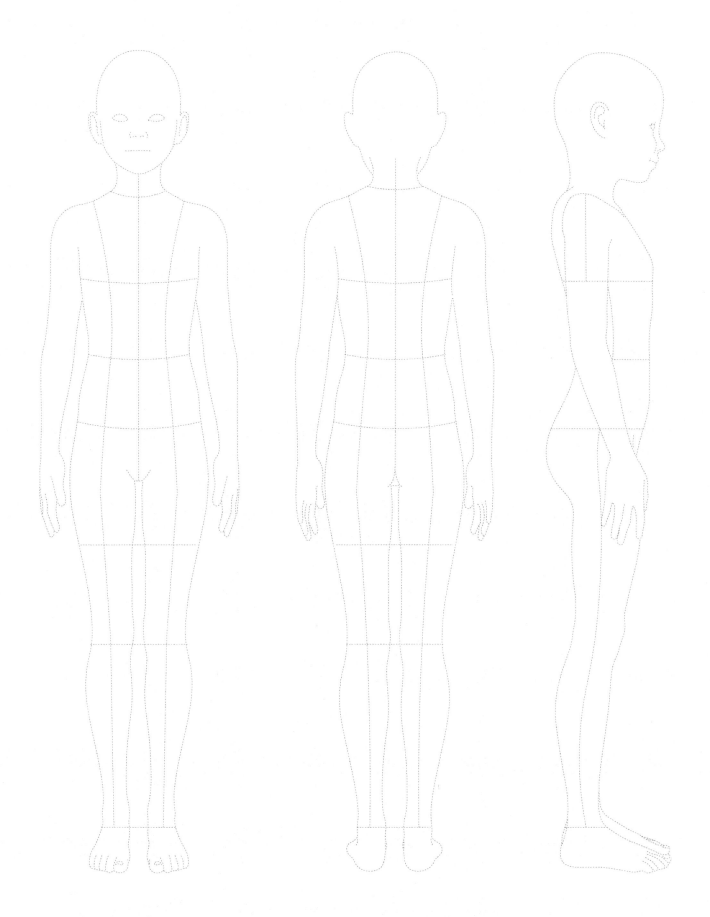

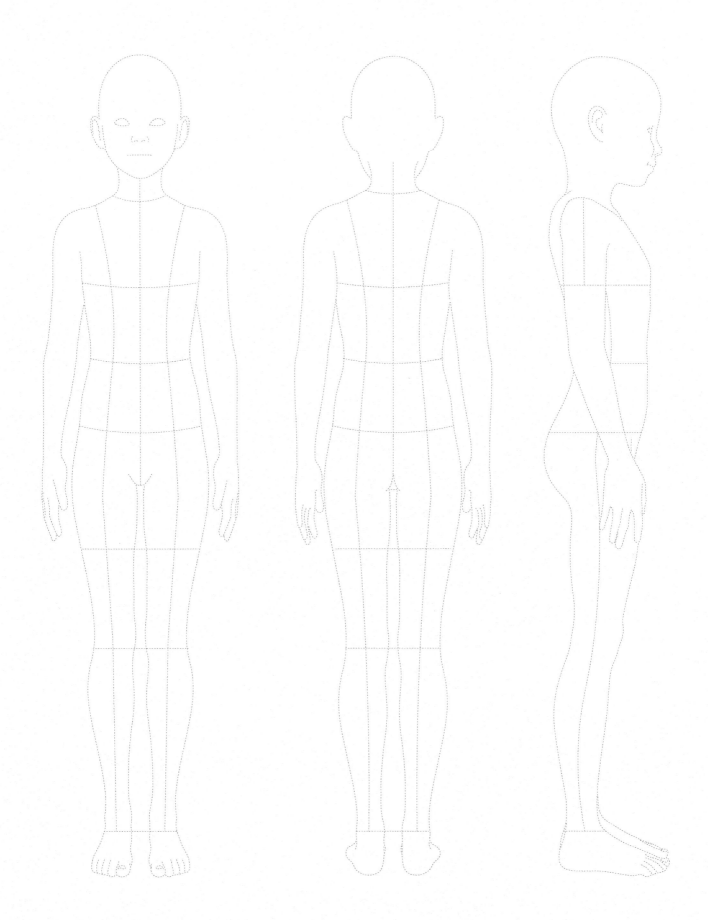

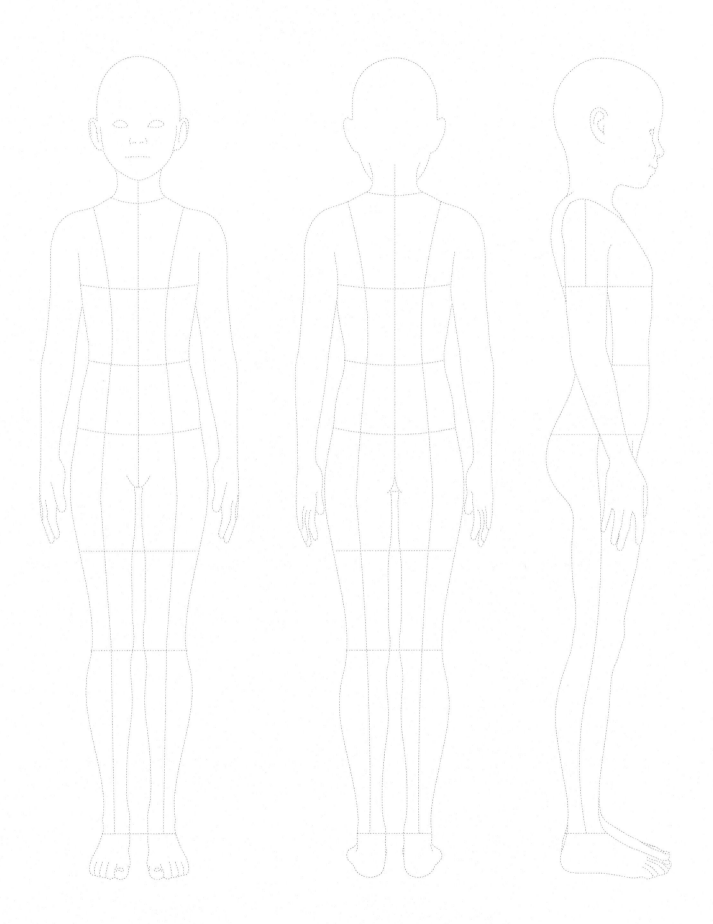

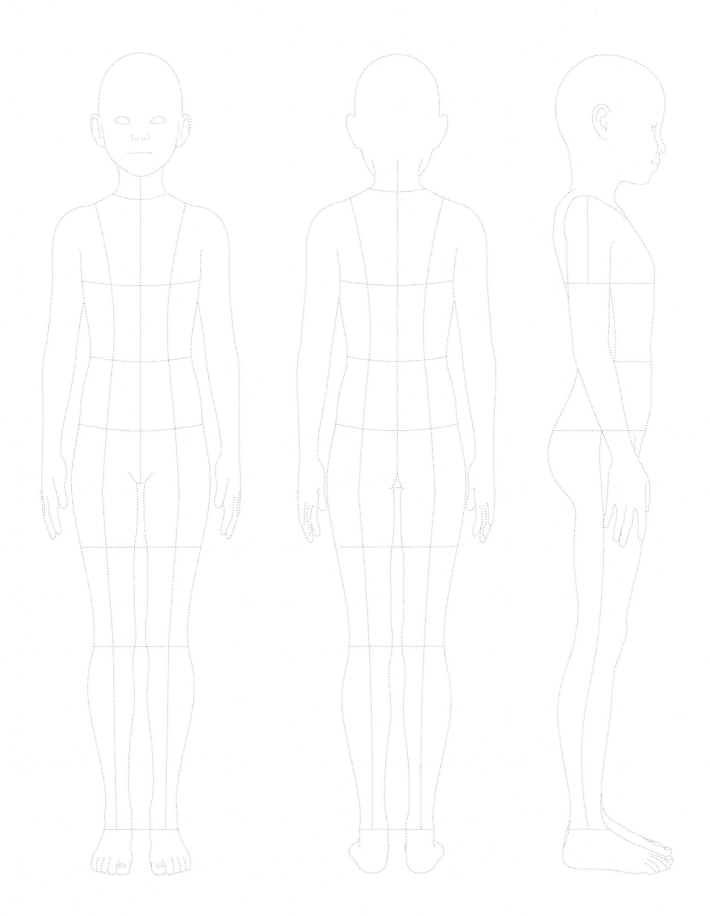

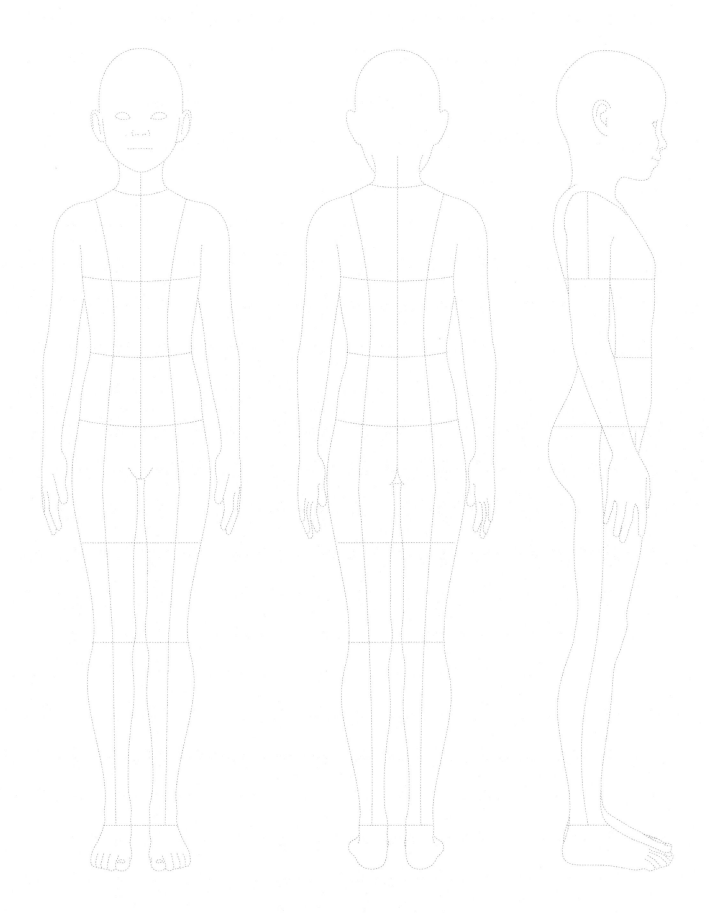

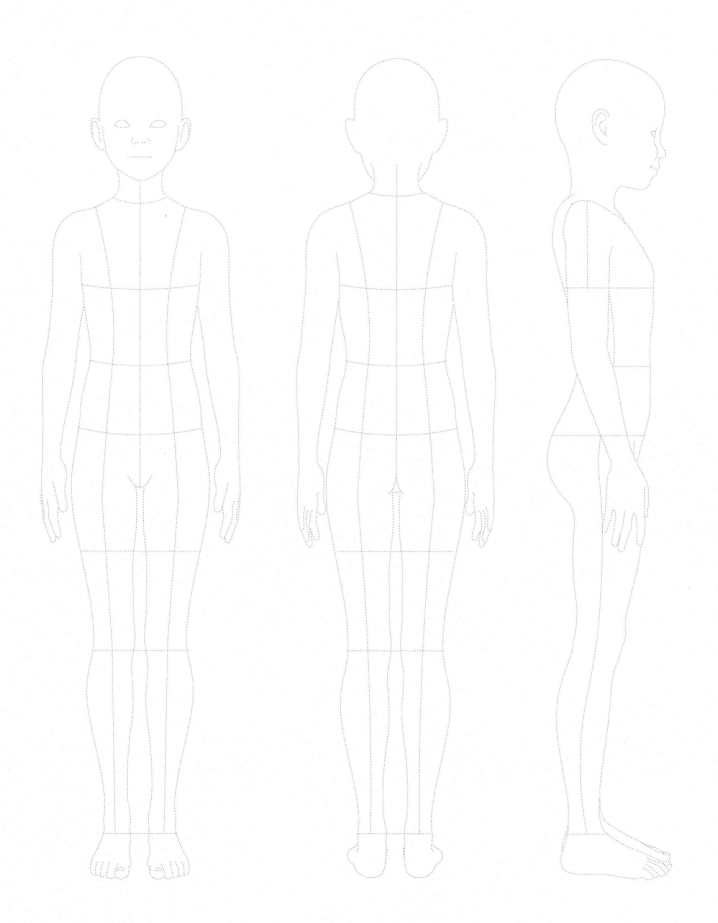

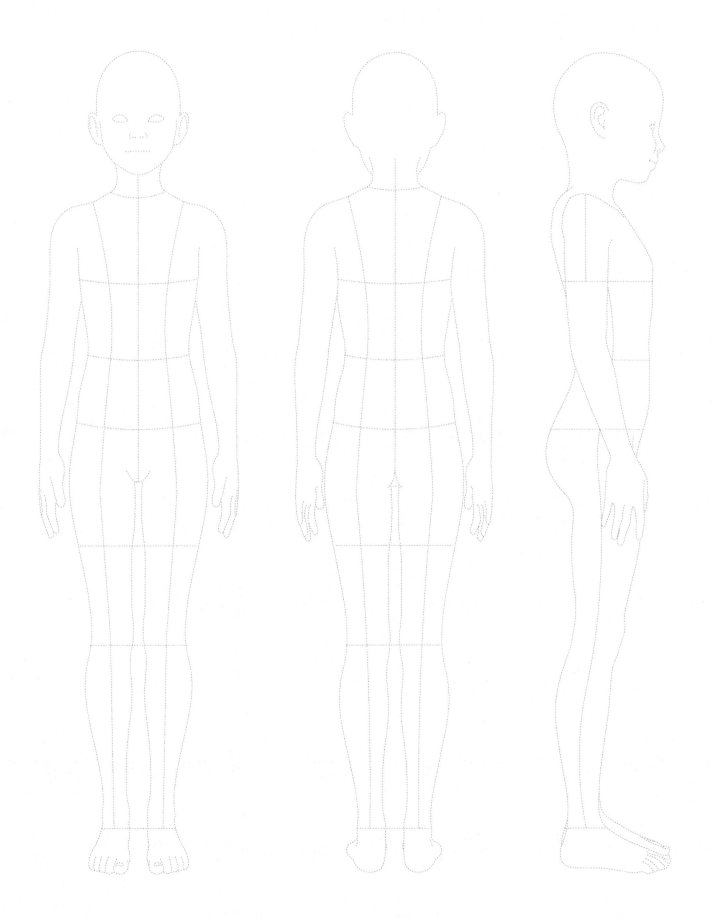

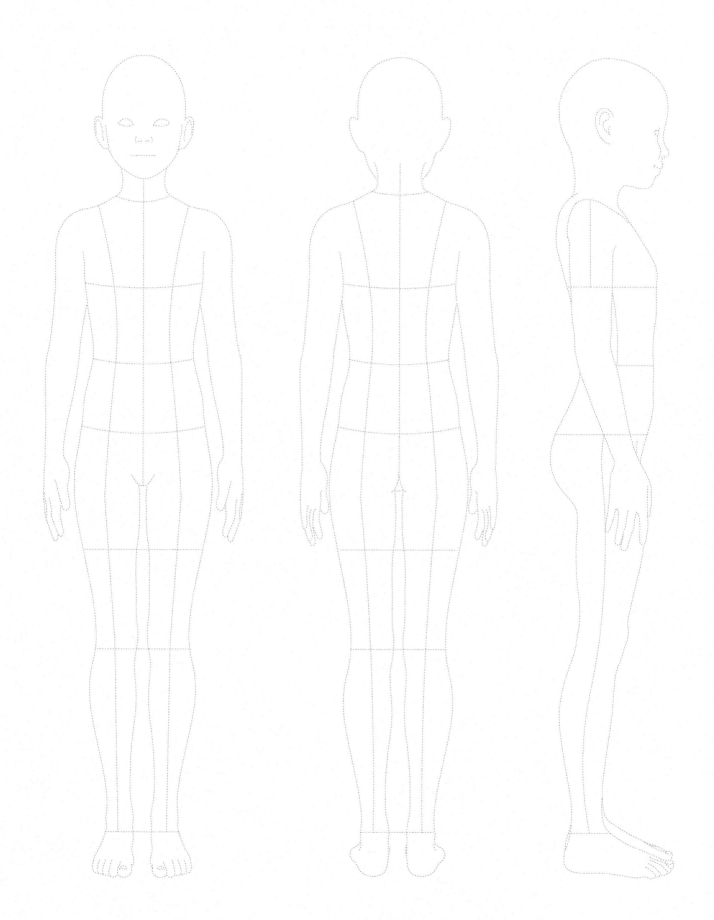

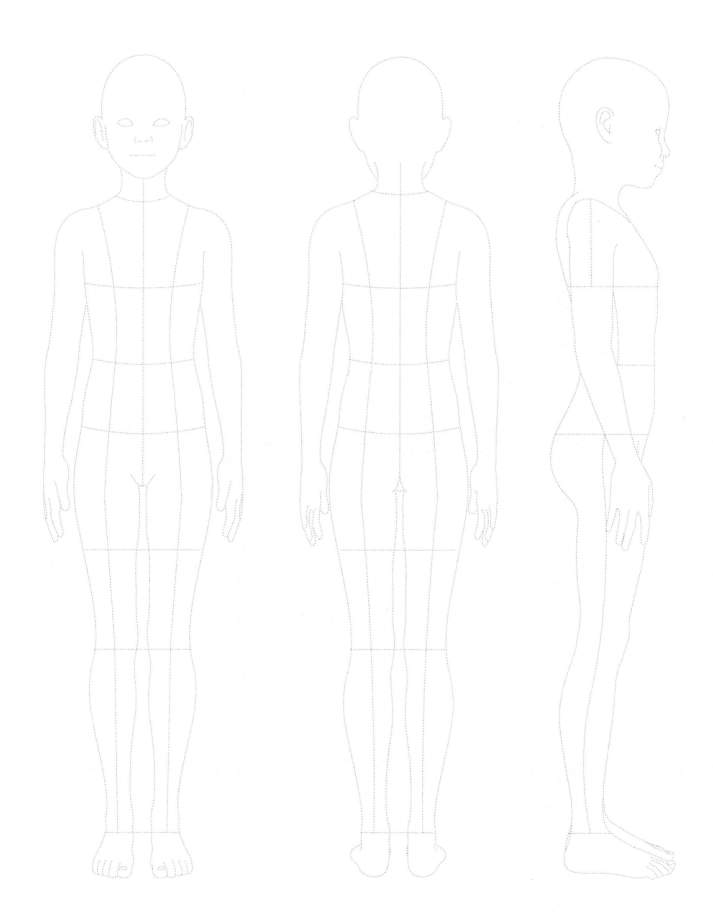

KIDS POSES

KIDS POSES OUTLINE

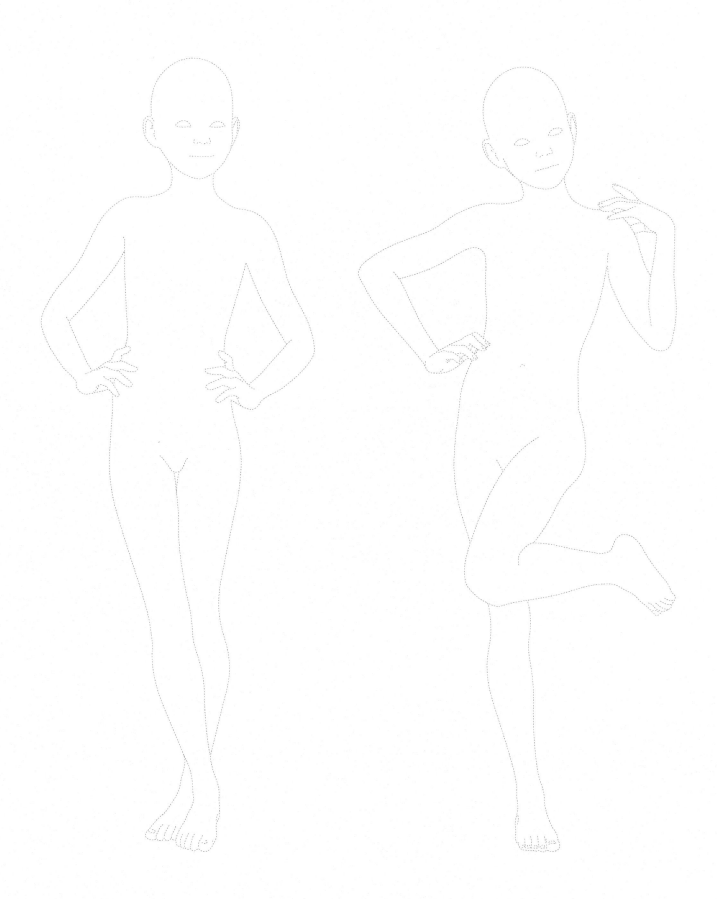

ACCESSORIES

HEAD & SHOULDERS ACCESSORIES DESIGN

JEWELRY

HEAD DISPLAY JEWELRY DESIGN

JEWELRY

HAND DISPLAY JEWELRY DESIGN

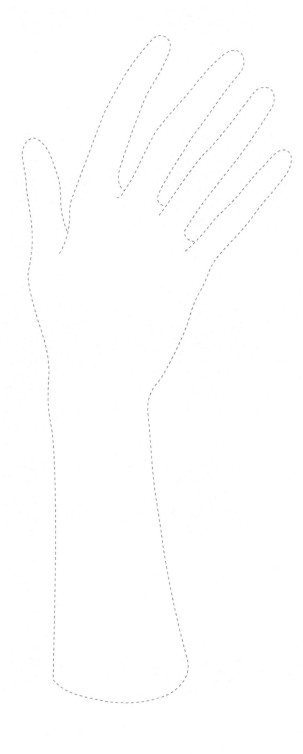

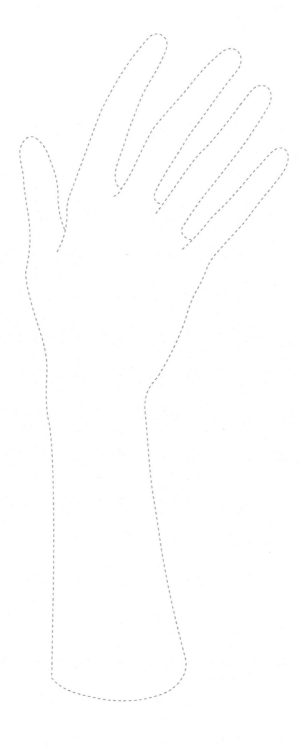

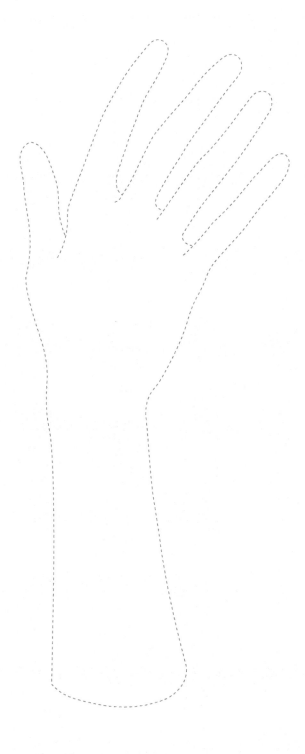

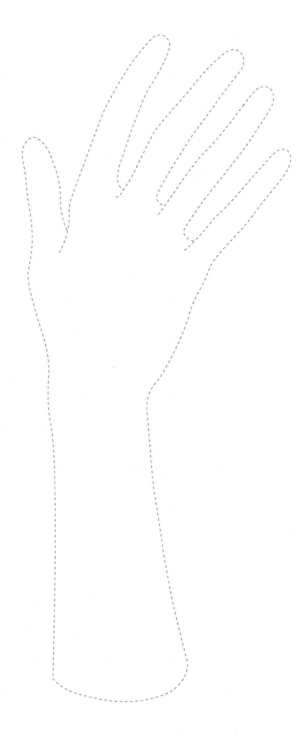

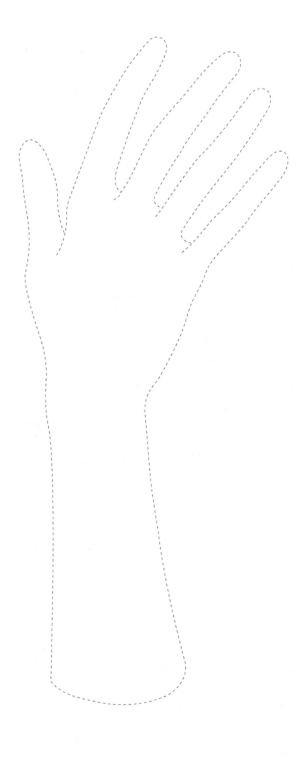

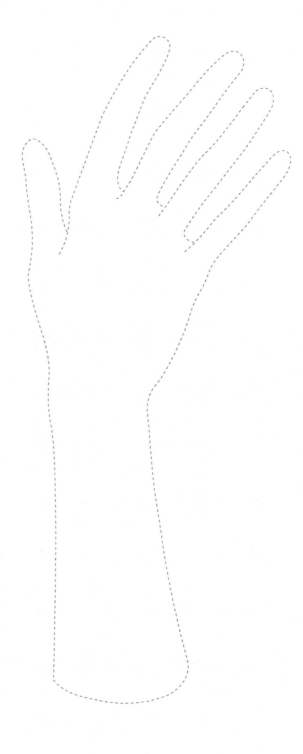

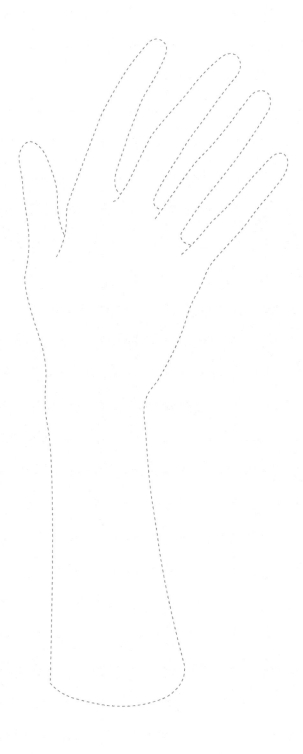

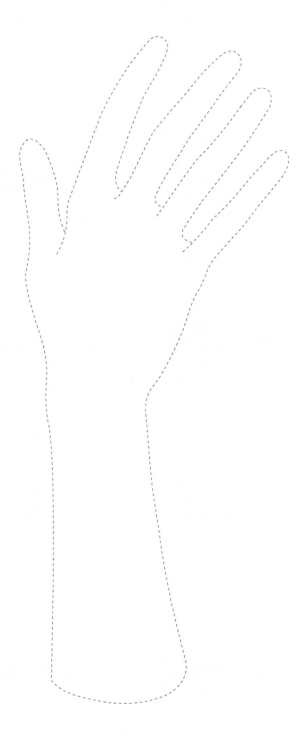

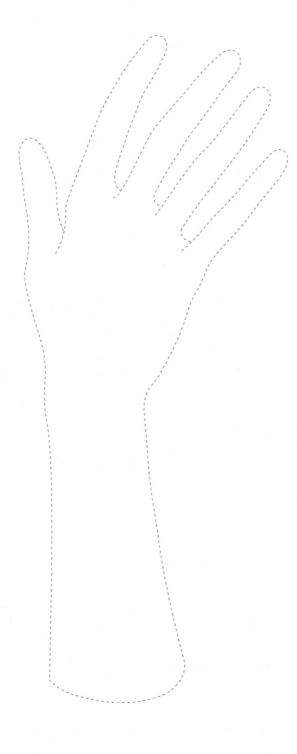

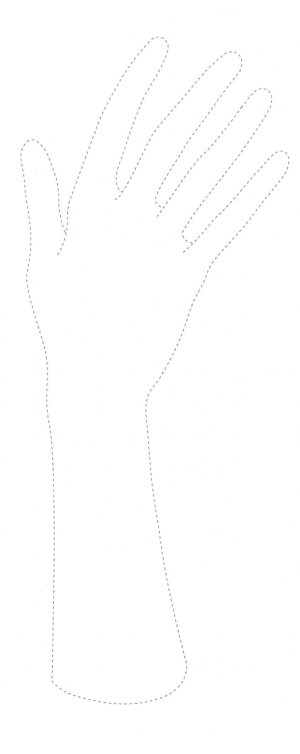

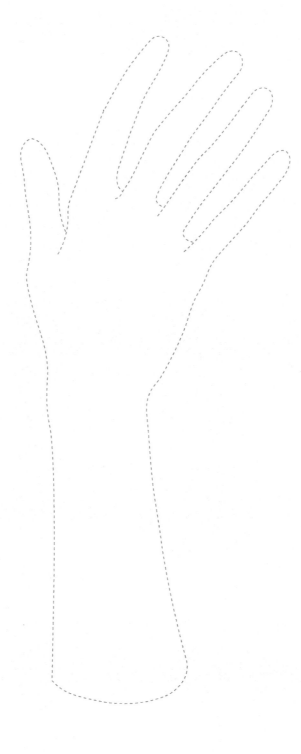

SHOE

SHOE LAST SHOE DESIGN

DETAILS:

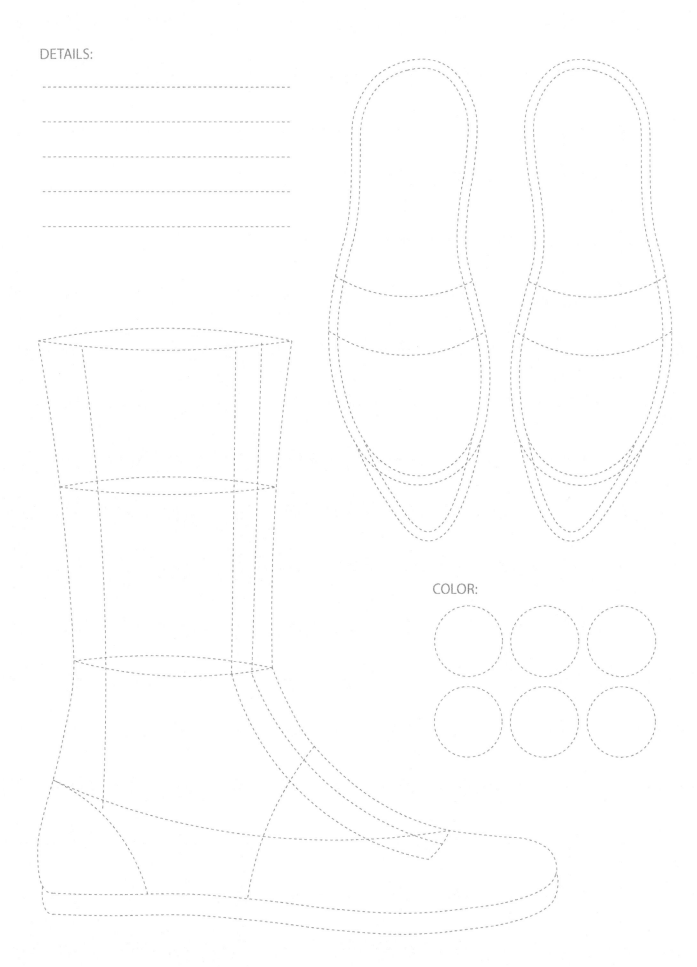

COLOR:

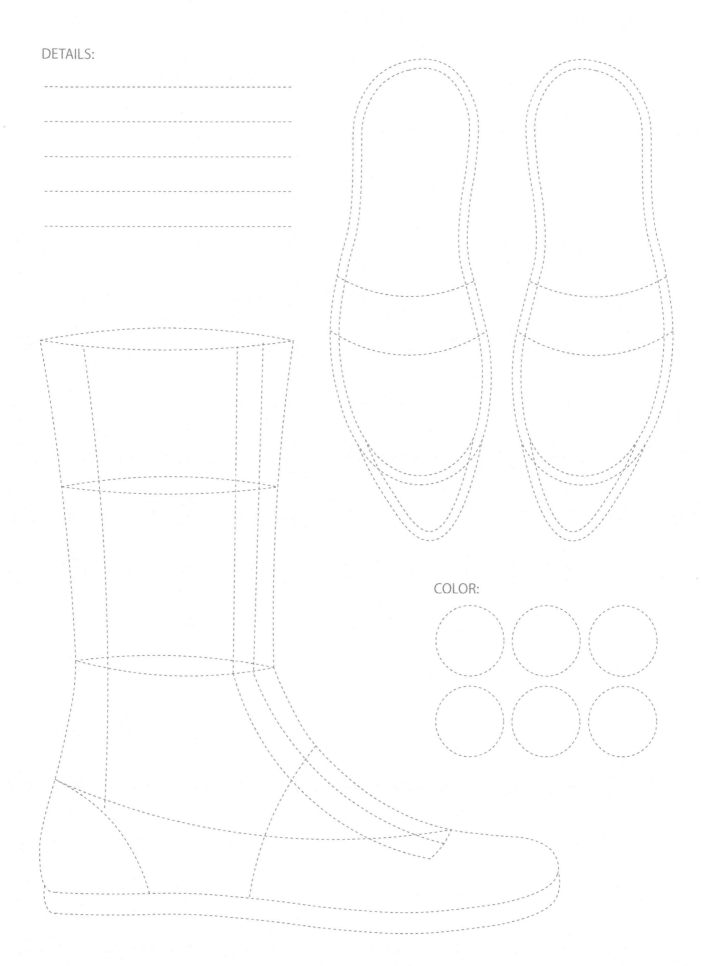

COLOR:

DETAILS:

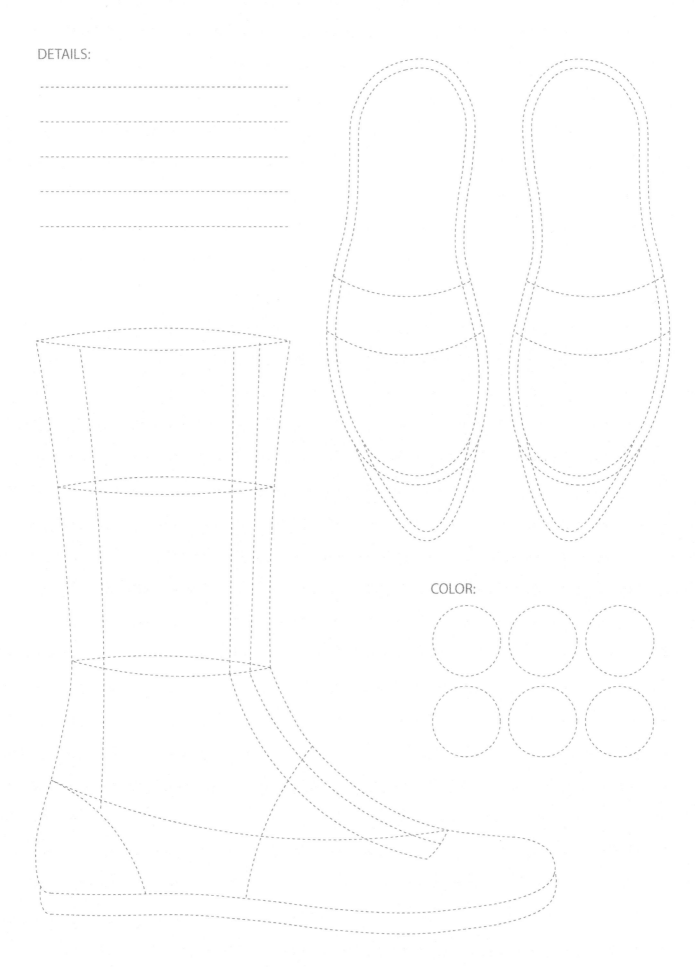

COLOR:

DETAILS:

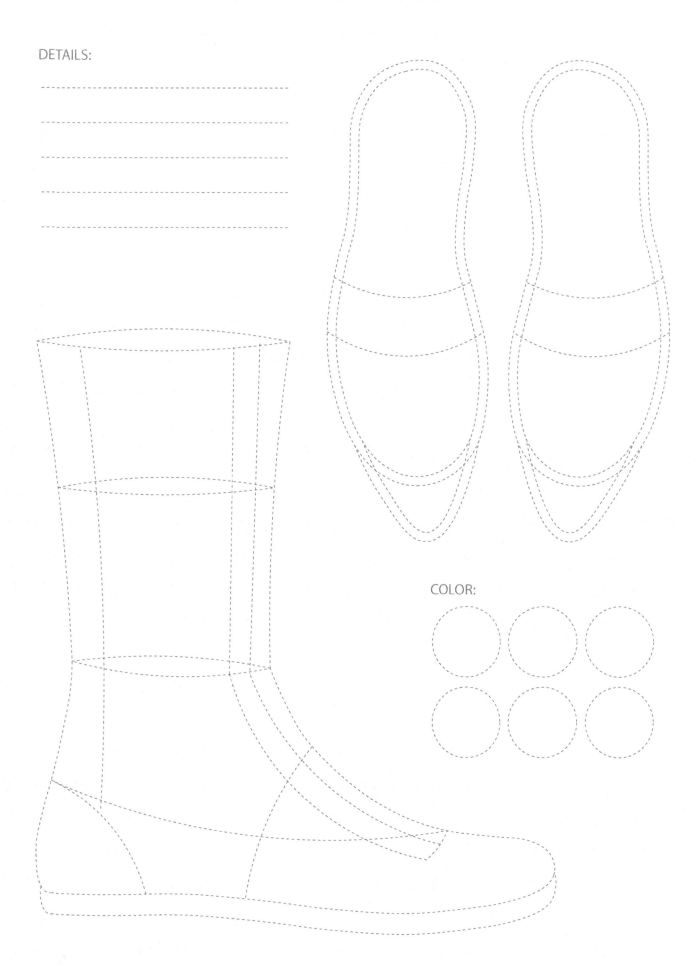

COLOR:

DETAILS:

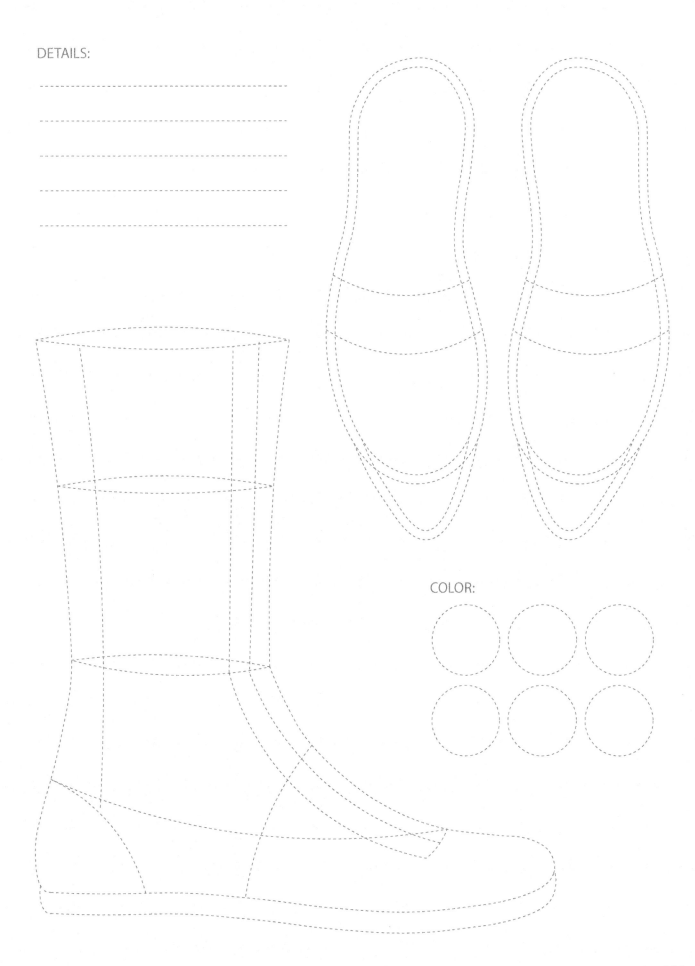

COLOR:

DETAILS:

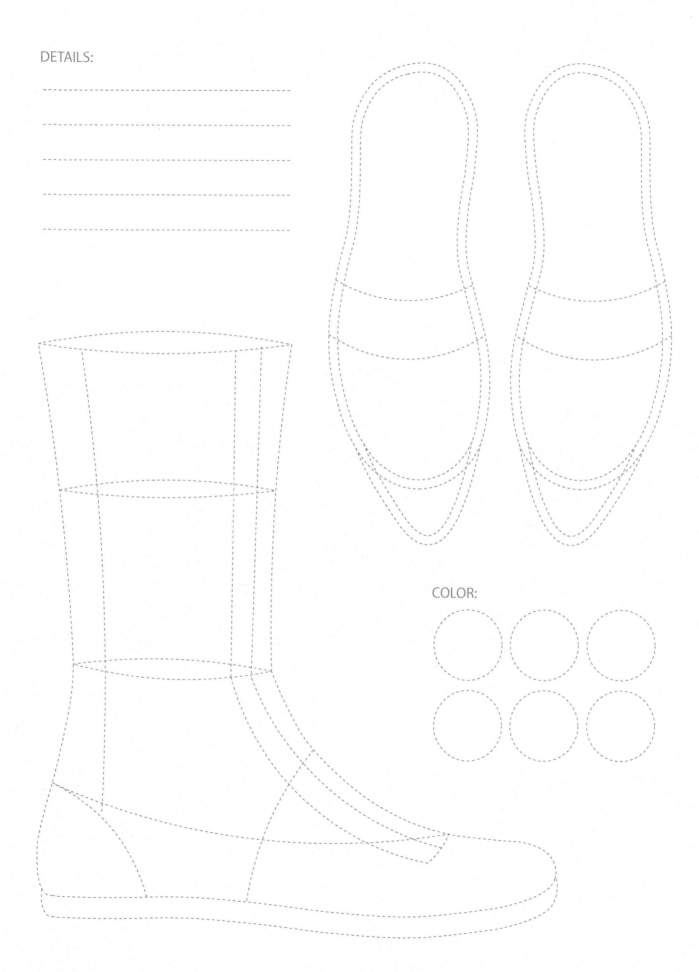

COLOR:

DETAILS:

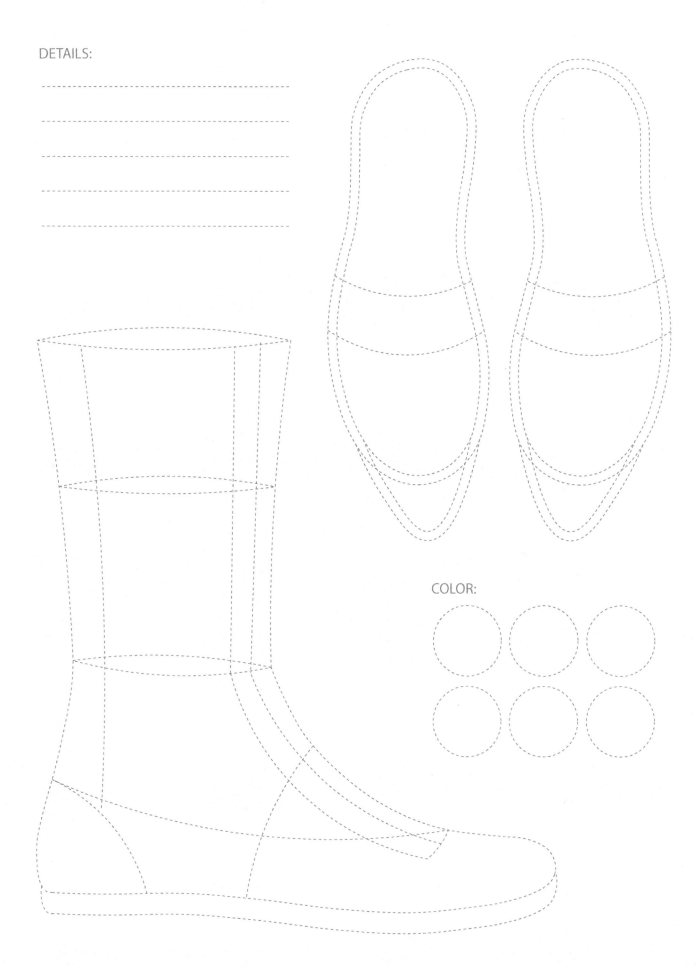

COLOR:

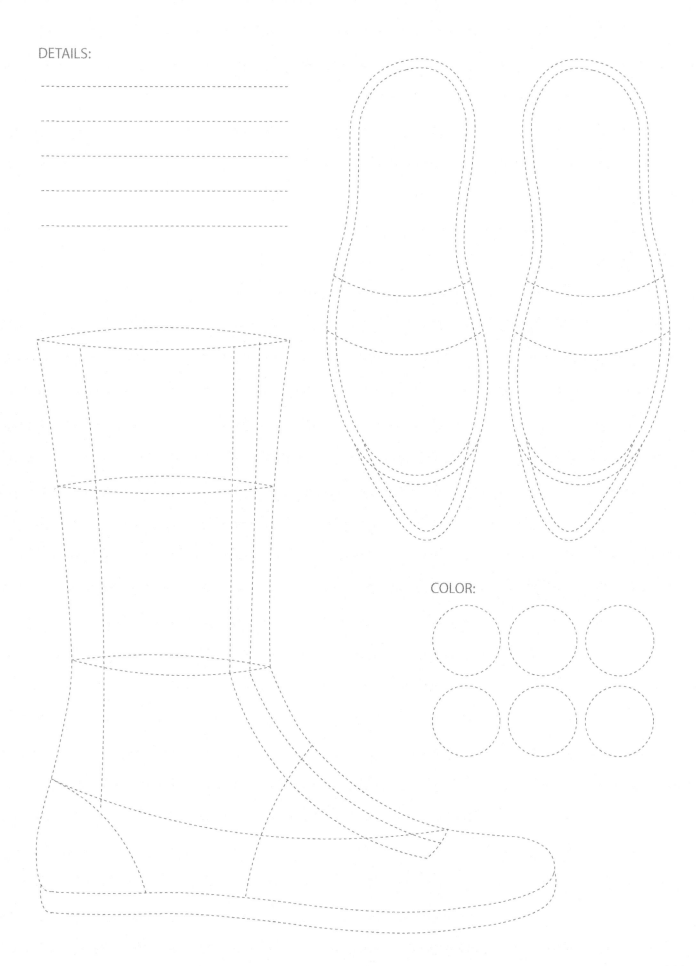

COLOR:

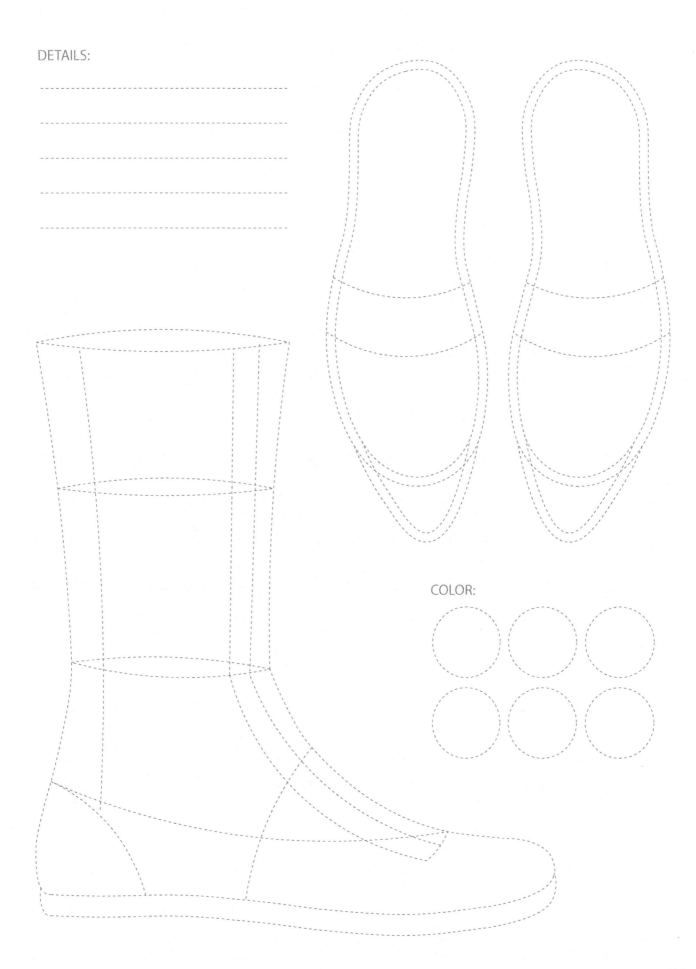

COLOR:

DETAILS:

COLOR:

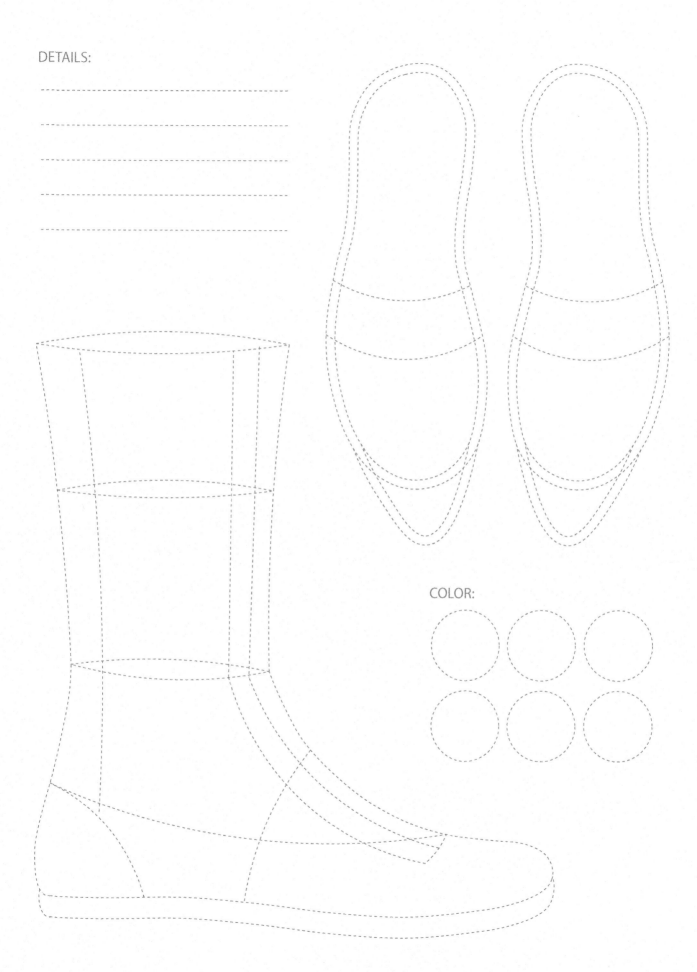

DETAILS:

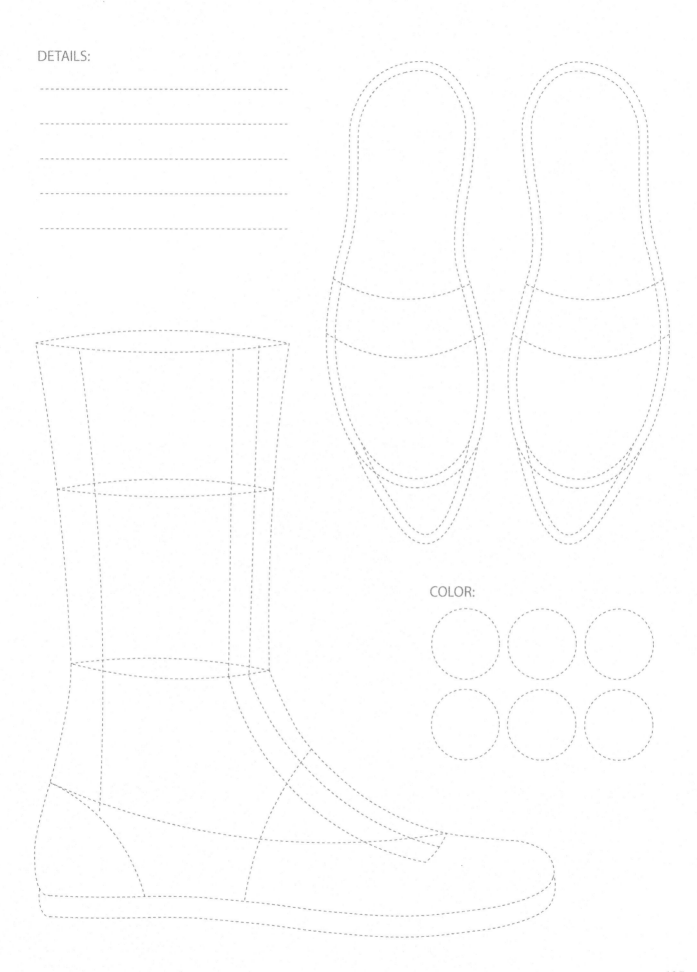

COLOR:

DETAILS:

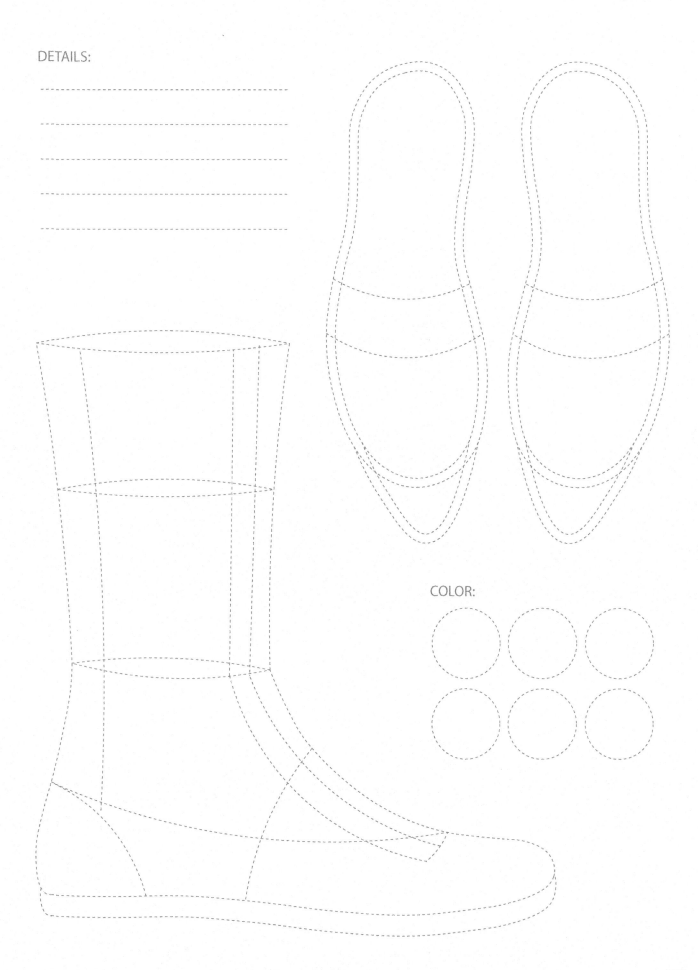

COLOR:

DETAILS:

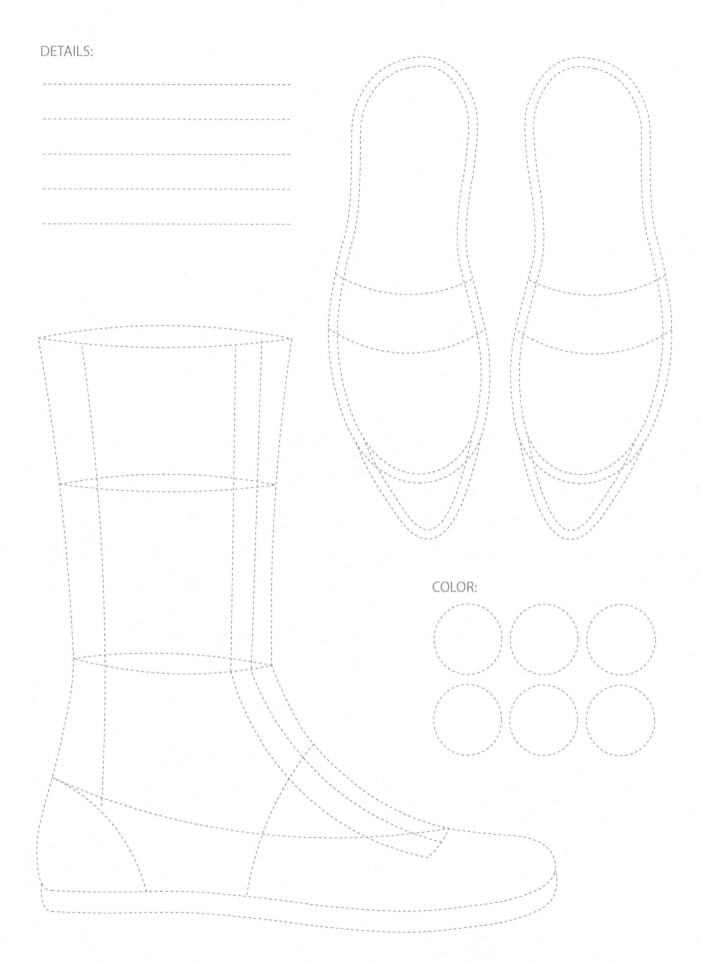

COLOR:

DETAILS:

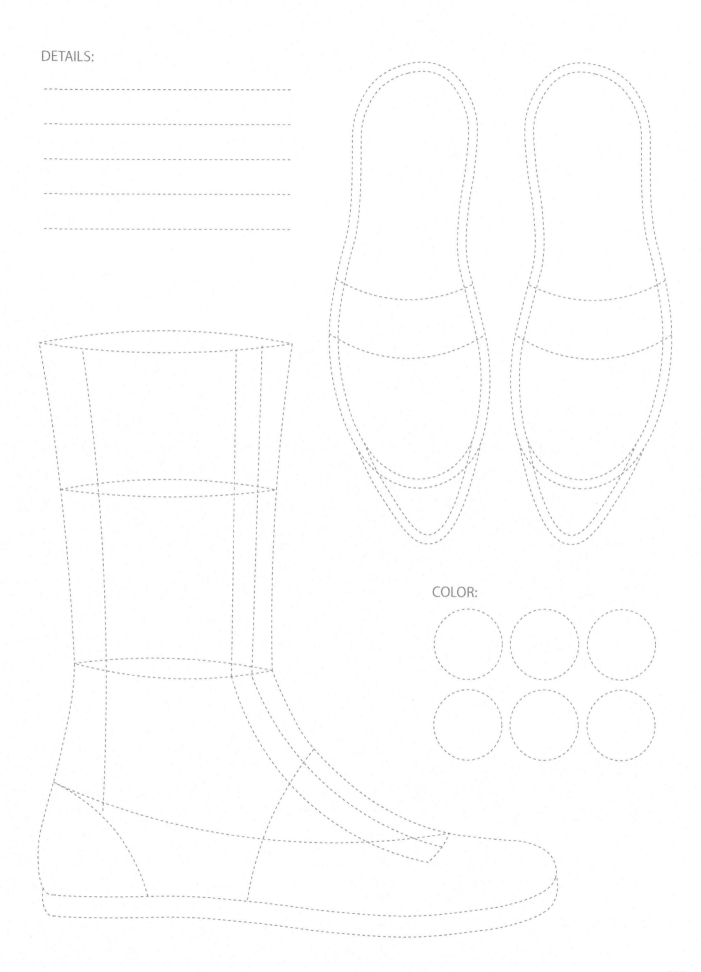

COLOR:

DETAILS:

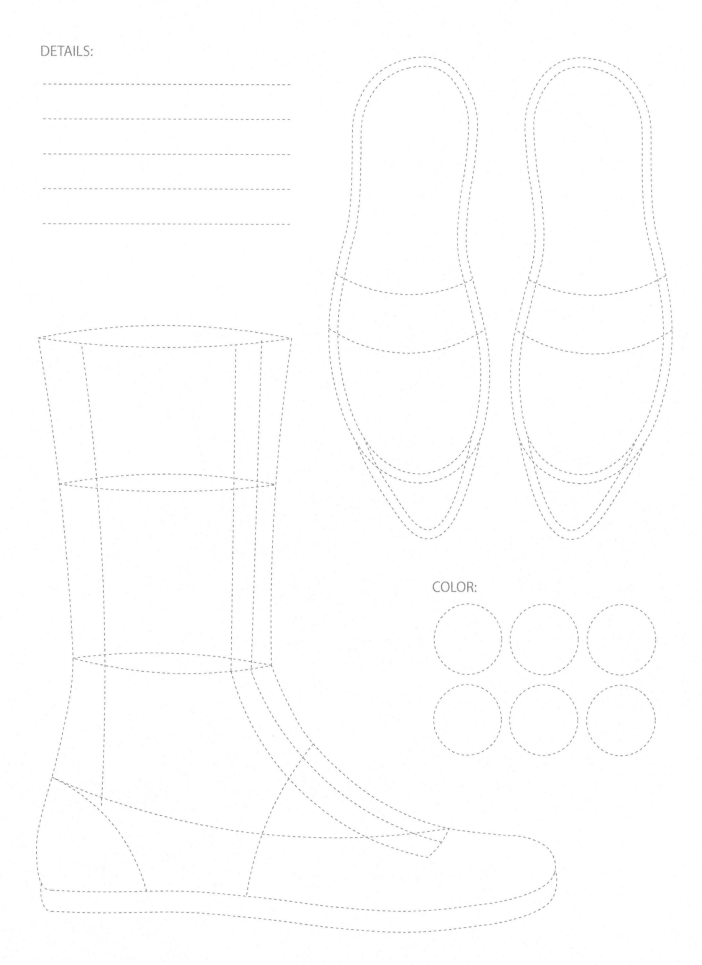

COLOR:

DETAILS:

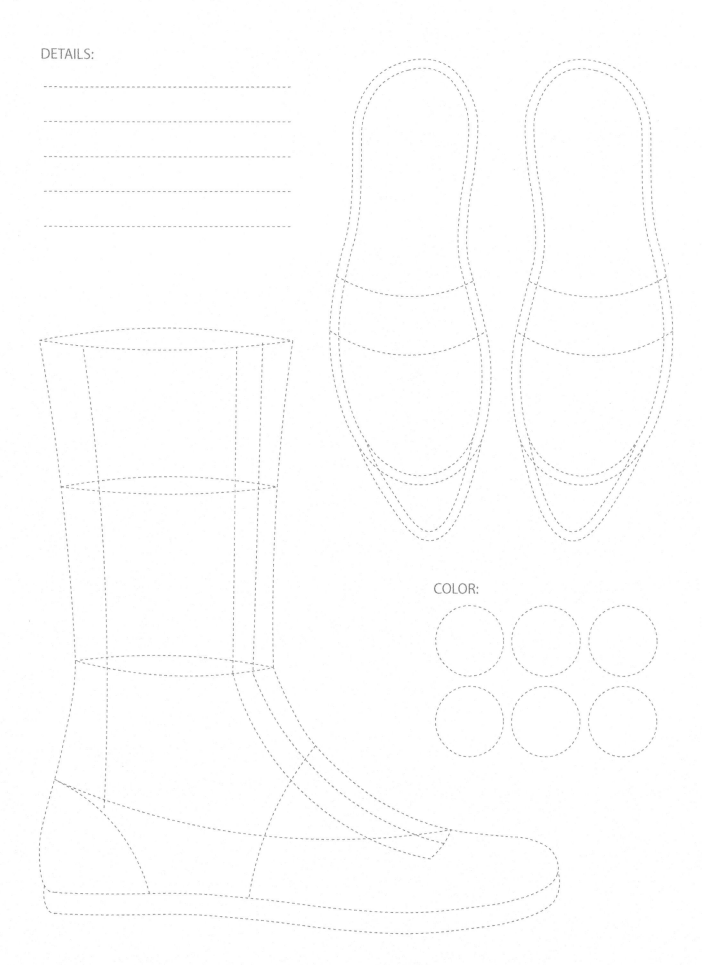

COLOR:

DETAILS:

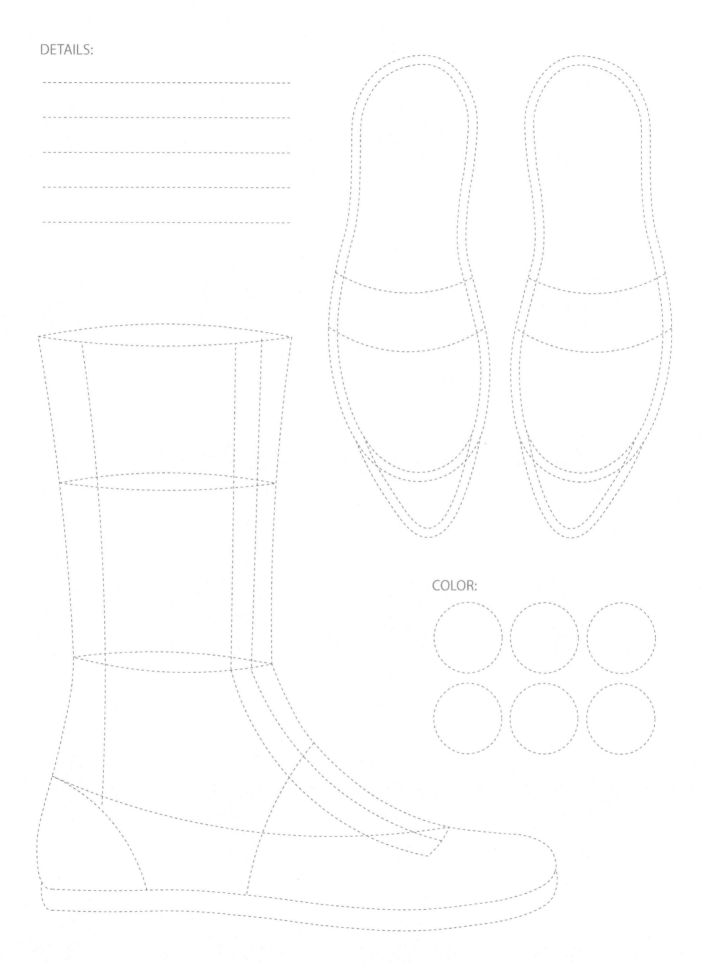

COLOR:

DETAILS:

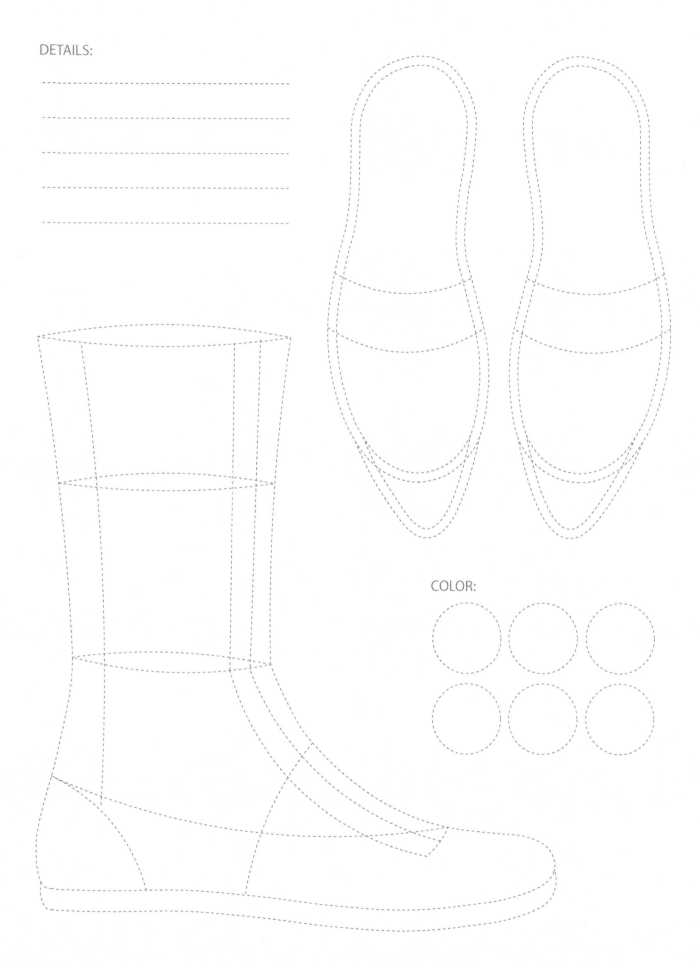

COLOR:

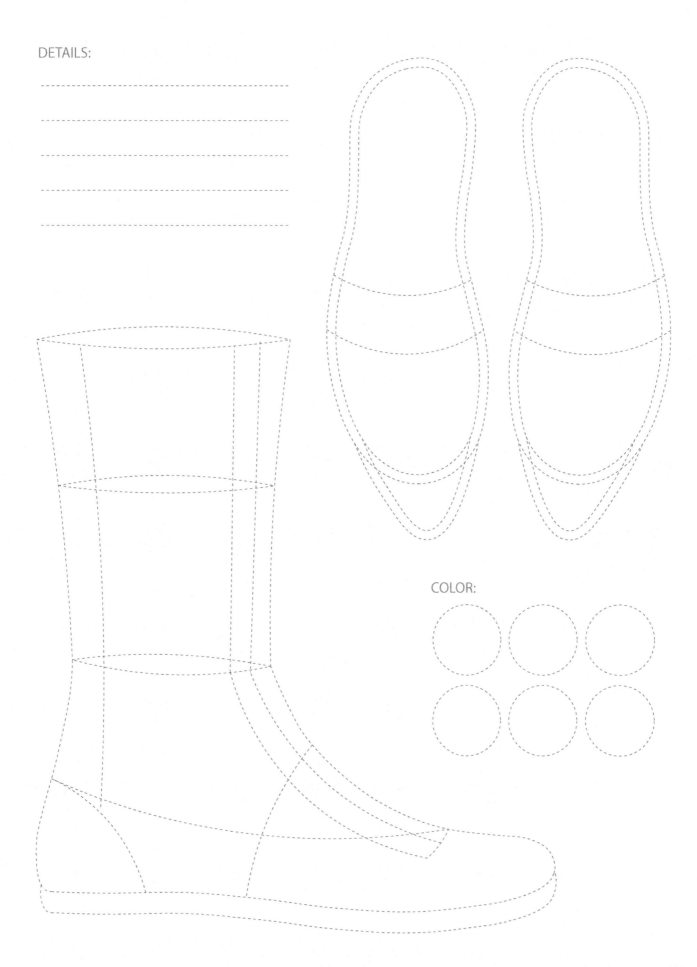

DETAILS:

COLOR:

DETAILS:

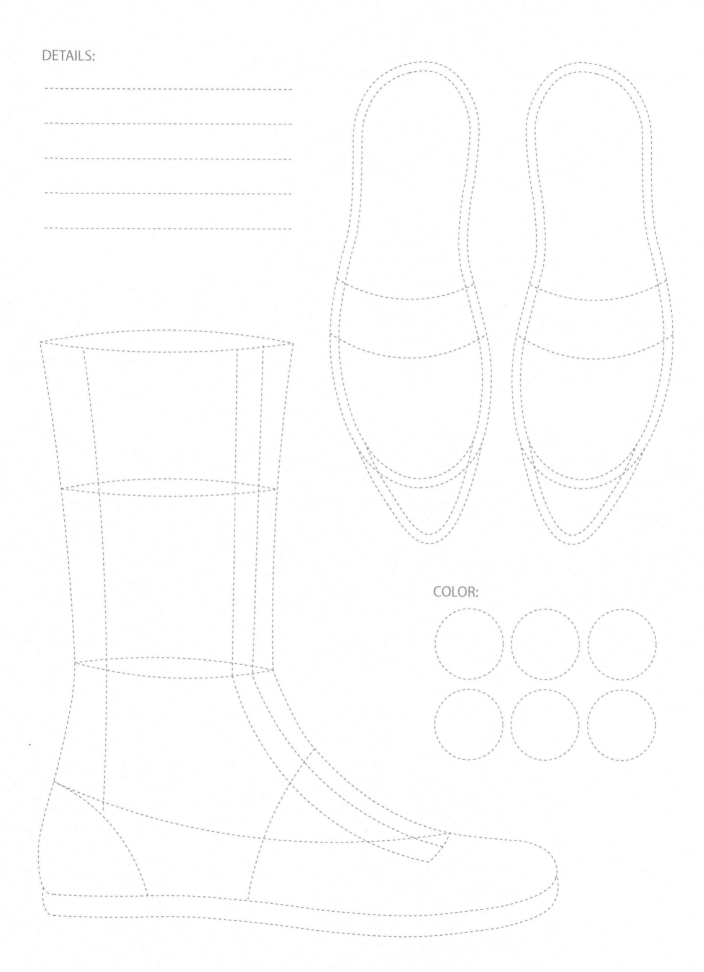

COLOR:

DETAILS:

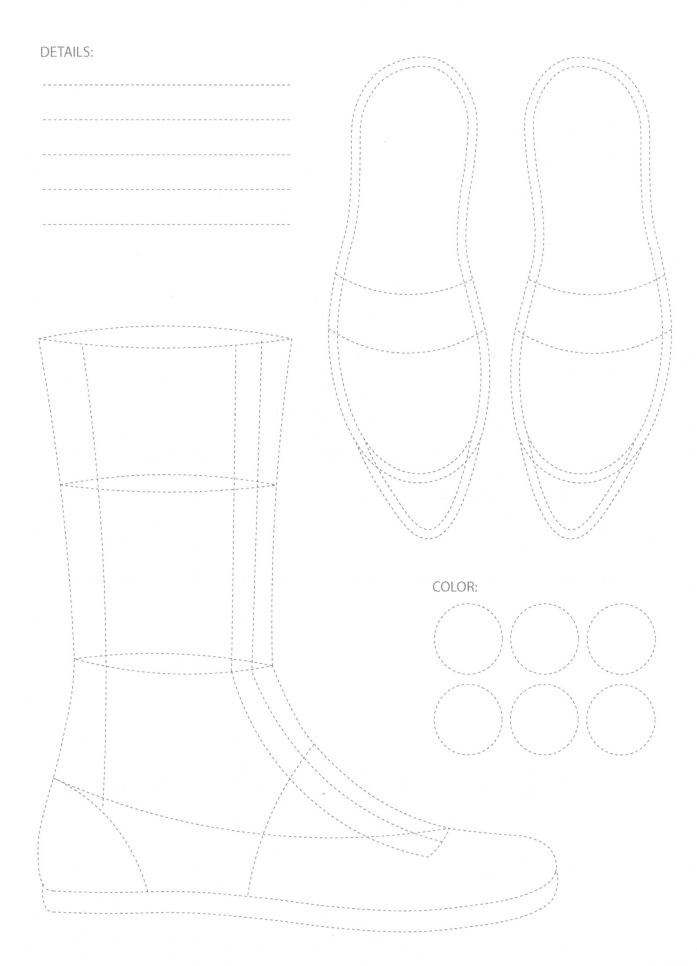

COLOR:

FASHION FIGURE

BONUS KIDS POSE OUTLINE

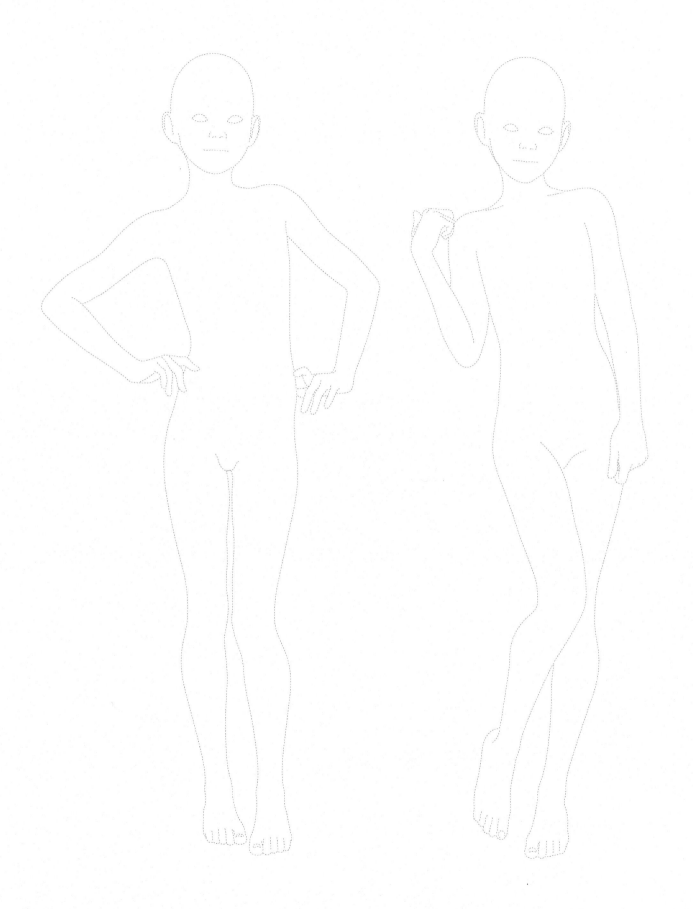

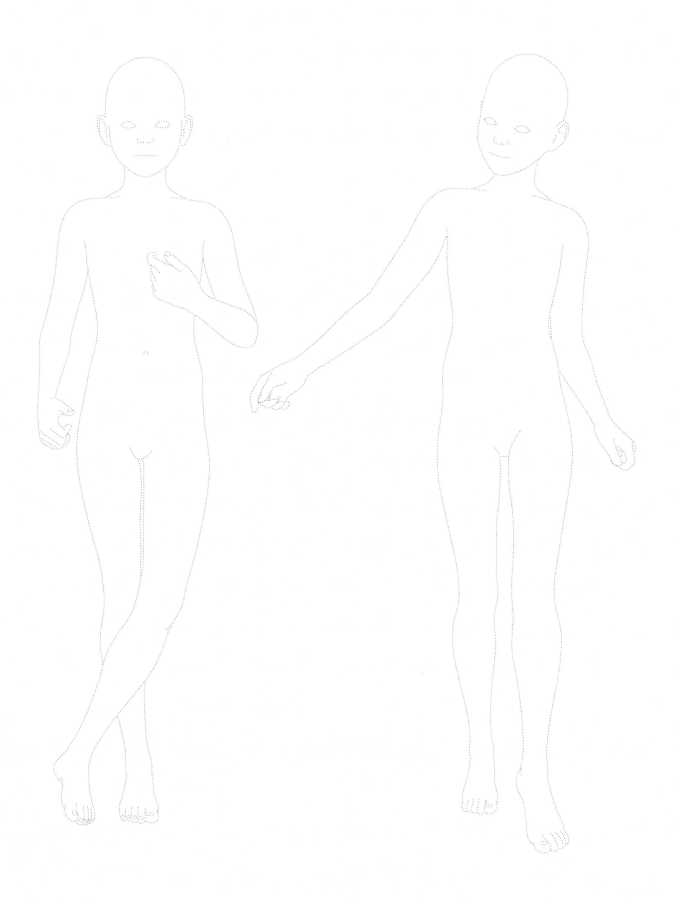

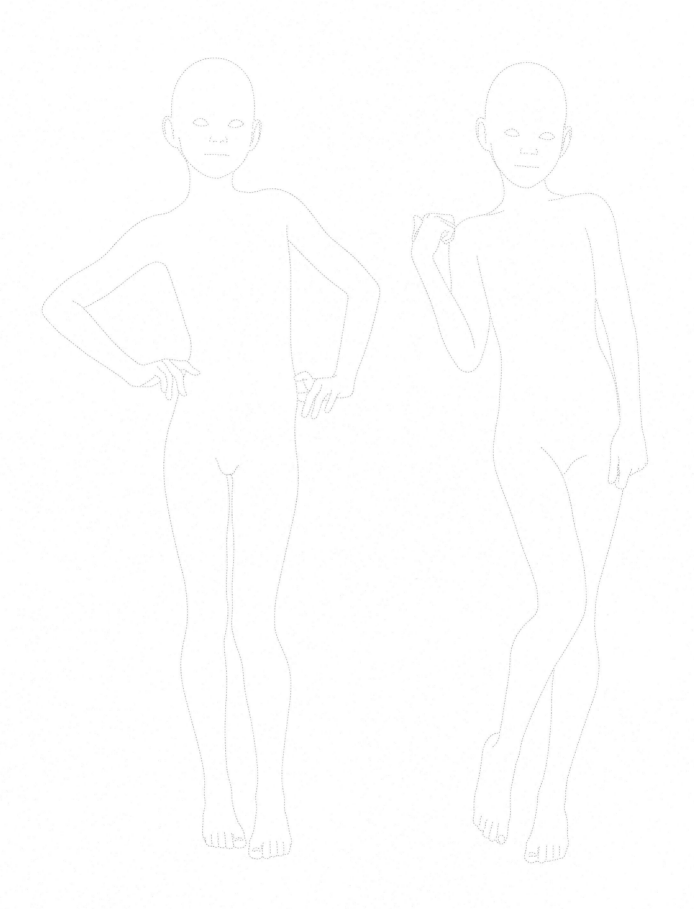

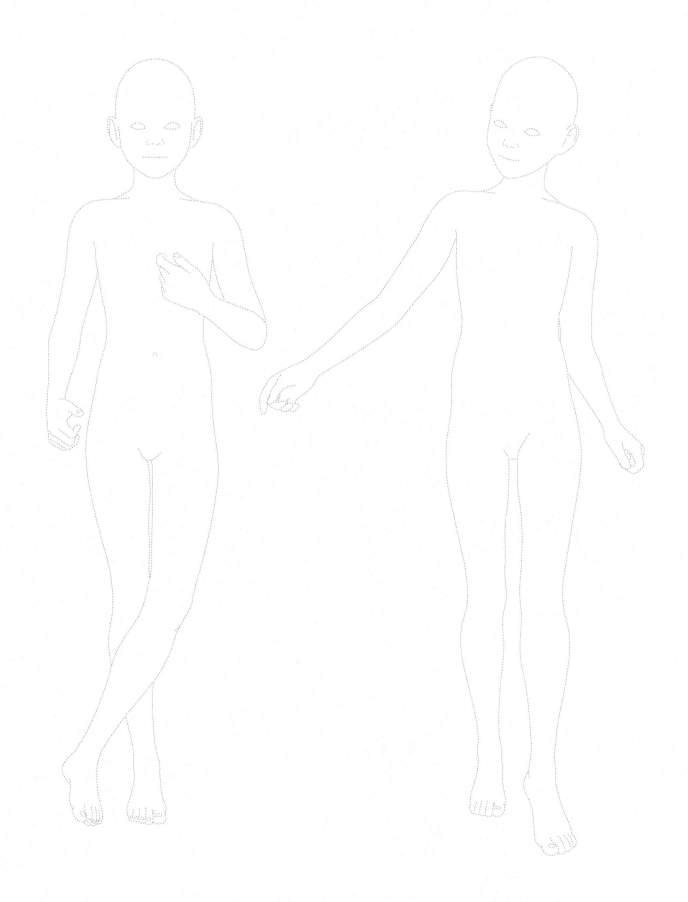

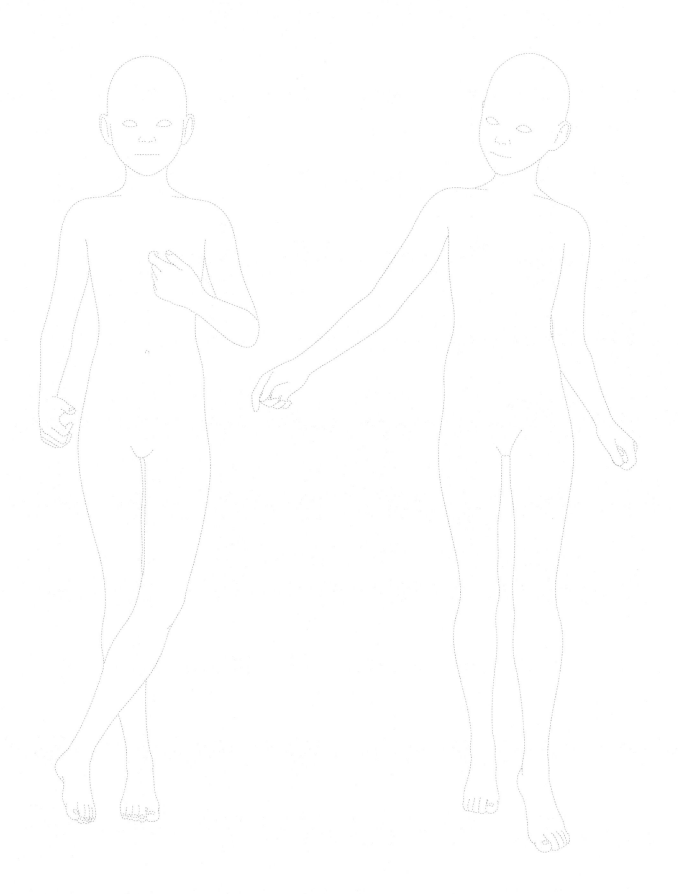

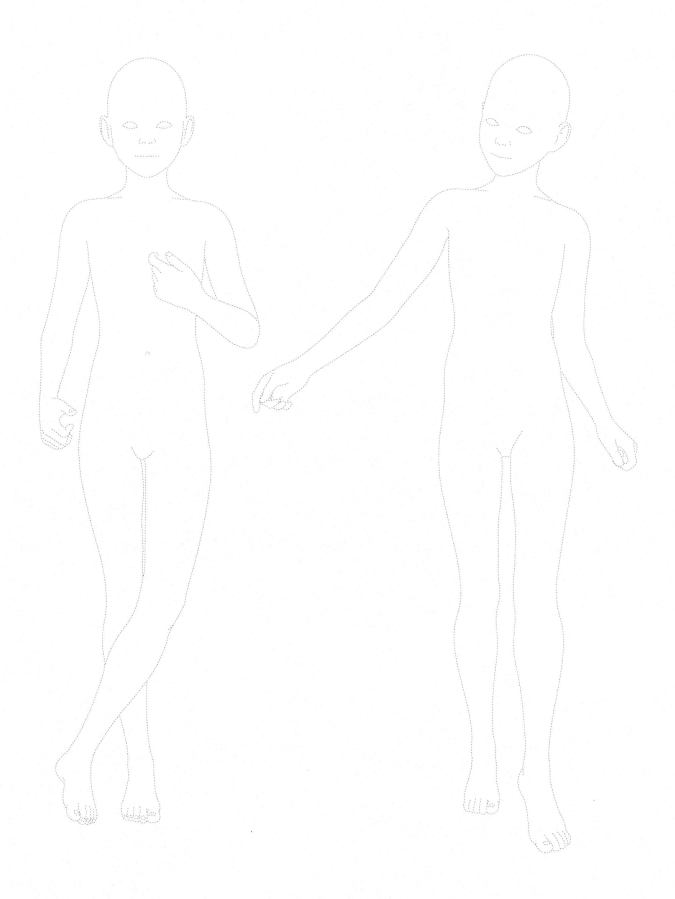

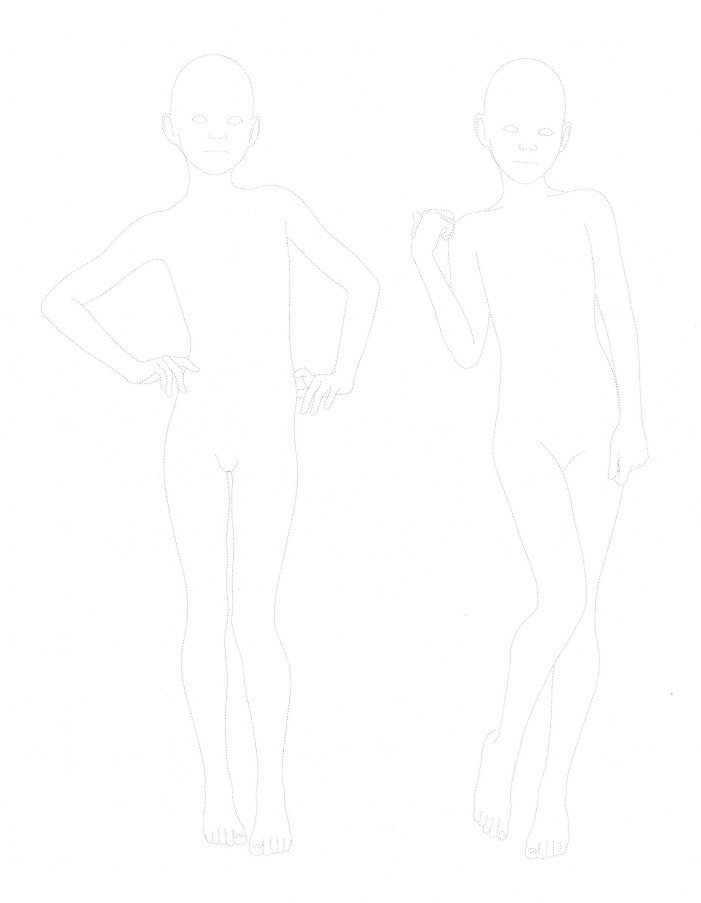

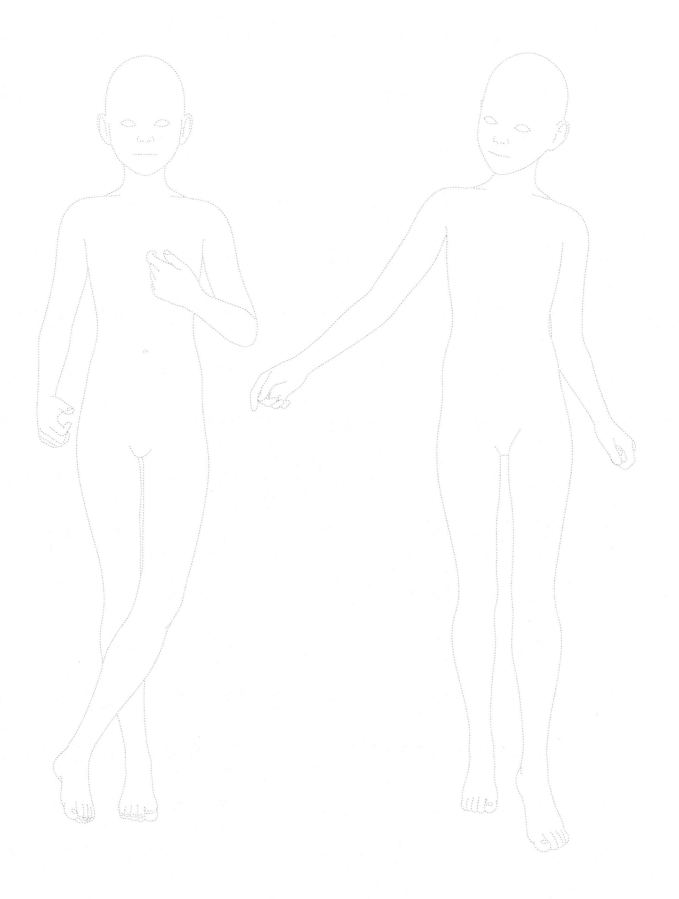

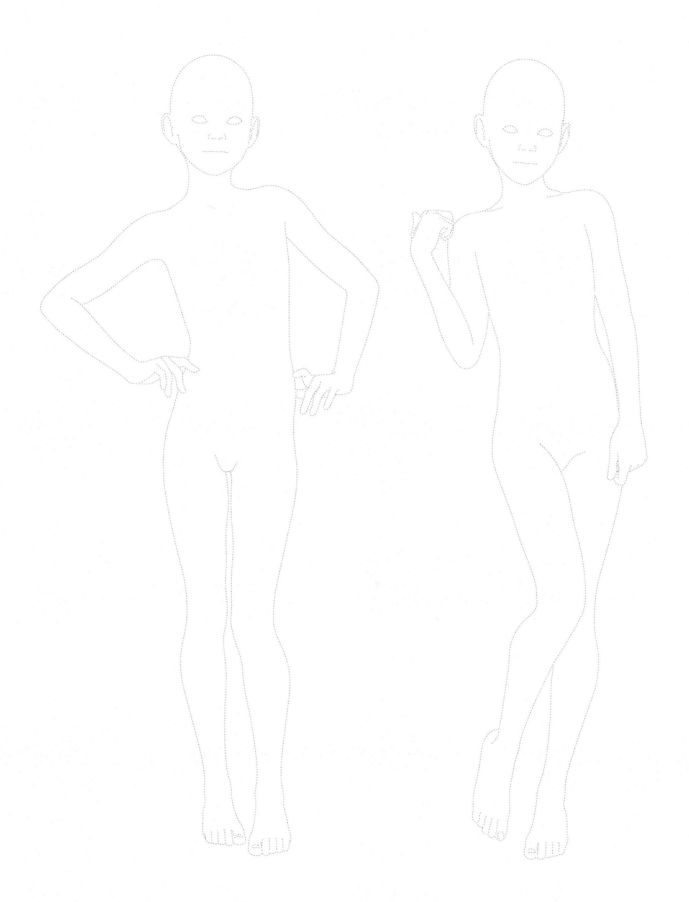

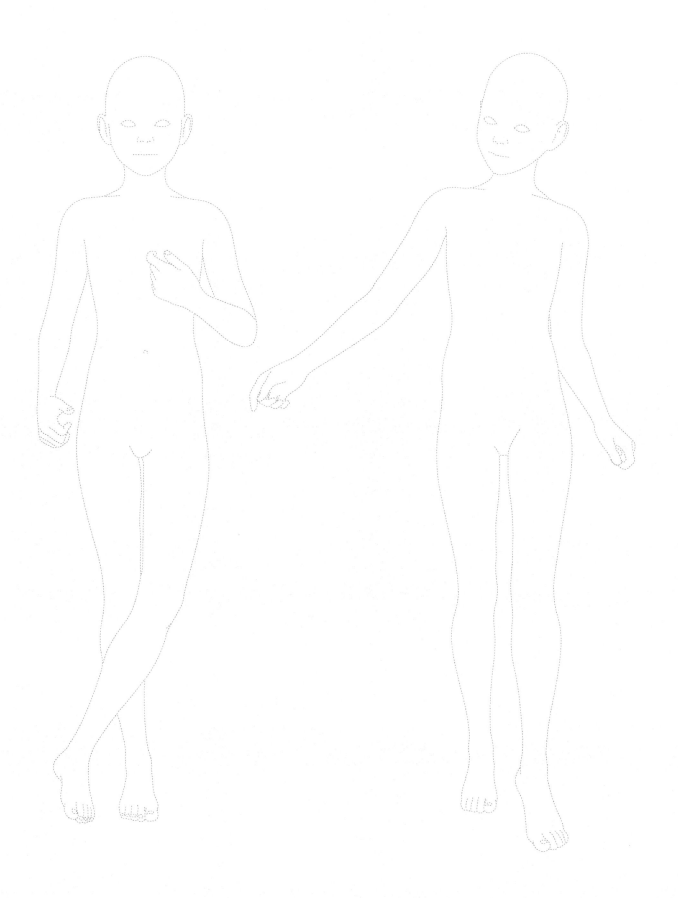

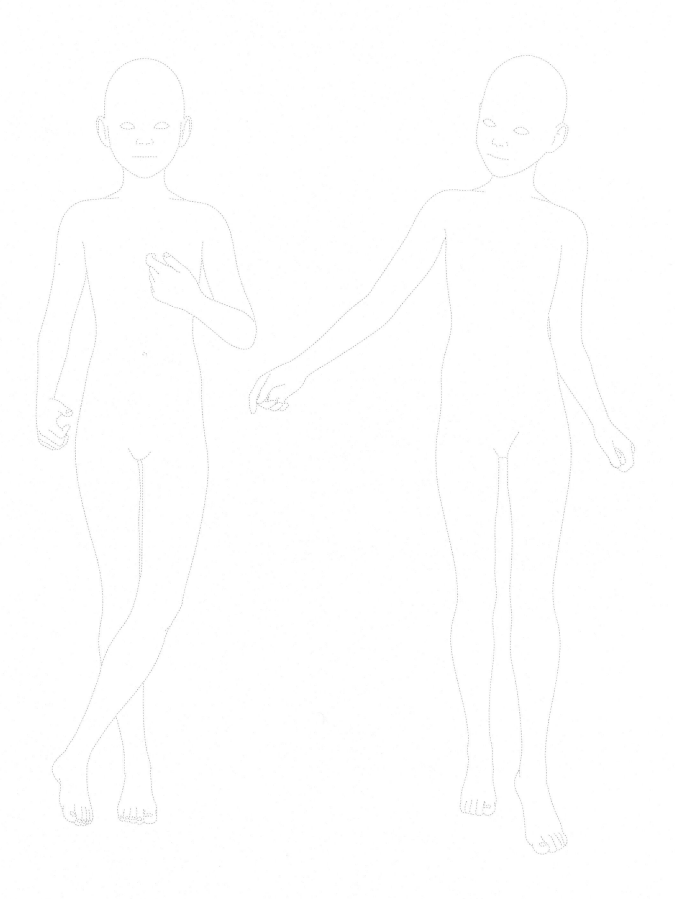

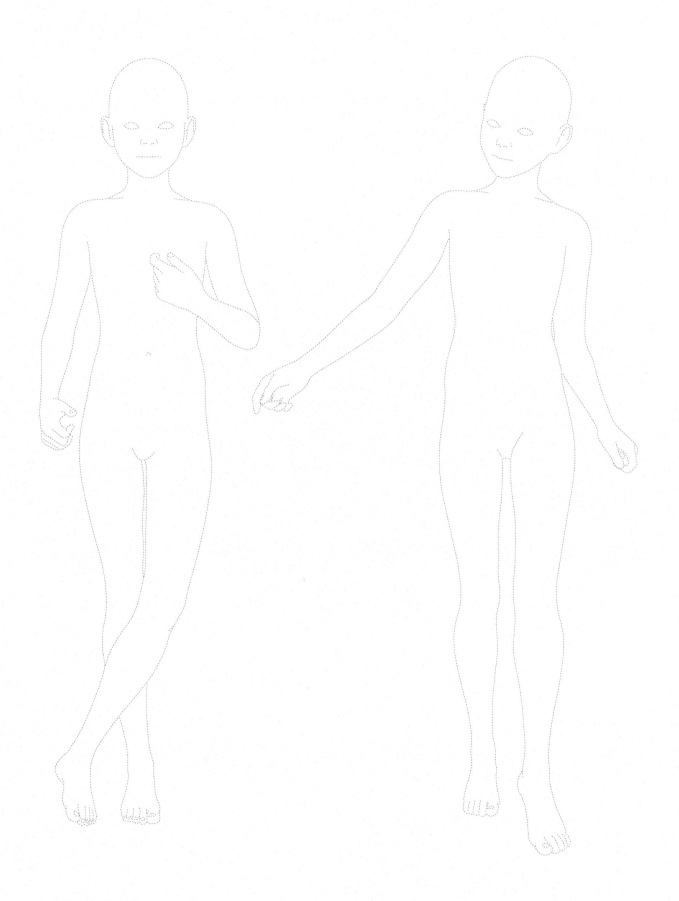

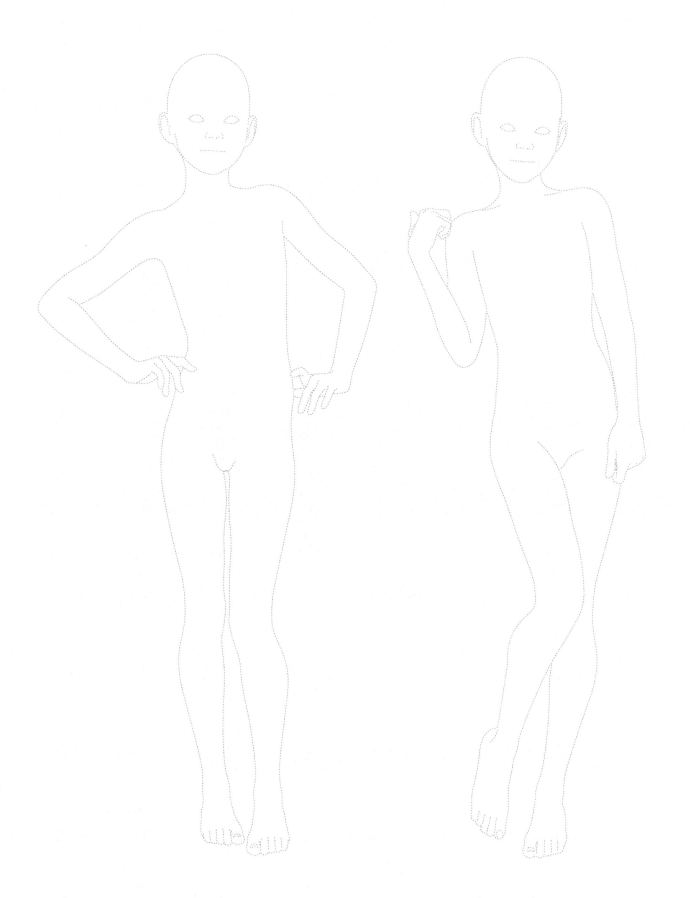

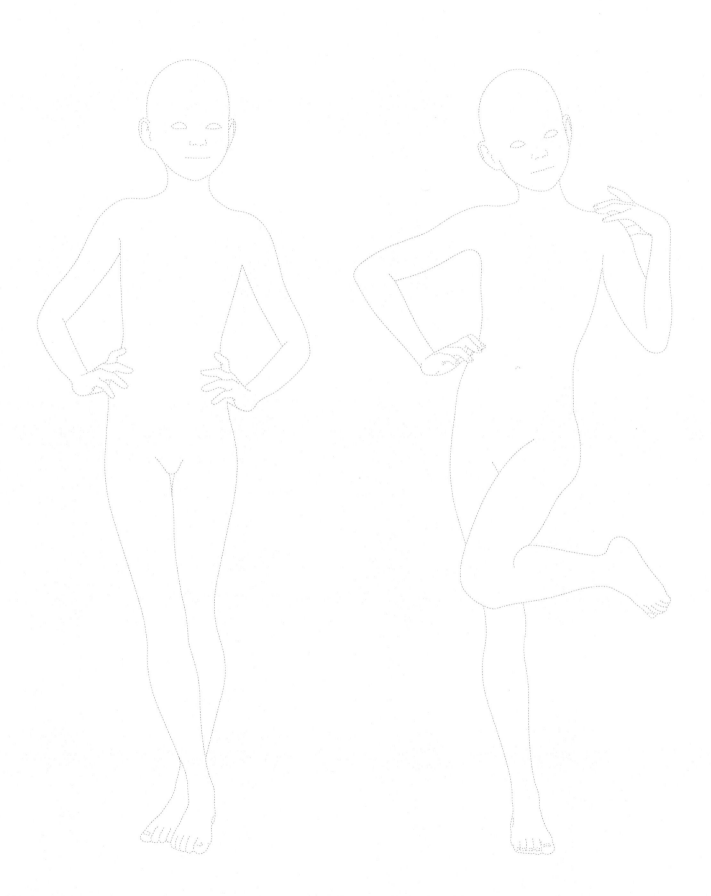

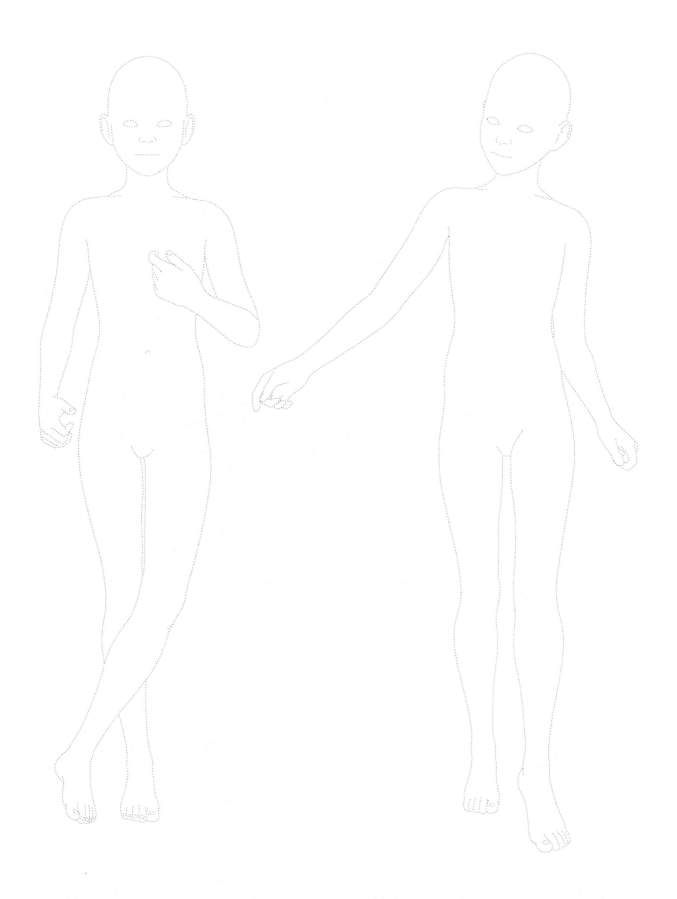

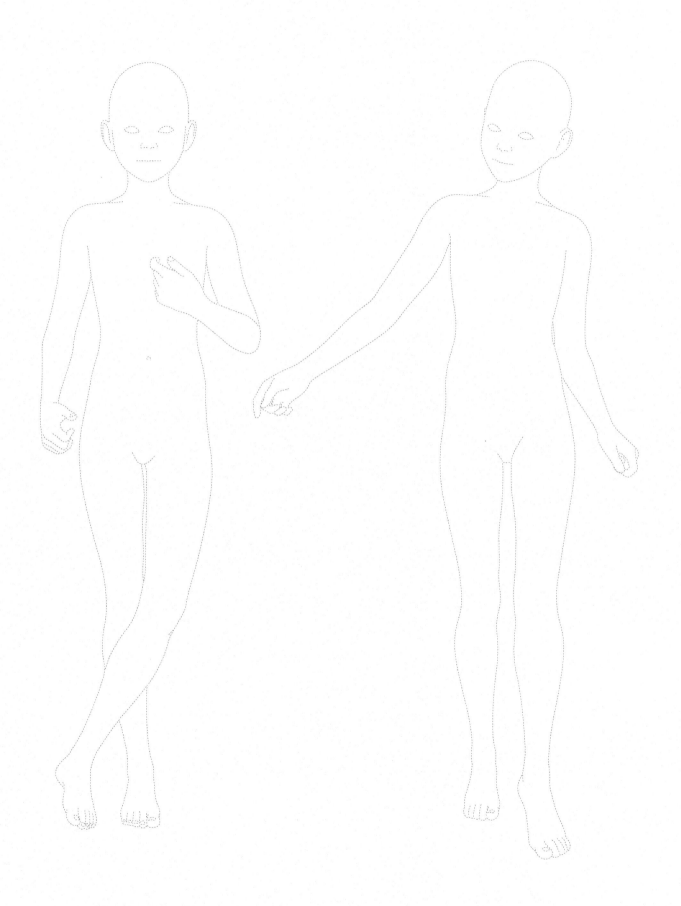

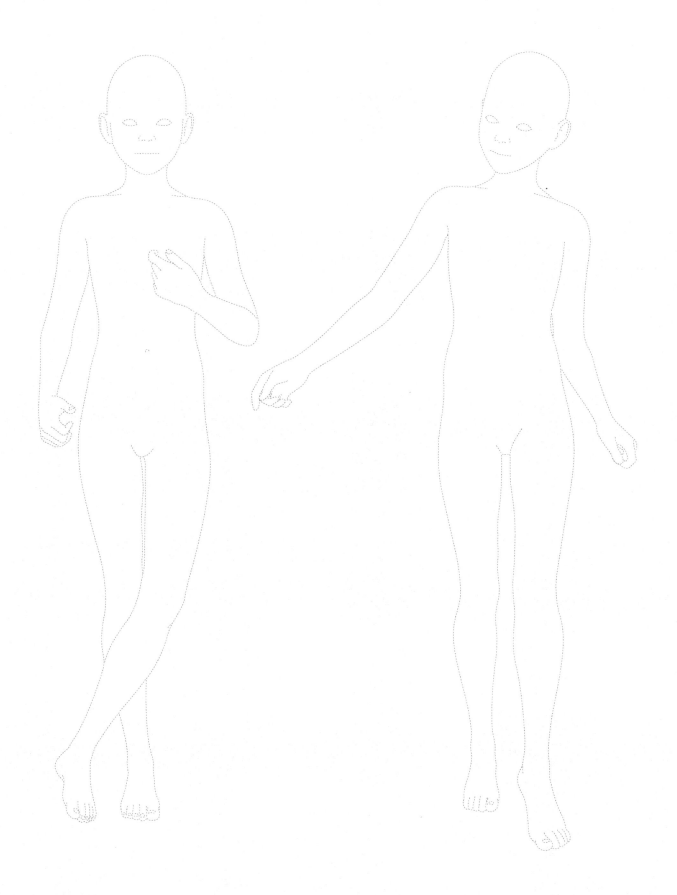

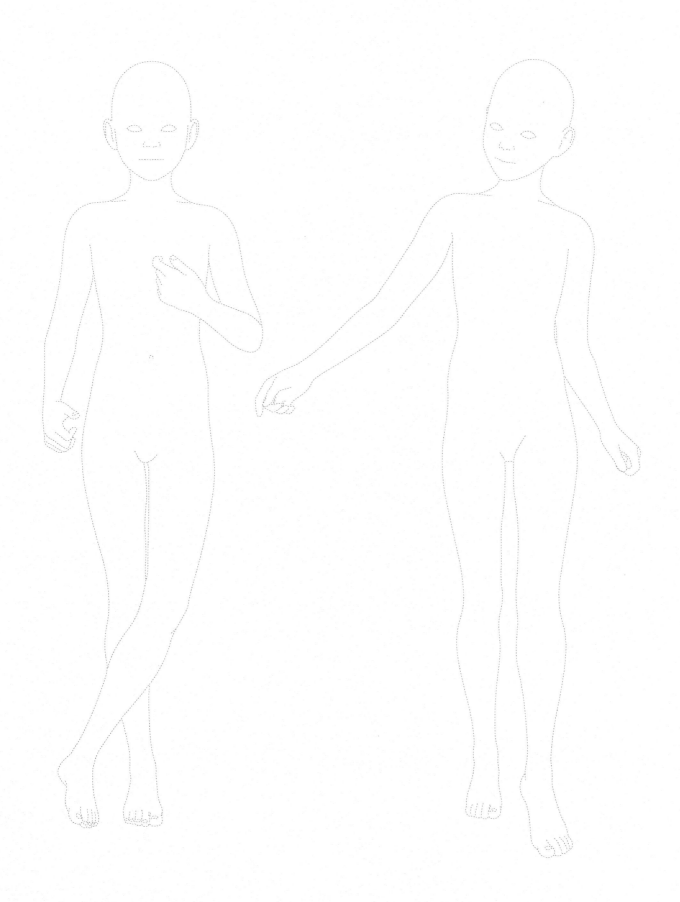

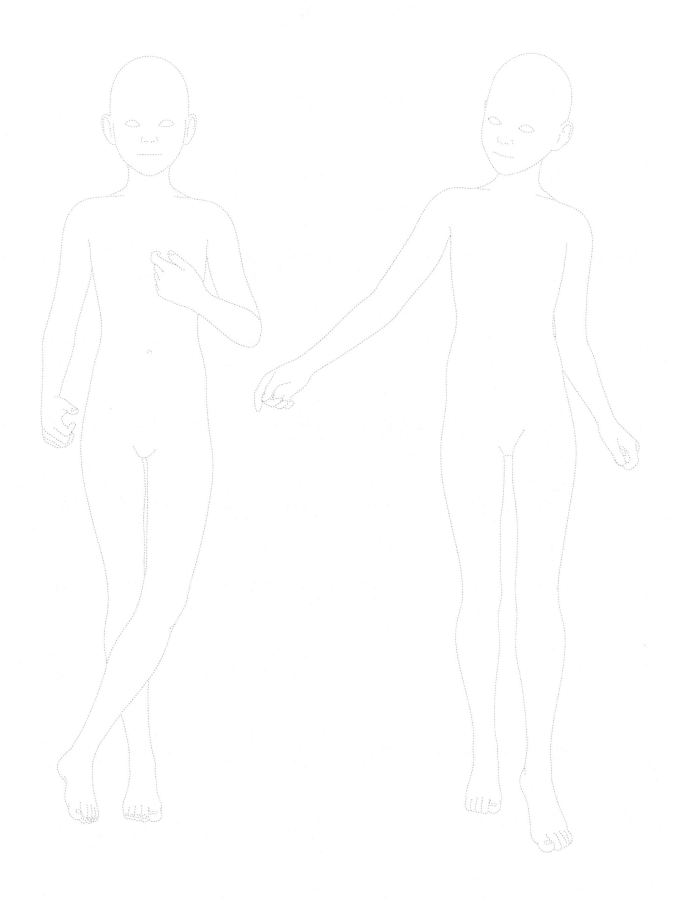

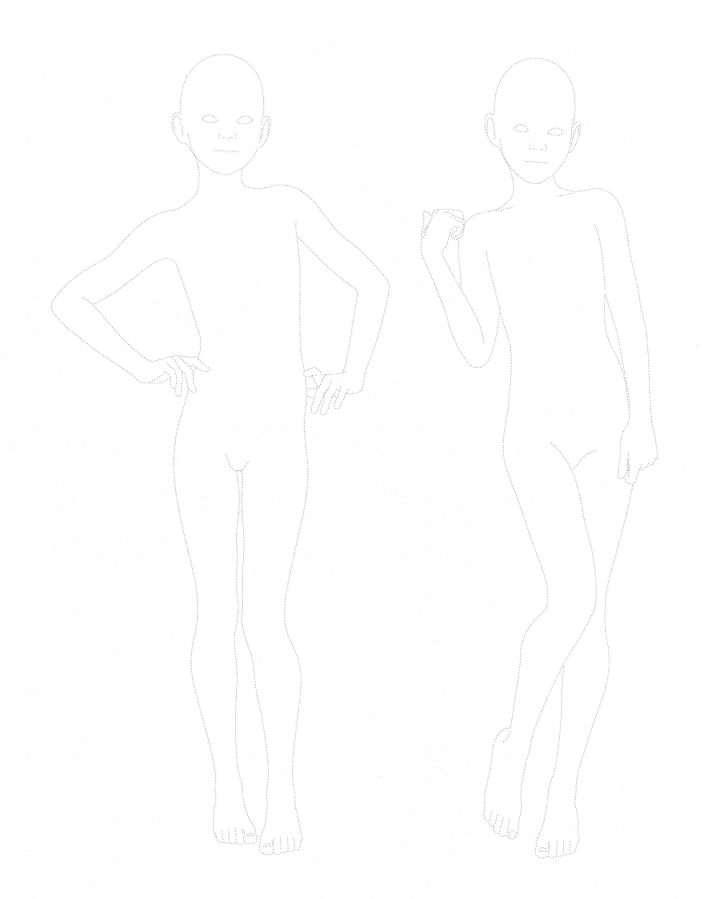

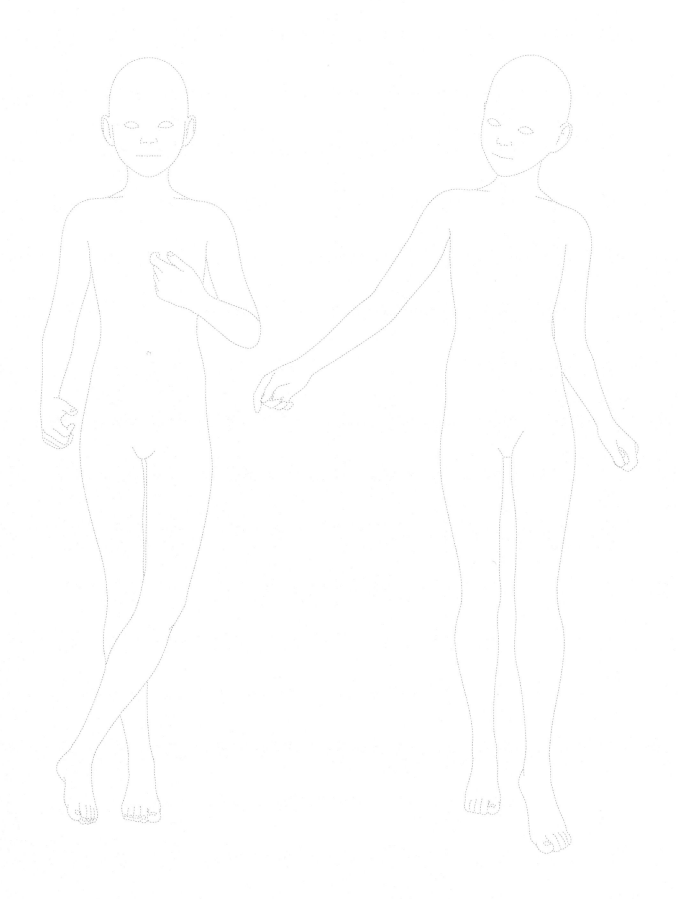

CROQUIS

FASHION CROQUIS OUTLINE

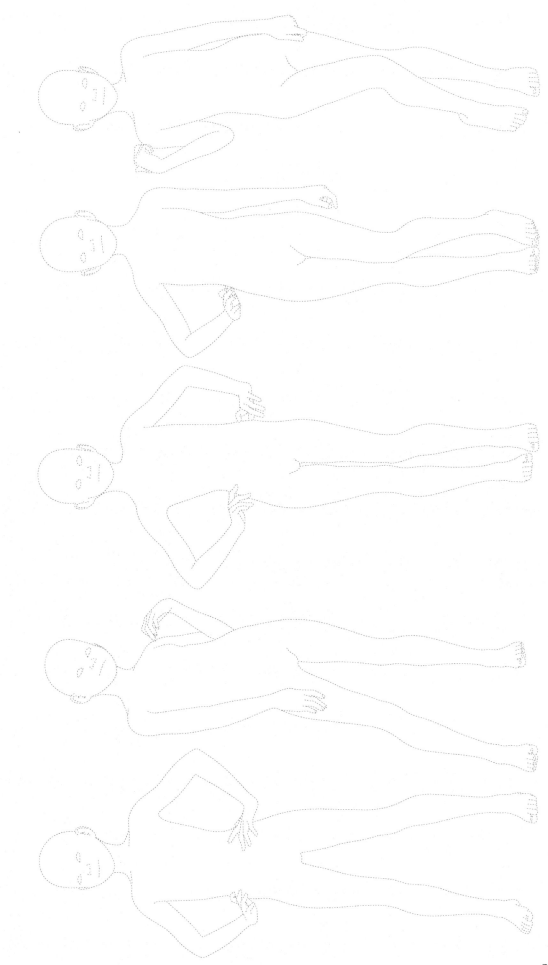

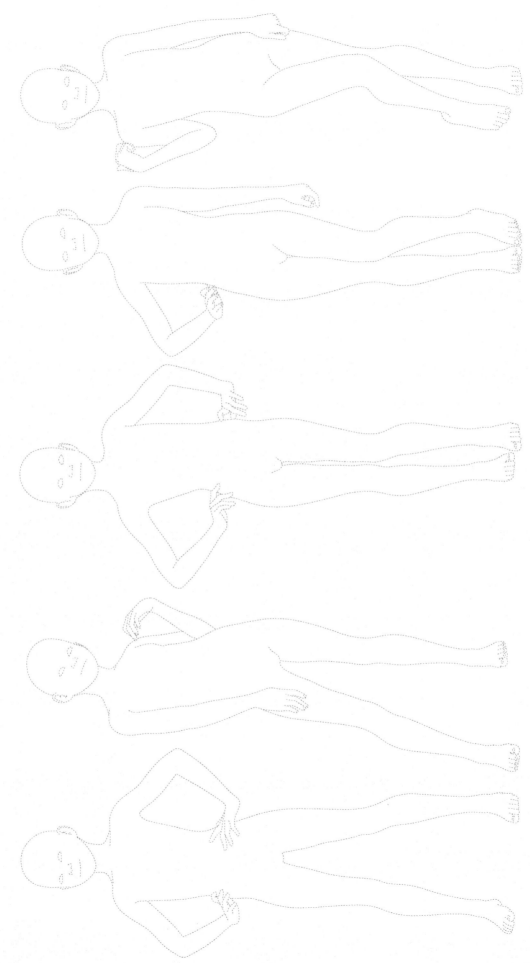

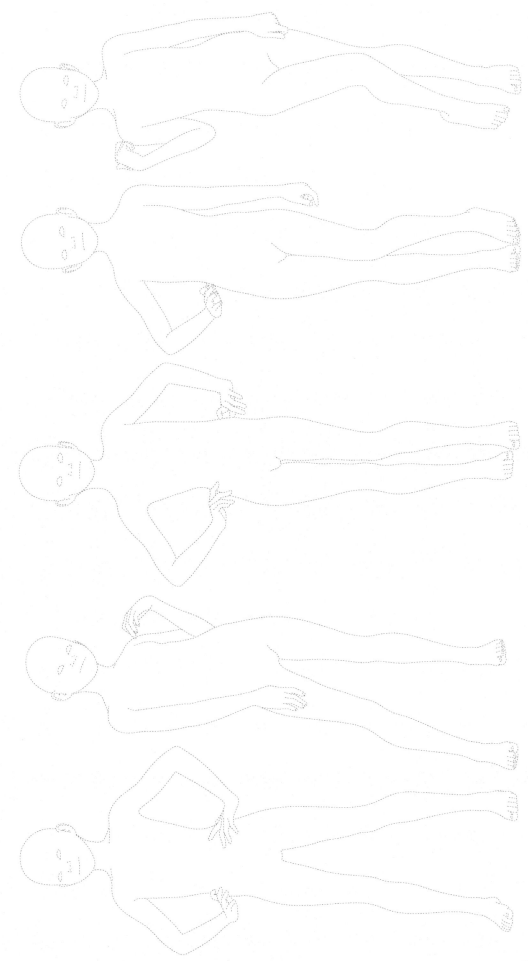

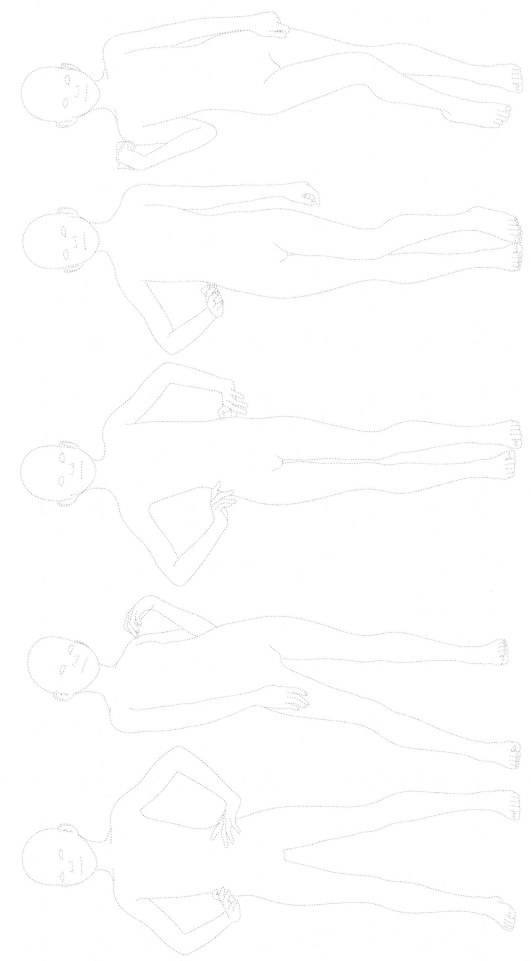

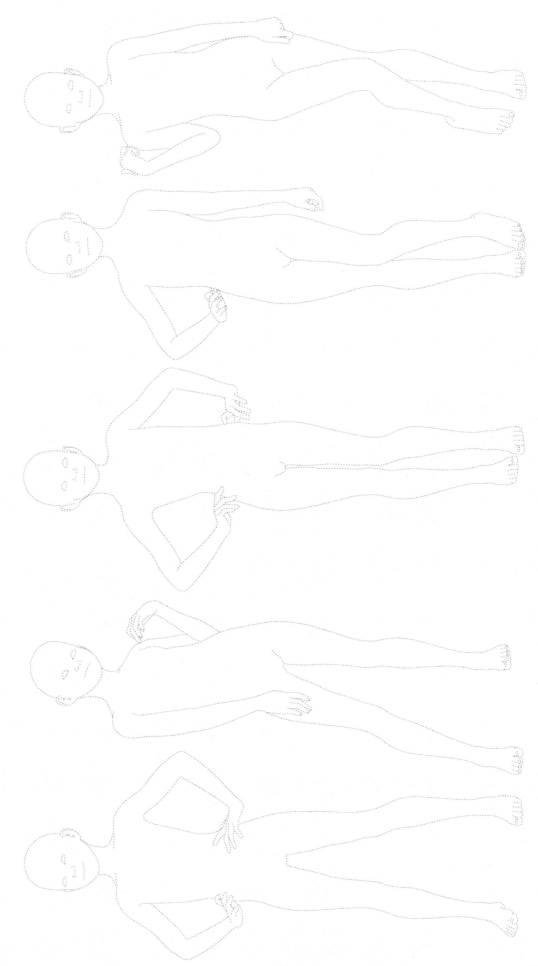

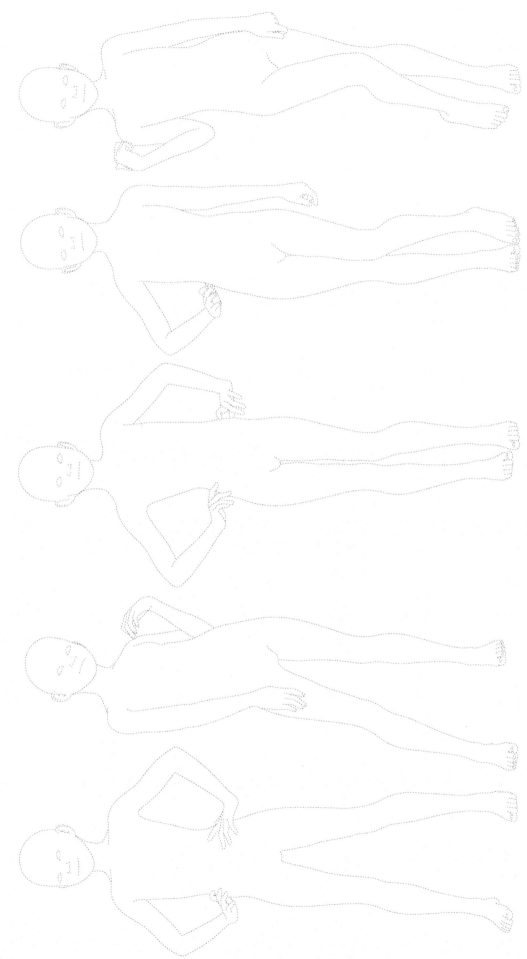

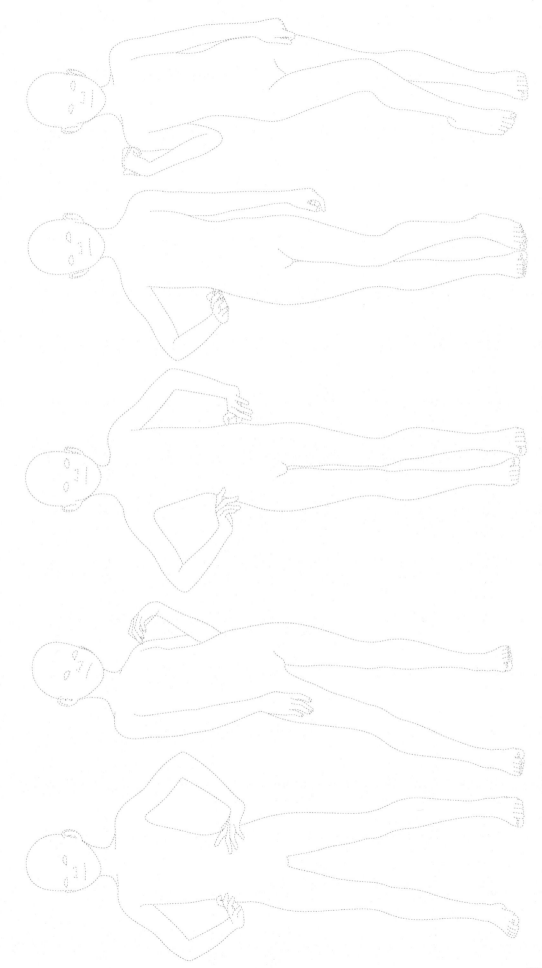

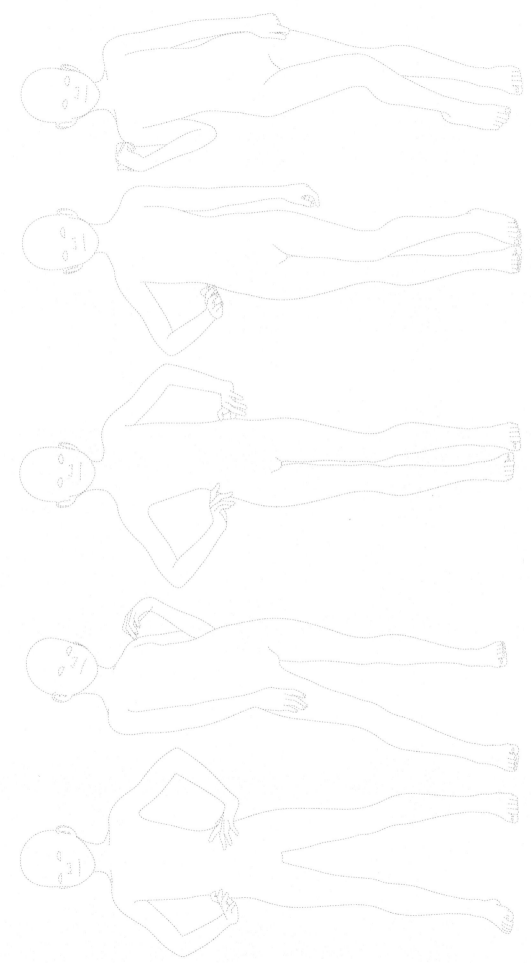

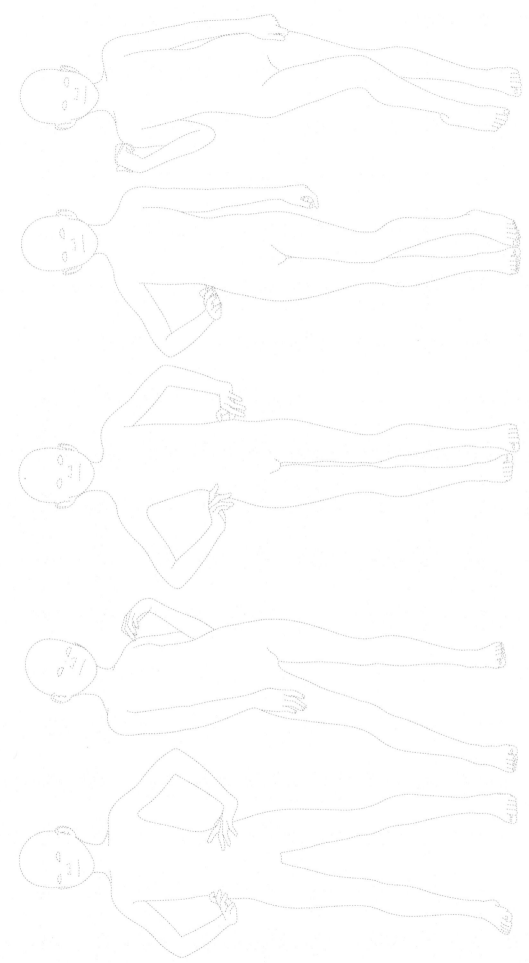

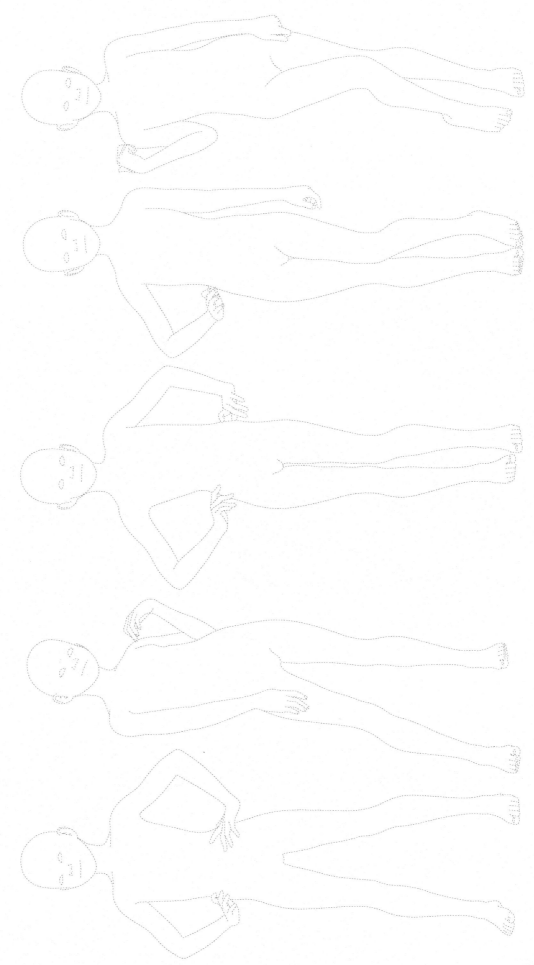

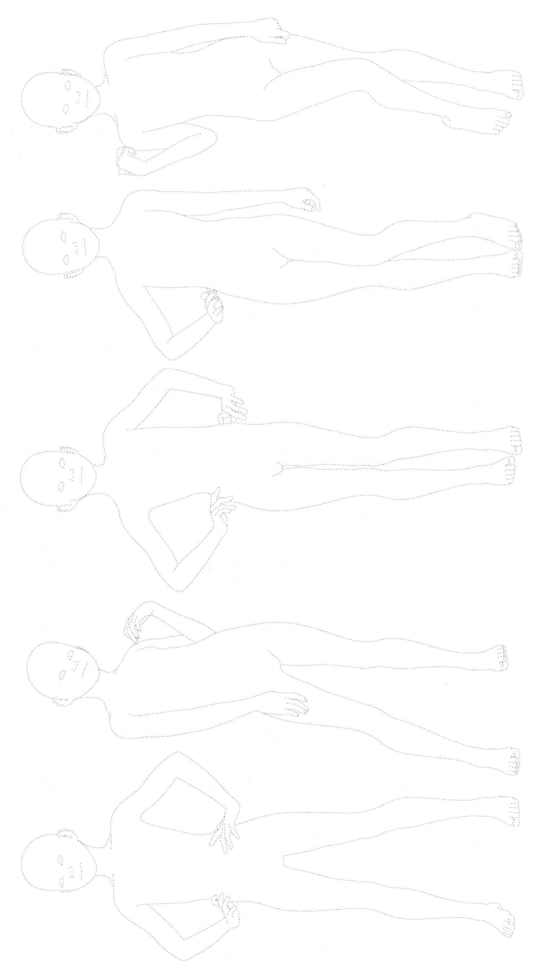

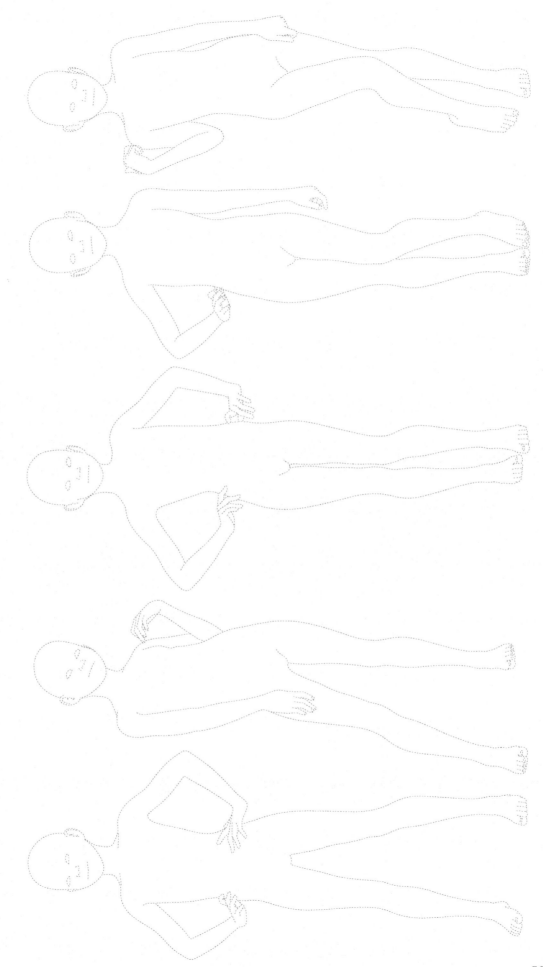

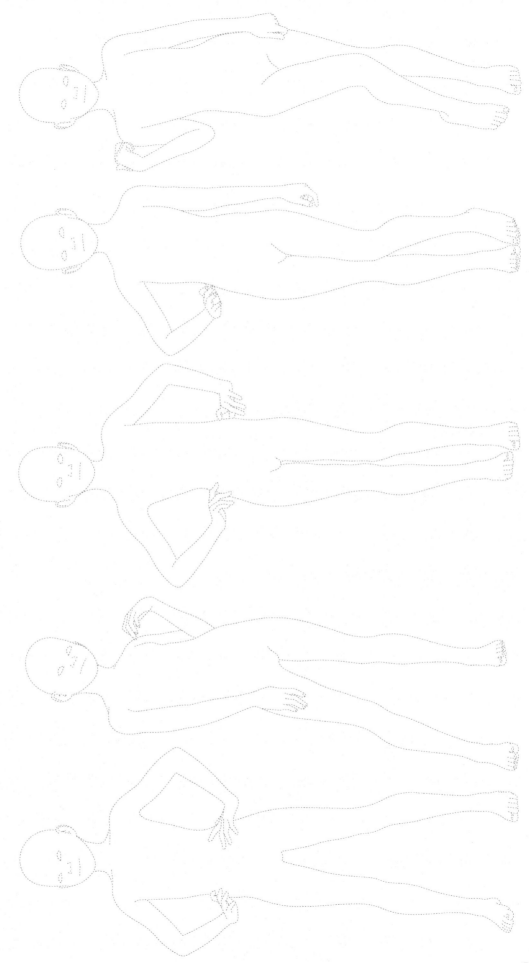

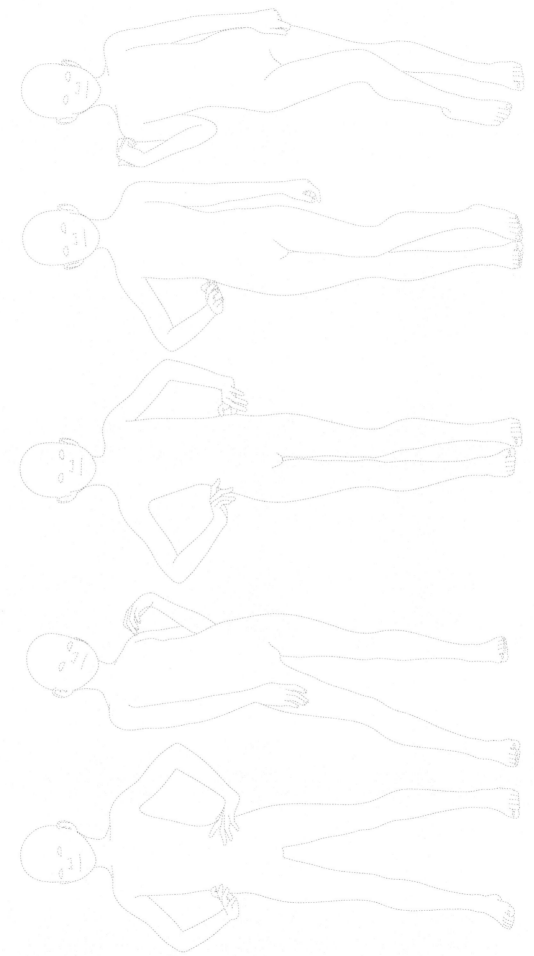

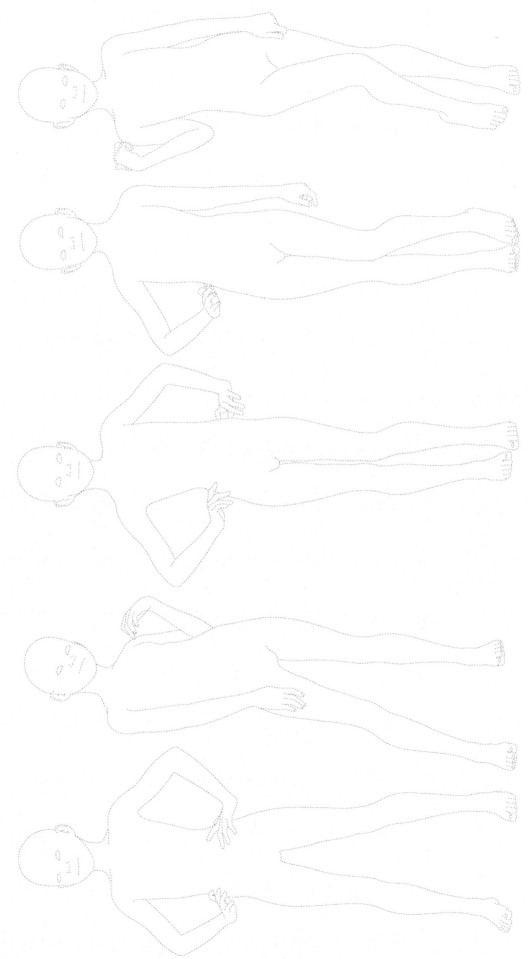

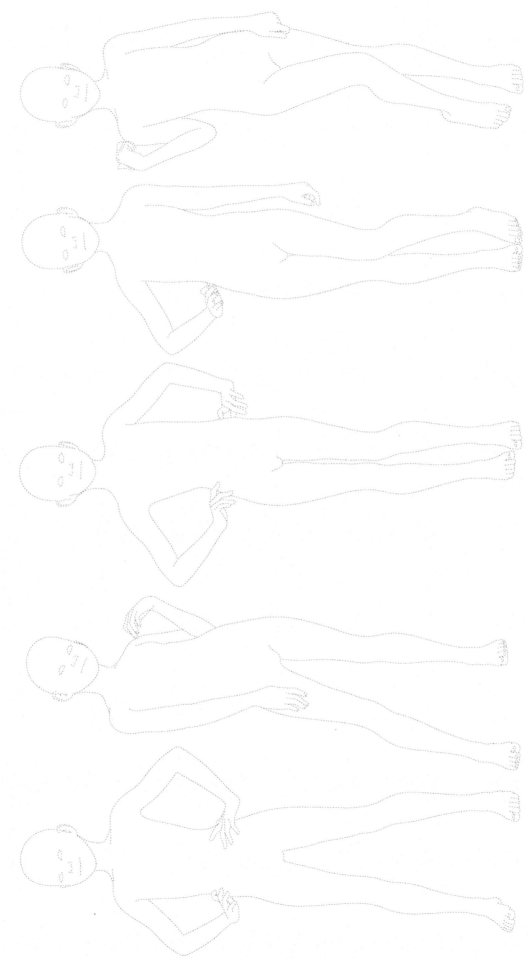

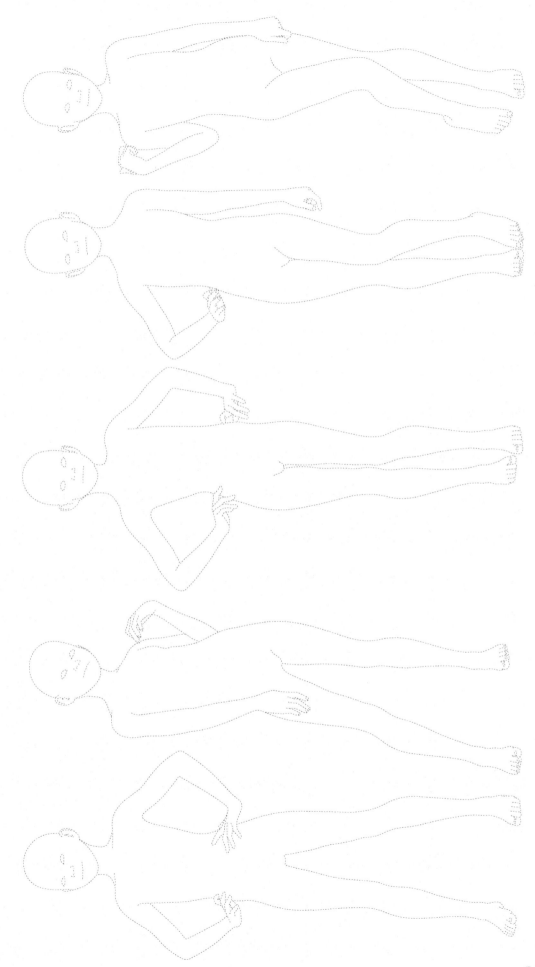

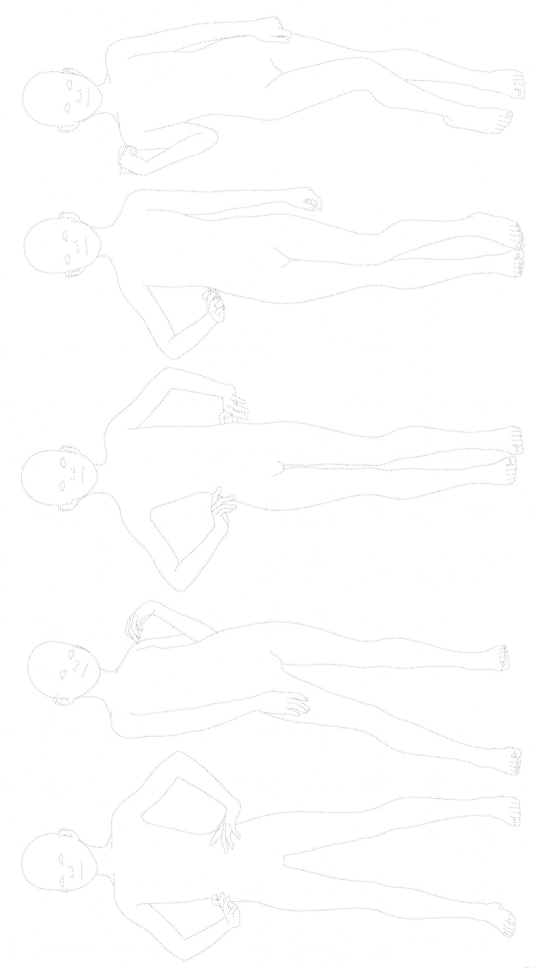

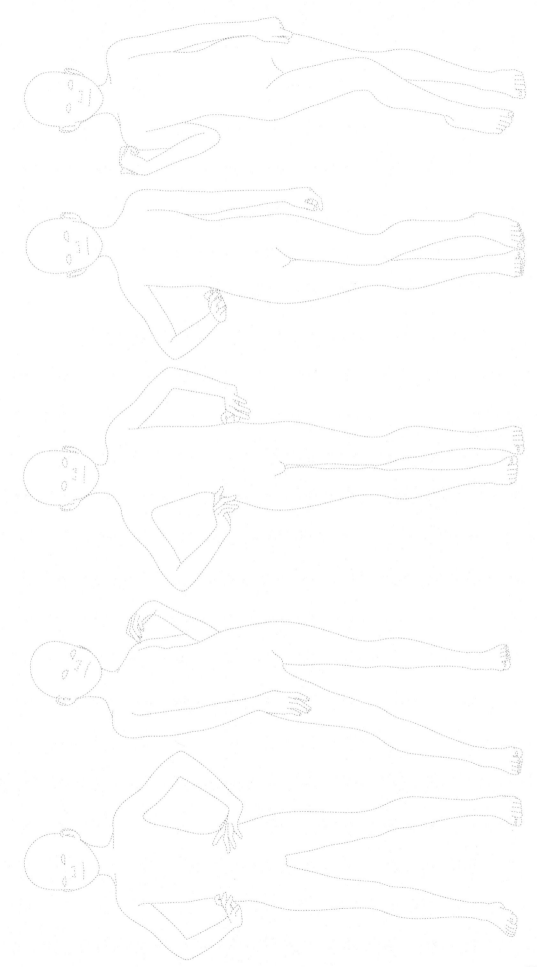

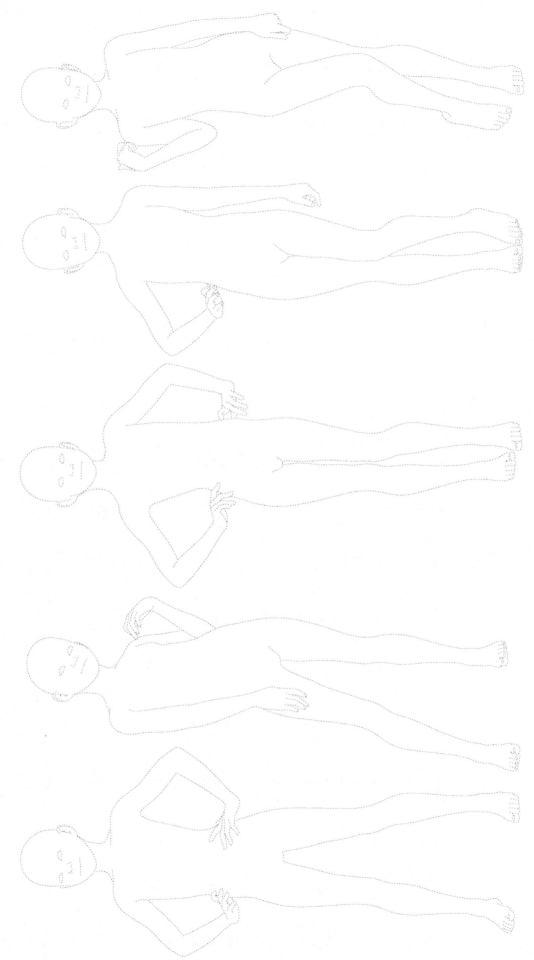

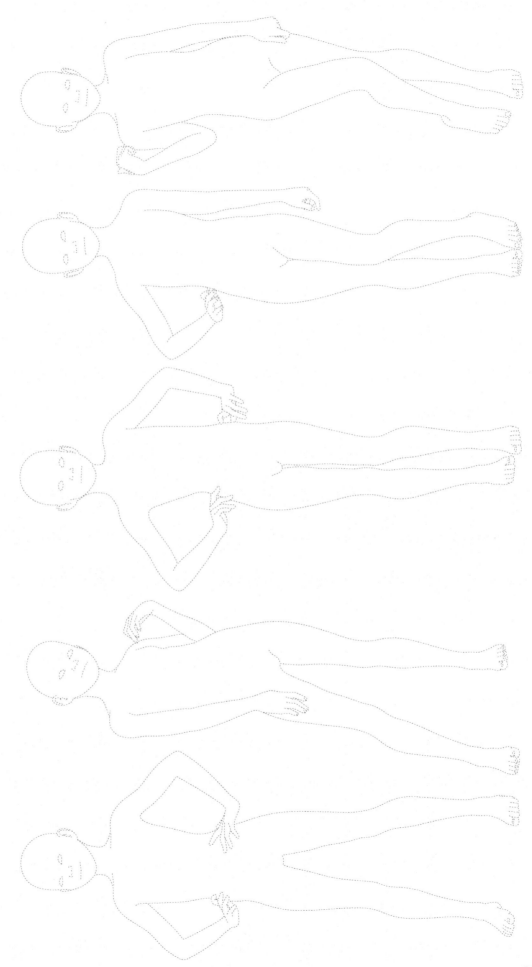

MEASUREMENTS

MEASUREMENTS

CHILDREN'S CLOTHING SIZES			
UK	**EUROPEAN**	**US**	**AUSTRALIA**
12 m	80 cm	12 - 18 m	
18 m	80 - 86 cm	18 - 24 m	18 m
24 m	86 - 92 cm	23 / 24 m	2
2 - 3	92 - 98 cm	2 T	3
3 - 4	98 - 104 cm	4 T	4
4 - 5	104 - 110 cm	5	5
5 - 6	110 - 116cm	6	6
6 - 7	116 - 122 cm	6 X -7	7
7 - 8	122 - 128 cm	7 to 8	8
8 - 9	128 - 134 cm	9 to 10	9
9 - 10	134 - 140 cm	10	10
10 - 11	140 - 146 cm	11	11
11 - 12	146 - 152 cm	14	12

CHILDREN'S SHOE SIZES			
UK	**EUROPEAN**	**US**	**AUSTRALIA**
4	20	4 ½ OR 4	12 ½
4 ½	21	5 OR 5 ½	13
5	21 OR 22	5 ½ OR 6	13 ½
5 ½	22	6	13 ½ OR 14
6	23	6 ½ OR 7	14 OR 14 ½
6 ½	23 OR 24	7 ½	14 ½ OR 15
7	24	7 ½ OR 8	15
7 ½	25	8 OR 9	15 ½
8	25 OR 26	8 ½ OR 9	16
8 ½	26	9 ½	16 ½
9	27	9 ½ OR 10	16 ½ OR 17
10	28	10 ½ OR 11	17 ½
10 ½ OR 11	29	11 ½ OR 12	18 OR 18 ½
11 ½	30	12 ½	18
12	31	13	19 OR 19 ½
12 ½	31	13 OR 13 ½	19 ½ OR 20
13	32	1	20
13 ½	32 ½	1 ½	20 ½
1	33	1 ½ OR 2	21
2	34	2 ½ OR 3	22

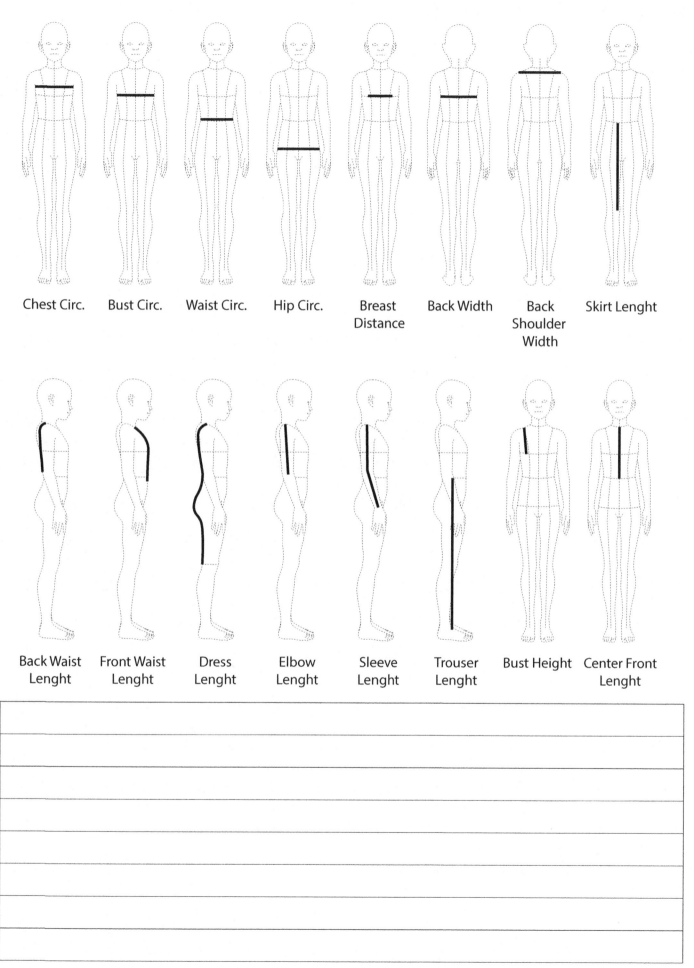

Chest Circ. Bust Circ. Waist Circ. Hip Circ. Breast Distance Back Width Back Shoulder Width Skirt Lenght

Back Waist Lenght Front Waist Lenght Dress Lenght Elbow Lenght Sleeve Lenght Trouser Lenght Bust Height Center Front Lenght

MEASUREMENTS

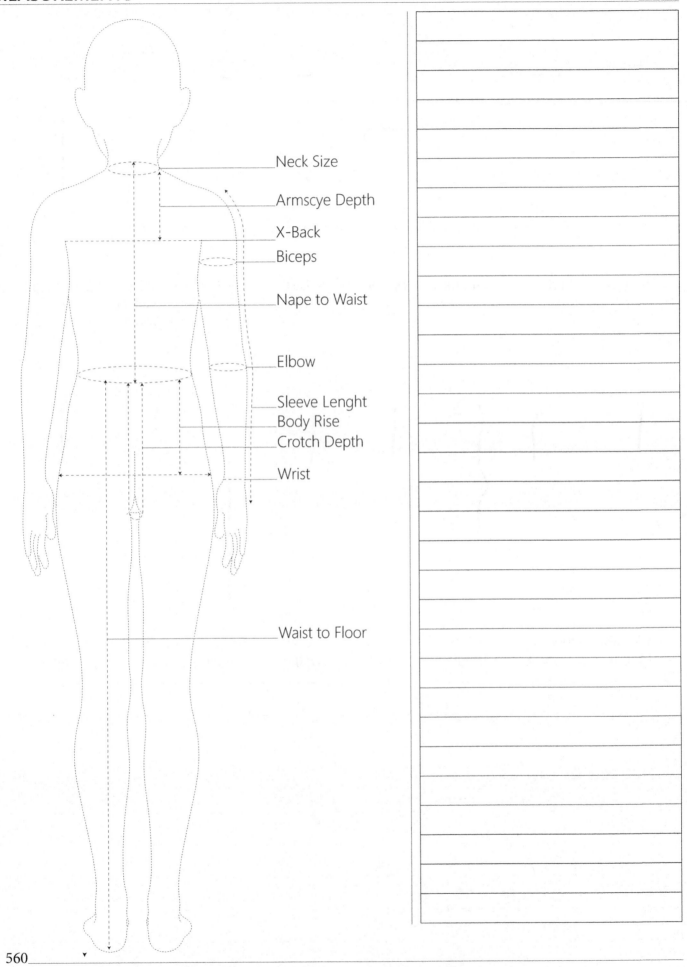

Neck Size

Armscye Depth

X-Back

Biceps

Nape to Waist

Elbow

Sleeve Lenght
Body Rise
Crotch Depth

Wrist

Waist to Floor

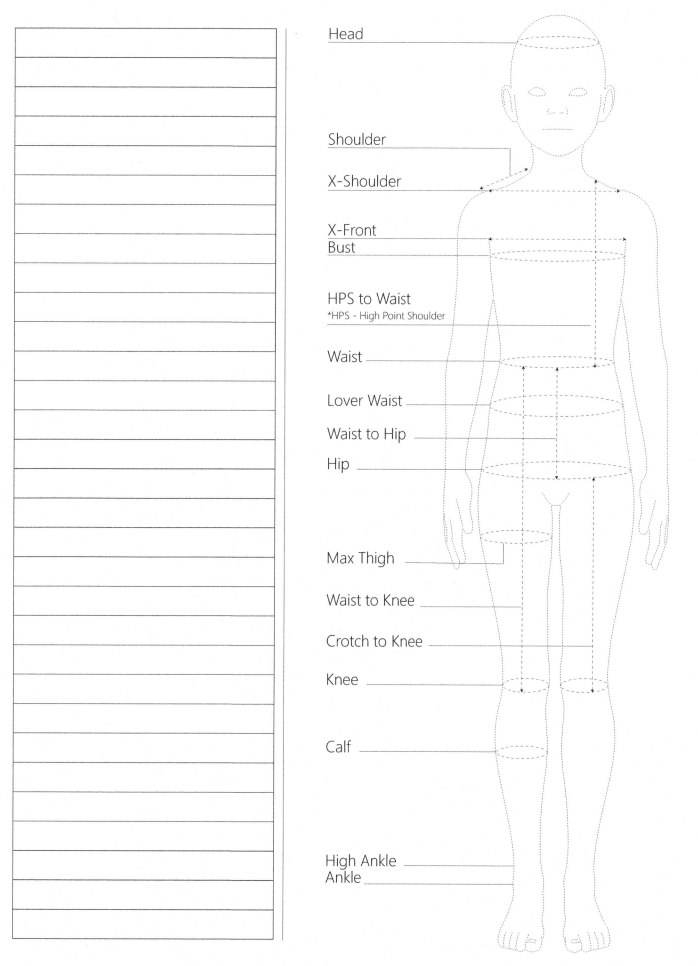

Head

Shoulder

X-Shoulder

X-Front
Bust

HPS to Waist
*HPS - High Point Shoulder

Waist

Lover Waist

Waist to Hip

Hip

Max Thigh

Waist to Knee

Crotch to Knee

Knee

Calf

High Ankle
Ankle

MEASUREMENTS

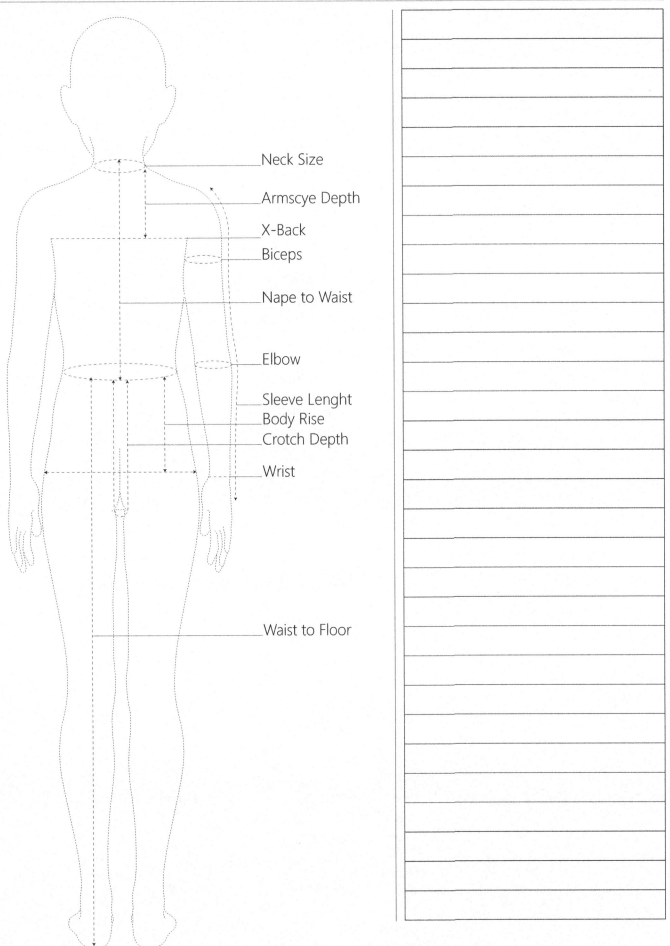

Neck Size

Armscye Depth

X-Back

Biceps

Nape to Waist

Elbow

Sleeve Lenght
Body Rise
Crotch Depth

Wrist

Waist to Floor

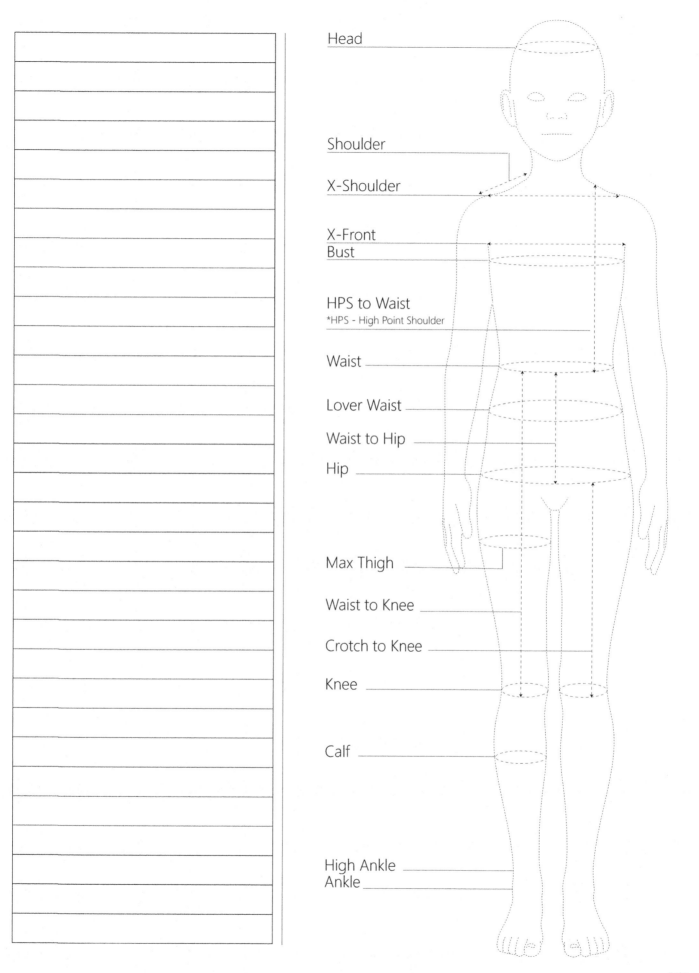

Head

Shoulder

X-Shoulder

X-Front
Bust

HPS to Waist
*HPS - High Point Shoulder

Waist

Lover Waist

Waist to Hip

Hip

Max Thigh

Waist to Knee

Crotch to Knee

Knee

Calf

High Ankle
Ankle

1. Coco Chanel	26. Ralph Rucci
2. Donna Karan	27. Salvatori Ferragamo
3. Giorgio Armani	28. Jimmy Choo
4. Calvin Klein	29. Alexandre Herchovitch
5. Donatella Versace	30. Mossimo Giannulli
6. Ralph Lauren	31. John Varvatos
7. Christian Dior	32. Daphne Guiness
8. Tom Ford	33. Jonathan Jony Ive
9. Pierre Cardin	34. Kate Spade
10. Yves Saint Laurent	35. Christian Audigier
11. Christian Louboutin	36. Allegra Versace
12. Karl Lagerfeld	37. Diane Von Furstenberg
13. Roberto Cavalli	38. Michael Kors
14. Marc Jacobs	39. Tory Burch
15. Betsey Johnson	40. Phoebe Philo
16. Sandy Powell	41. Oscar De La Renta
17. Domenico Dolce (R) & Stefano Gabbana	42. Zac Posen
18. Alexander Mcqueen	43. Riccardo Tischi
19. Valentino Garavani	44. Vera Wang
20. Miuccia Prada	45. Isabel Marant
21. Tommy Hilfiger	46. Esteban Cortázar
22. Carolina Herrera	47. Viviene Westwood
23. Jean-Paul Gaultier	48. Paul Smith
24. Herve Lager	49. Jil Sander
25. Stella McCartney	50. Anna Sui

A	
Adire	A cotton fabric that has been resist-dyed using indigo. The textile takes on a look similar to batik or shibori fabrics.
Aloe Vera Fabric	A fabric infused with thousands of aloe vera "capsules." These capsules are microscopic, airtight and waterproof. They open to release the gel only when the fabric is touched or rubbed. Essentially, every time an infused garment is worn, the aloe is applied to the skin. It is naturally anti-bacterial and combats body odor.
Aurvastra Fabrics	Natural, organic yarns are dyed by hand using plants that contain medicinal properties. The dye bath infuses the fibers with the lovely natural colors of these plants, along with their healing components. The yarns are then woven into fabric, and made into clothing or bedding.
Aramid	A manufactured fiber in which the fiber-forming substance is a long chain of synthetic polyamide in which at least 85% of the amide linkages are attached directly to two aromatic rings. Aramid fabrics are very strong and are resistant to high temperatures and extreme external forces. Aramid fabrics are used in thermally protective clothing; (i.e. coveralls, jackets, gloves, shirts, pants).
B	
Barathea	A closely woven fabric made of silk, rayon, cotton, or wool, having a pebbled surface. Barathea is mainly used for dresses, neckties, trimmings and suits.
Barkcloth	Originally, the term referred to a fabric found throughout the South Pacific and is made from the inner bark of certain trees. The bark is beaten into a paper-like fabric, then dyed or otherwise colored. Tapa cloth is one of the best known types of true barkcloth. Barkcloth is a term that also refers to a fabric, often cotton or rayon, with a somewhat crepe-like feel that is designed to resemble true barkcloth. This fabric is used extensively for draperies, slipcovers, and other home furnishings.
Batik	Batik describes a special technique of resist dyeing which was first used in Indonesia. Before dyeing the fabric is pile-spread with wax. The waxed areas remain in the original color while the rest of the fabric adopts the dyeing color. To get the typical veined effect to the design the wax is cracked. Today, it is largely produced in an industrial way.
Basket Weave	A variation of the plain weave construction, formed by treating two or more warp yarns and/or two or more filling yarns as one unit in the weaving process. Yarns in a basket weave are laid into the woven construction flat, and maintain a parallel relationship. Both balanced and unbalanced basket weave fabrics can be produced. Examples of basket weave construction includes monk cloth and oxford cloth.
Batiste	A medium-weight, plain weave fabric, usually made of cotton or cotton blends. End-uses include blouses and dresses.
Batting	Traditionally the middle layer, or stuffing, of a quilt. Batting can be made from cotton, polyester, silk, wool or a blend of these. Different types of batting vary in size and fiber content. Batting also helps conserve warmth. Beaded – This refers to any style of fabric that has beads embroidered into the design. Beading can be done at the time the fabric is made or can be re-embroidered after the fabric is made.
Bedford Cord	A cord cotton-like fabric with raised ridges in the lengthwise direction. Since the fabric has a high strength and a high durability, it is often used for upholstery and work clothes.
Bengaline	A ribbed fabric similar to faille, but heavier and with a coarser rib in the filling direction. It can be made of silk, wool, acetate, or rayon warp, with wool or cotton filling. The fabric was first made in Bengal, India, and is used for dresses, coats, trimmings, and draperies.
Berber Fleece	Berber fleece is made when the yarn is knitted into fabric, which is brushed with wire brushes to pull the material together and to fluff it up. The resulting material has a looped, soft pile, with large air pockets, which improve the insulating properties of the fabric. The pile is sheared to create an even length. Synthetic materials such as polyester are most frequently used to create Berber fleece, which tends to be strong, stretchy, and colorfast. In addition to being warm, Berber fleece is also designed to wick moisture away from the surface of the wearer. It will also not absorb moisture as readily as some natural fibers, since synthetics are water resistant. Berber fleece is a fabric that is very lightweight, warm, and soft. It is often compared to fur, because of the incredibly soft texture it has.
Birdseye	Fabric with a woven-in dobby design. The pattern has a center dot and resembles the eye of a bird. It is used in cotton diapers, pique, and wool sharkskin.
Boiled Wool	This is a felted knitted wool that it offers the flexibility of a knit with great warmth. Create your own by washing double the needed amount of 100% wool jersey in hot water and drying in a hot dryer. Expect 50% shrinkage. Appropriate for jackets, vests and stuffed animals.w

FABRIC GLOSSARY

Bonded	A fabric composed of 2 or more layers joined together with an adhesive, resin, foam, or fusible membrane.
Boucle	A knit or woven fabric made from a rough, curly, knotted boucle yarn. The fabric has a looped, knotted surface and is often used in sportswear and coats
Broadcloth	A plain weave tightly woven fabric, characterized by a slight ridge effect in one direction, usually the filling. The most common broadcloth is made from cotton or cotton/polyester blends.
Brocade	A heavy, exquisite jacquard type fabric with an all-over raised pattern or floral design. Common end-uses include such formal applications as upholstery, draperies, and eveningwear.
Brushed	A finishing process for knit or woven fabrics in which brushes or other abrading devices are used on a loosely constructed fabric to permit the fibers in the yarns to be raised to create a nap on fabrics or create a novelty surface texture.
Buckram	Mainly cotton and sometimes synthetic. A cheap, low-textured, loose weave, very heavily sized and stiff fabric. Also, 2 fabrics are glued together; one is open weave and the other much finer. Some is also made in linen in a single fabric. Also called crinoline book muslin or book binding. Buckram softens with heat and can be shaped while warm. Used for interlinings and all kinds of stiffening in clothes, book binding, and for millinery (because it can be moistened and shaped). Used to give stiffness to leather garments not as stiff and often colored is called "tarlatan". Buckram is originally from Bukhara a city in west Asia from whence the cloth was exported.
Bull Denim	A twill weave cotton denim fabric that is soft but tough as nails. Bull Denim is durable and heavier than regular denim. It takes dye well with very good results. Not stiff like canvas.
Bunting	Bunting is a loosely woven cloth traditionally made of wool, but now often made with polyester. Bunting is mainly used for flags and festive decorations. It is also known as banner cloth.
Burlap	A loosely constructed, heavy weight, plain weave fabric used as a carpet backing, and as inexpensive packaging for sacks of grain or rice. Also, as fashion dictates, burlap may also appear as a drapery fabric.
Burn-Out	A brocade-like pattern effect created on the fabric through the application of a chemical, instead of color, during the burn-out printing process. (Sulfuric acid, mixed into a colorless print paste, is the most common chemical used.) Many simulated eyelet effects can be created using this method. In these instances, the chemical destroys the fiber and creates a hole in the fabric in a specific design, where the chemical comes in contact with the fabric. The fabric is then over-printed with a simulated embroidery stitch to create the eyelet effect. However, burn-out effects can also be created on velvets made of blended fibers, in which the ground fabric is of one fiber like a polyester, and the pile may be of a cellulosic fiber like rayon or acetate. In this case, when the chemical is printed in a certain pattern, it destroys the pile in those areas where the chemical comes in contact with the fabric, but leave the ground fabric unharmed.
C	
Calico	A tightly-woven cotton type fabric with an all-over print, usually a small floral pattern on a contrasting background color. Common end-uses include dresses, aprons, and quilts.
Canton Flannel	Four harness warp-faced twill weave. Characteristics The filling yarn is a very loosely twisted and soft and later brushed to produced a soft nap on the back, the warp is medium in size. The face is a twill. Heavy, warm, strong and absorbent. Named for Canton, China where it was first made. Comes bleached, unbleached, dyed, and some is printed. Used in Interlinings, sleeping garments, linings, coverings, work gloves.
Canvas	Cotton, linen, or synthetic fabric made with a basic plain weave in heavy and firm weight yarns for industrial or heavy duty purposes. Also referred to as "duck", although the term "canvas" usually relates to the heavier coarser constructions.
Challis	A lightweight, soft plain weave fabric with a slightly brushed surface. The fabric is often printed, usually in a floral pattern. Challis is most often seen in fabrics made of cotton, wool, or rayon.
Chambray	A plain woven fabric that can be made from cotton, silk, or manufactured fibers, but is most commonly cotton. It incorporates a colored warp (often blue) and white filling yarns
Chantilly Lace	One of the most popular of bridal laces often used for the trimming on bridal veils. It is made by the bobbin method and has designs outlined by thick cords.
Chamois	Chamois cloth is woven to imitate the leather, usually has a slightly napped surface, and is usually yellow, as is the goat skin. It is used for gloves and as a cloth for washing autos. It is also used in clothing.
Charmeuse	Charmeuse is an opaque, shiny fabric that is similar to satin but lighter weight. Charmeuse also has a softer hand and a clingier look. Silk, polyester and rayon fabrics are commonly given a charmeuse finish.

Cheesecloth	A lightweight, sheer, plain-woven fabric with a very soft texture. It may be natural colored, bleached, or dyed. It usually has a very low yarn count. When dyed it may be called bunting and could be used for flags or banners.
Chenille	A specialty yarn, characterized by a pile protruding on all sides, resembling a caterpillar. The yarn is produced by first weaving a fabric with a cotton or linen warp and a silk, wool, rayon, or cotton filling. The warp yarns are taped in groups of tightly woven filling yarns, which have been beaten in very closely. After weaving, the fabric is cut into strips between the yarn groups. Each cutting produces a continuous chenille yarn, which is then twisted, creating the chenille yarn, and giving the pile appearance on all sides of the yarn. The chenille yarn is used mainly for decorative fabrics, embroidery, tassels, and rugs.
Chiffon	A plain woven lightweight, extremely sheer, airy, and soft silk fabric, containing highly twisted filament yarns. The fabric, used mainly in evening dresses and scarves, can also be made from rayon and other manufactured fibers.
China Silk	A plain weave silk of various weights. This silk is the "hand" or touch that many people identify as silk. There are various weights of China silk from light, used for linings and many "washable silks" with the wrinkled look, to heavy for shirts and dresses.
China Twill	A lightweight cotton twill fabric. China Twill is 6-7 ounces per yard and is typically used for blouses, shirts and light weight skirts. See Twill.
Chintz	Glazed plain weave cotton fabric with a tightly spun fine warp and a coarser slack twist filling, often printed with brightly colored flowers or stripes. Named from Hindu word meaning spotted. Several types of glazes are used in the finishing process. Some glazes wash out in laundering, but others such as resin finishes are permanent. Unglazed chintz is called cretonne. Chintz end-uses include draperies, slipcovers, skirts, and summer dresses, and shirts.
Cire	A finishing process that produces a high gloss on the surface on the fabric by passing it through heavy rollers (calendering). Fabrics made of thermoplastic fibers like nylon or polyester are cired by calendering with heat and pressure alone. Other fabrics like rayons or silks are calendered with wax or other compounds. Cire fabrics have a much higher shine than glazed fabrics and are usually somewhat slippery.
Clips	A fabric decorated with small woven spots of extra warp or filling yarn-the floating threads between the spots being clipped or sheared in finishing. Also known as clip-spot fabric.
Cloque	Term used to describe a fabric with a raised effect Jacquard, usually knitted from two colors, and often used interchangeably with matelasse and blister. Cotton cloque is frequently popular for summer dress and jacket or coat costumes.
Coated	Fabrics that have been coated with a lacquer, varnish, rubber, plastic resin of polyvinyl chloride or polyethylene, or other substance to make them longer lasting or impervious to water or other liquids.
Coating	A term used to describe a fabric suitable for outerwear, such as coats, as in coating fabric. Also, something applied to a finished fiber or fabric, such as a rubber coating to make a fabric impervious to water. Coating suggests a thicker layer of the substance than does the word finish. A rubber-coated fabric is probably more resistant to water than one that has been treated with a water-resistant finish.
CoolMax®	CoolMax® is the brand name of a series of high-performance fabrics designed and marketed mainly for sportswear .that are designed to wick moisture away from the skin. CoolMax® was created using four channel polyester fibers that are woven together in cross sections to allow air to flow through the fabric. The fabrics employ specially-engineered polyester fibers to improve "breathability" compared to natural fibers like cotton. CoolMax® is a lightweight, durable fabric that is temperature regulating and keeps the skin dry and warm. It is comfortable and form fitting which makes it ideal for layering
Coolmax™ EcoTech™	This ultimate performance fabric delivers the same high-performance, quick-dry benefits and comfort as the original Coolmax® fabric, but has the added benefit of being made from recycled resources. The process for making Coolmax™ EcoTech™ fiber begins with post-consumer bottles made of polyethylene terephthalate, or PET.
Corduroy	A fabric with a pile that is usually in rows that are parallel to the selvedge. The pile is formed by weaving the fabric with two types of picks – binder picks that 'hold the fabric together', and pile picks that go over an number of warps on the face side of the fabric. The pile picks are sliced open after weaving in a process known as cutting. The ridges are built so that clear lines can be seen when the pile is cut. The fabric is then desized and bleached, and then brushed to develop the pile into uniform races that are known as wales. Corduroy is classified by the number of wales or cords to the inch. The foundation of the fabric can be either a plain or twill weave. It is traditionally made of cotton but may be cotton blends or other fibers as well. Of all cotton fabrics, corduroy is the warmest because its wales form an insulated cushion of air. It is common in men's women's and children's apparel especially trousers.

FABRIC GLOSSARY

Coutil	Coutil (or Coutille) is woven cloth created specifically for making corsets. It is woven tightly to inhibit penetration of the corset's bones and resist stretching. Coutil has a high cotton content. Cotton has good dimensional stability, or a resistance to stretching, which makes it a good choice for such a stressed garment. Coutil may be plain (similar to 100% cotton facing), satin, or brocade. It is also common for coutil to have a herringbone texture, or a similar woven texture.
Covert	Made with two shades of color e.g. (Medium and light brown). The warp is 2 ply (1 light; 1 dark) and filling 1 ply (dark or same as warp). Very rugged and closely woven. Has a mottled or speckled effect. First used as a hunting fabric. Has a clear finish and hard texture. Wears exceptionally well and has a smart appearance. Light in weight. Used for over coating for both men and women. It is also made waterproof and used a great deal in rain water.
Crash	Typically made of Linen. It is very rugged and substantial in feel. Come in white or natural shades or could be dyed, printed, striped, or checked. The yarn is strong, irregular in diameter but smooth. Has a fairly good texture. Used for toweling, suitings, dresses, coats.
Crepe	A lightweight fabric of silk, rayon, cotton, wool, man-made, or blended fibers, and characterized by a crinkled surface. This surface is obtained through the use of crepe yarns (yarns that have such a high twist that the yarn kinks), and by chemical treatment with caustic soda, embossing, or weaving (usually with thicker warp yarns and thinner filling yarns). Although crepe is traditionally woven, crepe yarns are now used to produce knit crepes.
Crepe-Back Satin	A satin fabric in which highly twisted yarns are used in the filling direction. The floating yarns are made with low twist and may be of either high or low luster. If the crepe effect is the right side of the fabric, the fabric is called satin-back crepe.
Crepe De Chine	Traditionally, a very sheer, pebbly, washable silk with the fabric degummed to produce crinkle. Today, it is a sheer, flat crepe in silk or man-made fibers. It is used for lingerie, dresses, and blouses.
Crepon	Crêpe effect appears in direction of the warp and achieved by alternate S and Z, or slack, tension, or different degrees of twist. Originally a wool Crêpe but now made of silk and rayon. It is much stouter and more rugged than the average Crêpe. Has a wavy texture with the "waves" running in a lengthwise direction. Mostly used for prints. Used for dresses and blouses.
Crewel	Crewel is a hand embroidery technique in which fine, loosely twisted yarn is chain stitched on cotton cloth. Imperfections, color variations, irregularities, natural black specks, dye marks, and dirt spots are characteristics that identify crewel as genuine. Most crewel designs are outlines of flowers, vines or leaves.
Crinkle	A fabric with an uneven surface, created by use of caustic soda that causes it to shrink unevenly. Plisse is an example of a crinkle crepe fabric. Crinkle crepe and plisse usually have a larger pattern to surface irregularities than crepe.
Crinoline	A lightweight, plain weave, stiffened fabric with a low yarn count (few yarns to the inch in each direction).
Crushed	Any fabric that has been treated so as to have a permanently crinkled, crushed or rumpled appearance.
Crushed Velvet	Any velvet with an irregular pattern of nap going in different directions. The pattern gives the fabric a "crushed or rumpled" appearance.
D	
Damask	A glossy jacquard fabric, usually made from linen, cotton, rayon, silk, or blends. The patterns are flat and reversible. The fabric is often used in napkins, tablecloths, draperies, and upholstery.
Dazzle	A type of polyester fabric that is widely used in making clothes like basketball uniforms, football uniforms, rugby ball uniforms and even casual clothing because it absorbs moisture quickly. It is a lightweight fabric that easily allows the body to receive ventilation during workouts, playing sports and engaging in just about any outside activity. Dazzle fabric is distinguished by the pattern of tiny holes in the weave of the material. To the touch, dazzle is soft and somewhat like silk, although it is far more sturdy than silk. Dazzle is extremely durable due to the tightly woven polyester fibers, which makes it nearly impossible to tear.
Denim	True denim is a twill weave cotton-like fabric made with different colored yarns in the warp and the weft. Due to the twill construction, one color predominates on the fabric surface.
Dobby Weave	A decorative weave, characterized by small figures, usually geometric, that are woven into the fabric structure. Dobbies may be of any weight or compactness, with yarns ranging from very fine to coarse and fluffy. Standard dobby fabrics are usually flat and relatively fine or sheer. However, some heavyweight dobby fabrics are available for home furnishings and for heavy apparel.

Doeskin	Generally used to describe a type of fabric finish in which a low nap is brushed in one direction to create a soft suede-like feel on the fabric surface. End-uses include billiard table surfaces and men's' sportswear.
Donegal Tweed	A medium to heavy, plain or twill weave fabric in which colorful yarn slubs are woven into the fabric. The name originally applied to a hand-woven thick woolen tweed fabric made in Donegal, Ireland. End-uses include winter coats and suits.
Dotted Swiss	A lightweight, sheer cotton or cotton blend fabric with a small dot flock-like pattern either printed on the surface of the fabric, or woven into the fabric. End-uses for this fabric include blouses, dresses, baby clothes, and curtains
Double Faced	A fabric construction, in which two fabrics are woven on the loom at the same time, one on top of the other. In the weaving process, the two layers of woven fabric are held together using binder threads. The woven patterns in each layer of fabric can be similar or completely different.
Double Knit	A fabric knitted on a circular knitting machine using interlocking loops and a double stitch on a double needle frame to form a fabric with double thickness. It is the same on both sides. Today, most double knits are made of 150 denier polyester, although many lightweight versions are now being made using finer denier yarns and blends of filament and spun yarns.
Double Weave	A woven fabric construction made by interlacing two or more sets of warp yarns with two or more sets of filling yarns. The most common double weave fabrics are made using a total of either four or five sets of yarns.
Drill	A heavy, strong, durable twilled fabric of cotton or man-made fibers, similar to denim that has a diagonal 2×1 weave running up to the left selvage. When strength of fabric is essential, drill is suitable for slacks, uniforms, overalls, and work shirts.
Dryflex	Dryflex is a "high performance" knit fabric blended with Lycra. It is a wind resistant and moisture-wicking fabric that is soft and very comfortable. Dryflex will stretch up to 250% without memory loss over a lifetime of wear. Dryflex is the perfect fabric for activewear as it is quick dry and easy to care for.
Duchess Satin	One of the heaviest and richest looking satins. It is usually made of silk. It is important for such formal clothing as wedding gowns.
Duck	A tightly woven, heavy, plain-weave, bottom-weight fabric with a hard, durable finish. The fabric is usually made of cotton, and is widely used in men's and women's slacks, and children's play clothes.
Dupioni	Silk that comes from the fiber formed by two silk worms that spun their cocoons together in an interlocking manner. The yarn is uneven, irregular, and larger than regular filaments. It is used to make shantung and dupioni.
E	
Embossed	A calendering process in which fabrics are engraved with the use of heated rollers under pressure to produce a raised design on the fabric surface.
Embroidered	An embellishment of a fabric or garment in which colored threads are sewn on to the fabric to create a design. Embroidery may be done either by hand or machine.
End-On-End	A closely woven fabric with alternating fine colored yarn and a white yarn creating a mini checkered effect with a smooth texture. The weave is commonly found in men's shirts.
Eyelash	Term used to describe clipped yarns that lie on the surface of a fabric, giving the effect of eyelashes.
Eyelet	A type of fabric which contains patterned cut-outs, around which stitching or embroidery may be applied in order to prevent the fabric from raveling.
F	
Faille	A glossy, soft, finely-ribbed silk-like woven fabric made from cotton, silk, or manufactured fibers
Faux Fur	A slang term for pile fabrics and garments that imitate animal pelts. The most popular fake furs are probably those made from modacrylic fiber.
Faux Leather	A term used for imitation leathers. More correctly, these should be described by their actual construction, such as vinyl-coated fabric.
Faux Suede	A fabric with a short nap and a soft finish that suggests animal suede.

Felt	A non-woven fabric made from wool, hair, or fur, and sometimes in combination with certain manufactured fibers, where the fibers are locked together in a process utilizing heat, moisture, and pressure to form a compact material.
Fishnet	Fishnet is an open, diamond shaped knit fabric.
Flannel	A medium-weight, plain or twill weave fabric that is typically made from cotton, a cotton blend, or wool. The fabric has a very soft hand, brushed on both sides to lift the fiber ends out of the base fabric and create a soft, fuzzy surface. End-uses include shirts and pajamas.
Flannelette	A medium-weight, plain weave fabric with a soft hand, usually made from cotton. The fabric is usually brushed only on one side, and is lighter weight than flannel. End-uses include shirts and pajamas.
Fleece	A lightweight fabric with a thick, heavy fleece-like surface. It may be a pile or napped fabric, and either woven or knit construction. End uses include coats, jackets, blankets, etc. Fleece fabrics are available in a variety of constuctions: Polarfleece® is the original fleece fabric, developed in 1979, by Malden Mills. It is typically used for non-technical garments, and it is only available at Malden Mills®; Polartec®, also developed by Malden Mills, was created for today's high-performance technical garments, which provides enhanced durability warmth, wind resistance, breathability and weather protection.
Flocked	A type of raised decoration applied to the surface of a fabric in which an adhesive is printed on the fabric in a specific pattern, and then finely chopped fibers are applied by means of dusting, air-brushing, or electrostatic charges. The fibers adhere only to the areas where the adhesive has been applied, and the excess fibers are removed by mechanical means.
Foil	Foil is a high gloss mylar usually in metallic colors that pulls away from the clear backing. Sometimes it is referred to as foil paper and other times it is referred to as foil sheets. The foil is applied to the fabric using very high heat.
Foulard	A lightweight twill-weave fabric, made from filament yarns like silk, acetate, polyester, with a small all-over print pattern on a solid background. The fabric is often used in men's ties.
Four-Ply Crepe	Four ply crepe is a heavier version of regular crepe made with four ply yarn. A four ply yarn is made from twisting together four individual yarn strands. The resulting fabric is medium to heavy weight, smooth and flat, with a crepe finish and a good deal of lustre. The fabric tailors and drapes beautifully and is a favorite for bridal usage. 4 ply silks are most frequently used for bridal gowns, semi fitted garments, dresses and suits. Fabric sews easily, but shows pin holes and ravels fairly easily.
Four-Way Stretch	A fabric that stretches both on the crosswise and lengthwise grains of the fabric. It is the same as two-way stretch.
French Terry	A knit jersey with loops on one side. Sometimes napped to make fleece.
G	
Gabardine	A tightly woven, twilled, worsted fabric with a slight diagonal line on the right side. Wool gabardine is known as a year-round fabric for business suiting. Polyester, cotton, rayon, and various blends are also used in making gabardine.
Gauze	A thin, sheer plain-weave fabric made from cotton, wool, silk, rayon, or other manufactured fibers. End-uses include curtains, apparel, trimmings, and surgical dressings.
Gazar	A silk or wool fabric with crisp hand and flat, smooth texture. Plain weave with high-twist double yarns interlaced as one.
Georgette	A sheer lightweight fabric, often made of silk or from such manufactured fibers as polyester, with a crepe surface. End-uses include dresses and blouses.
Gingham	A medium weight, plain weave fabric with a plaid or check pattern. End-uses include dresses, shirts, and curtains.
GORE-TEX®	GORE-TEX® fabrics are created by laminating GORE-TEX® membranes to high-performance textiles, then sealing them with an innovative solution for guaranteed waterproof protection. GORE-TEX® is designed to be durably waterproof, windproof, and breathable and maintain its performance for the life of the end product. GORE-TEX® is best known for its use in protective, yet breathable, rainwear fabrics.
Gossamer	Gossamer is a very light, sheer, gauze-like fabric, popular for white wedding dresses and decorations.
Greige Goods	The state of a fabric as it comes from the loom or knitting machine (after it has been constructed) but before it has been colored, finished or processed.

H	
Habutai	Soft, lightweight silk dress fabric originally woven in the gum on hand looms in Japan. It is sometimes confused with China silk, which is technically lighter in weight.
Heather	A yarn that is spun using pre-dyed fibers. These fibers are blended together to give a particular look. (For example, black and white may be blended together to create a grey heathered yarn.) The term, heather, may also be used to describe the fabric made from heathered yarns.
Herringbone	A fabric in which the pattern of weave resembles the skeletal structure of the herring. It is a twill weave in which the wale runs in one direction for a few rows and then re verses, forming a "V" pattern. It is made with a broken twill weave that produces a balanced, zigzag effect and is used for sportswear, suits, and coats.
Hopsack	Popular suiting fabric made from a 2-and-2 or a 3-and-3 basket weave. Generally appear as small squares. A coarse, open woven fabric which got its name from the plain weave fabric used for sacking in which hops were gathered. The hopsack weave is found in silk, cotton, wool, linen, rayon, hemp, and jute.
Houndstooth	A variation on the twill weave construction in which a broken check effect is produced by a variation in the pattern of interlacing yarns, utilizing at least two different colored yarns.
I	
Ikat	a style of weaving that uses a resist dyeing process similar to tie-dye on either the warp or weft before the threads are woven to create a pattern or design. A Double Ikat is when both the warp and the weft are tie-dyed before weaving. Through common usage, the word has come to describe both the process and the cloth itself. Ikats have been woven in cultures all over the world. In Central and South America, Ikat is still common in Argentina, Bolivia, Ecuador, Guatemala and Mexico.
Illusion	A very fine sheer net fabric usually of nylon or silk. Used for veils.
Interfacing	Fabrics used to support, reinforce and give shape to fashion fabrics in sewn products. Often placed between the lining and the outer fabric, it can be made from yarns or directly from fibers, and may be either woven, non-woven, or knitted.
Interlining	Interlining is a layer of fabric inserted between the face and the lining of a garment, drapery, or quilt. Interlining is similar to batting, a thick layer of fiber designed to provide insulation, loft, and body to quilts, pillow toppers, and heavy winter jackets. Depending on the application, interlining materials can be woven, knitted, or created by fusing fibers together. Silk, wool, and artificial fibers with good insulating qualities are common choices for interlining. Some interlinings are designed to be fused, while others are intended to be sewn to one or both layers of the textile. As an inner lining within textiles, interlining is used in a number of applications. In many cases, interlining serves as an additional layer of insulation. For example, drapes are often interlined with flannel or a similarly thick material to keep rooms warmer in winter and cooler in summer, while many winter coats and pants use a thick layer of interlining to protect the wearer from the elements.
Interlock	The stitch variation of the rib stitch, which resembles two separate 1 x 1 ribbed fabrics that are inter-knitted. Plain (double knit) interlock stitch fabrics are thicker, heavier, and more stable than single knit constructions.
Irridescent	Fabric woven with yarns of one color in the warp and another color in the filling so that the fabric seems to change color as the light strikes it. Other names for this type of fabric are changeable and shot.
J	
Jacquard	Woven fabrics manufactured by using the Jacquard attachment on the loom. This attachment provides versatility in designs and permits individual control of each of the warp yarns. Thus, fabrics of almost any type or complexity can be made. Brocade and damask are types of jacquard woven fabrics.
Jersey	The consistent interlooping of yarns in the jersey stitch to produces a fabric with a smooth, flat face, and a more textured, but uniform back. Jersey fabrics may be produced on either circular or flat weft knitting machines.
K	

L	
Lace	A decorated openwork fabric created by looping, interlacing, braiding, or twisting threads. [t is made (either on a background fabric of net or without a background fabric) with a design formed by a net work of threads made by hand or on special lace machines, with bobbins, needles, or hooks. The pattern in lace is usually open and most often floral in design. Machine-made lace is most commonly seen today and many patterns formerly only made by hand, are imitated by machine. Lace is the traditional bridal fabric, but it is also used for other non-formal clothing such as sports clothes. The following entries are some of the major types of lace.
Lamé	A woven fabric using flat silver or gold metal threads to create either the design or the background in the fabric. Lame is usually gold or silver in color; sometimes copper lamé is seen. Lamé comes in different varieties, depending on the composition of the other threads in the fabric. Common examples are tissue lamé, hologram lamé and pearl lamé. An issue with lamé is that it is subject to seam or yarn slippage, making it less than ideal for garments with frequent usage. Lamé is often used in evening and dress wear; and in theatrical and dance costumes.
Laminated	A term used to describe fabrics which have been joined together through the use of a high-strength reinforcing scrim or base fabrics between two plies of flexible thermoplastic film. It can a bonded utilizing either foam itself, or some other material, such as adhesives, heat, or chemical bonding agents.
Lawn	A light, fine cloth made using carded or combed, linen or cotton yarns. The fabric has a crease-resistant, crisp finish. Linen lawn is synonymous with handkerchief linen. Cotton lawn is a similar type of fabric, which can be white, solid colored, or printed.
Leno	A construction of woven fabrics in which the resulting fabric is very sheer, yet durable. In this weave, two or more warp yarns are twisted around each other as they are interlaced with the filling yarns; thus securing a firm hold on the filling yarn and preventing them from slipping out of position. Also called the gauze weave. Leno weave fabrics are frequently used for window treatments, because their structure gives good durability with almost no yarn slippage, and permits the passage of light and air.
Lining	Fabric made in the same shape as the outer fabric, a lining supports and protects the outer fabric and hides seams as well. Linings are found not only in apparel, but also in draperies and occasionally curtains and bedspreads. Items that are lined tend to wear better and last longer than unlined items and the appearance of a lined item is usually better than that of an unlined one.
Liquid Lamé	A slinky, slippery light weight metallic with the feel of silk. Liquid Lamé has a satiny sheen, and a slight stretch.
Loden	Loden is a water-resistant greasy wool used in heavy coatings.
M	
Madras	A lightweight plain weave cotton fabric with a striped, plaid, or checked pattern. A true madras will bleed when washed. This type of fabric is usually imported from India. End-uses are men's and women's shirts and dresses.
Marocain	A ribbed fabric with a wavy look, resembling Crêpe. It is made of silk, wool and manufactured fibers. Used mainly for suits and dresses.
Matelassé	A medium to heavyweight luxury fabric made in a double cloth construction to create a blistered or quilted surface. Common end-uses are upholstery, draperies, and evening dresses.
Matka	a heavy weight silk made from very thick yarns. The yarns are obtained from short ends of silk from Mulberry silkworms (Bombyx Mori) and spun by hand without removing the gum (sericin). As such, there are slubs and irregularities that give the fabric a unique character. It looks something like a tweed, but the fibers are all the same color. Matka is good for suits and jackets.
Matte Jersey	Tricot knit with a dull surface made with fine crepe yarn.
Melton	A thick to medium thick tightly woven wool with heavily brushed nap giving the fabric a smooth finish with no warp or weft yarns visible. Wool Melton is used mainly for jackets, coats and blankets.
Mesh	A type of fabric characterized by its net-like open appearance, and the spaces between the yarns. Mesh is available in a variety of constructions including wovens, knits, laces, or crocheted fabrics.
Metallic	An inorganic fiber made from minerals and metals, blended and extruded to form fibers. The fiber is formed from a flat ribbon of metal, coated with a protective layer of plastic, which reduces tarnishing. Metal used in apparel fabric is purely decorative.

Minky	Minky is an incredibly soft and plush "micro-fiber" fabric. Minky is a modern "micro-fiber" fabric that is amazingly soft. It rivals cashmere in softness and resembles real mink in touch. It is quick-drying, highly absorbent, and actually quite strong.
Moiré/Watermarked	A corded fabric, usually made from silk or one of the manufactured fibers, which has a distinctive water-marked wavy pattern on the face of the fabric.
Moleskin	Moleskin is a heavy, strong (usually cotton) fabric woven with coarse, carded yarns that give it a velvety nap. The feel of moleskin is smooth and solid, reminiscent of suede. The reverse has a satiny look and feel. Generally, it will contain 2-4% spandex. Moleskin is great for pants, jackets and heavy shirts.
Monk's Cloth	A heavy weight cotton fabric utilizing the basket weave variation of the plain weave. Used for draperies and slip covers, monk's cloth is an example of 4 x 4 basket weave. It has poor dimensional stability and tends to snag.
Moss Crepe	A vegetable fiber obtained from the inside of the woody stalk of the flax plant. It is one of the oldest fabrics known. It is strong, and today's man-made fibers are often blended with it to improve its wrinkle resistance and give the fabric other desirable qualities. Linen is woven in various weights for different purposes and is occasionally used in knit blends.
Mouseline	The name for a broad category of fabrics, usually fairly sheer and lightweight and made in a variety of fibers, including man-mades, silk, cotton, and wool. Mousseline usually has a crisp hand. The word mousseline is often used today for a fabric resembling de soie.
Mudcloth	Also known as Bògòlanfini or bogolan, it is a handmade, cotton textile that is traditionally dyed with fermented mud. It originates from Mali, West Africa.
Muslin	An inexpensive, medium weight, plain weave, low count (less than 160 threads per square inch) cotton sheeting fabric. In its unfinished form, it is commonly used in fashion design to make trial garments for preliminary fit.
N	
Napped	A fuzzy, fur-like feel created when fiber ends extend from the basic fabric structure to the fabric surface. The fabric can be napped on either one or both sides.
Netting	An open mesh fabric of rayon, nylon, cotton, or silk; made in a variety of geometric-shaped meshes of different sizes and weights, matched to various end-uses. The net is made by knotting the intersections of thread or cord to form the mesh.
Noil	A silk fabric that is sportier in appearance and created by short fibers, often from the innermost part of the cocoon. Has the look of hopsack but much softer. Silk Noil (sometimes incorrectly called raw silk) has a nubby feel and a low sheen. Noil somewhat resembles cotton in surface texture, and sews easily. The nubby texture of noil comes from the use of very short fibers that are used to weave the fabric. When these short fibers are spun into yarns, the resulting yarns have occasional slubs and loose ends. Nubs vary between different weaves. Noil which has not been completely de-gummed (had the natural sericin removed), may easily attract dirt and odors.
O	
Oil Cloth	Originally, textiles such as cotton were coated in oil to create resistance to moisture. Now, resins from plastics are used instead of oil. Olefin is a very versatile fiber with excellent flexibility. Used for waterproof garments, book bags, belts, bibs, pencil cases, luggage, surgical supplies.
Organdy	A stiffened, sheer, lightweight plain weave fabric, with a medium to high yarn count. End-uses include blouses, dresses, and curtains/draperies.
Organza	A crisp, sheer, lightweight plain weave fabric, with a medium to high yarn count, made of silk, rayon, nylon, or polyester. The fabric is used primarily in evening and wedding apparel for women.
Osnaburg	A tough medium to heavyweight coarsely woven plain weave fabric, usually made of a cotton or cotton/poly blend. Lower grades of the unfinished fabric are used for such industrial purposes as bags, sacks, pipe coverings. Higher grades of finished osnaburg can be found in mattress ticking, slipcovers, workwear, and apparel.
Ottoman	A tightly woven plain weave ribbed fabric with a hard slightly lustered surface. The ribbed effect is created by weaving a finer silk or manufactured warp yarn with a heavier filler yarn, usually made of cotton, wool, or waste yarn. In the construction, the heavier filler yarn is completely covered by the warp yarn, thus creating the ribbed effect. End uses for this fabric include coats, suits, dresses, upholstery, and draperies.

Oxford	A fine, soft, lightweight woven cotton or blended with manufactured fibers in a 2 x 1 basket weave variation of the plain weave construction. The fabric is used primarily in shirtings.
P	
Panné	A type of lustrous, lightweight velvet fabric, usually made of silk or a manufactured fiber, in which the pile has been flattened in one direction. Panné velvet has a longer or higher pile than regular velvet, but shorter than plush. It is pressed flat and has a high luster made possible by a tremendous roller-press treatment given the material in finishing. It is now often made as knit fabric.
Parachute	A compactly woven, lightweight fabric comparable with airplane cloth. It is made of silk, nylon, rayon, cotton, or polyester.
Peachskin	Peachskin is a smooth finish applied to finely woven Micro Fiber fabric. The soft, sueded finish results from sanding or chemical treatment of the fabric. This finish allows suits and dresses to flow with movement and drape beautifully. The feel of peachskin is soft, smooth and moderately wrinkle-resistant. It is a medium weight fabric that has a fuzzy, suede like feel.
Peau de Soie	A medium to heavy weight smooth and silky fabric with a satiny, lustrous finish. Looks like Charmeuse, but Peau de Soie has a moderately stiff drape. Those who cannot pronounce Peau de Soie (French for 'skin of silk') call this Duchess Satin. It can be made of silk or manufactured fibers, and used mainly for bridal gowns and eveningwear.
Percale	A medium weight, plain weave, low to medium count (180 to 250 threads per square inch) cotton-like fabric. End-uses include sheets, blouses, and dresses.
Performance	Fabrics made for a variety of end-use applications, which provide functional qualities, such as moisture management, UV protection, anti-microbial, thermo-regulation, and wind/water resistance.
Pile	A fabric in which certain yarns project from a foundation texture and form a pile on the surface. Pile yarns may be cut or uncut in the fabric. Corduroy and velveteen are examples of cut filling pile fabrics.
Pincord	A medium-weight fabric, either knit or woven, with raised dobby designs including cords, wales, waffles, or patterns. Woven versions have cords running lengthwise, or in the warp direction. Knitted versions are double-knit fabric constructions, created on multi-feed circular knitting machines.
Pleather	The term pleather ("plastic leather") is a slang term for synthetic leather made out of plastic. A portmanteau of plastic and leather, the term is sometimes used derogatorily, implying use as a substitute for genuine animal hide to cut costs. Besides cost, pleather may also be preferred because it is lighter than leather, or as an alternative to real leather citing reasons of animal cruelty. Pleather, being made of plastic, will not decompose as quickly. Not all pleathers are the same. Polyurethane is washable, can be dry-cleaned and allows some air to flow through the garment. PVC pleather in contrast does not "breathe" and is difficult to clean. PVC cannot be dry-cleaned because the cleaning solvents can make the PVC unbearably stiff.
Plissé	A lightweight, plain weave, fabric, made from cotton, rayon, or acetate, and characterized by a puckered striped effect, usually in the warp direction. The crinkled effect is created through the application of a caustic soda solution, which shrinks the fabric in the areas of the fabric where it is applied. Plissé is similar in appearance to seersucker. End-uses include dresses, shirtings, pajamas, and bedspreads.
Plush	A compactly woven fabric with warp pile higher than that of velvet. Plush (from French peluche) is a textile having a cut nap or pile the same as fustian or velvet. Originally the pile of plush consisted of mohair or worsted yarn, but now silk by itself or with a cotton backing is used for plush. Modern plush is commonly manufactured from synthetic fibres such as polyester. Brushed or sheared fabrics are also sometimes referred to as plush. One of the largest uses of this fabric is in the production of toys, with small stuffed animals made from plush fabric, such as teddy bears, known as plushies. The French term for "teddy bear" is ours en peluche. Plush is also one of the main materials for the construction of designer toys.
Point d'Esprit	Mainly cotton, sometimes silk, a leno, gauze, knotted, or mesh woven fabric. Point d'Esprit was first made in France in 1834. as a dull surfaced net with various sized holes. Has white or colored dots individually spaced or in groups. Used for curtains, bassinets, evening gowns.
Pointelle	A Very feminine, delicate-looking, rib-knit fabric made with a pattern of openings. Pointelle is a drop needle knit fabric. It is a textured fabric with holes forming a design in the fabric.
Pongee	The most common form is a naturally colored lightweight, plain weave, silk-like fabric with a slubbed effect. End-uses include blouses, dresses, etc.
Ponte di Roma	A fabric made in a double knit construction, usually produced in one color rather than color patterns. This plain fabric has an elastic quality with a slight horizontal line. The fabric looks the same on both sides.

Poplin	A fabric made using a rib variation of the plain weave. The construction is characterized by having a slight ridge effect in one direction, usually the filling. Poplin used to be associated with casual clothing, but as the "world of work" has become more relaxed, this fabric has developed into a staple of men's wardrobes, being used frequently in casual trousers.
Pucker	The uneven surface caused by differential shrinkage in the two layers of a bonded fabric during processing, dry cleaning, or washing.
Q	
Quilted	A fabric construction in which a layer of down or fiberfill is placed between two layers of fabric, and then held in place by stitching or sealing in a regular, consistent, all-over pattern on the goods.
R	
Raschel	A warp knitted fabric in which the resulting knit fabric resembles hand crocheted fabrics, lace fabrics, and nettings. Raschel warp knits contain inlaid connecting yarns in addition to columns of knit stitches.
Reversible	A fabric that can be used on either side. Generally, the term reversible is applied to two quite different fabrics joined together by such methods as laminating or double cloth construction. Reversible fabrics frequently are used for coats, less frequently for other garments.
Rib Knit	A basic stitch used in weft knitting in which the knitting machines require two sets of needles operating at right angles to each other. Rib knits have a very high degree of elasticity in the crosswise direction. A 1 x 1 rib has one rib up and one down. A 2 x 1 rib has two ribs up and one down. This knitted fabric is used for complete garments and for such specialized uses as sleeve bands, neck bands, sweater waistbands, and special types of trims for use with other knit or woven fabrics. Lightweight sweaters in rib knits provide a close, body-hugging fit.
Ripstop	A lightweight, wind resistant, and water resistant plain weave fabric. Large rib yarns stop tears without adding excess weight to active sportswear apparel and outdoor equipment such as sleeping bags and tents.
S	
Sailcloth	Any heavy, plain-weave canvas fabric, usually made of cotton, linen, polyester, jute, nylon, etc. that is used for sails and apparel (i.e. bottomweight sportswear).
Sateen	A fabric made from yarns with low luster, such as cotton or other staple length fibers. A variation of the satin weave, produced by floating fill yarns over warp yarns. The fabric has a soft, smooth hand and a gentle, subtle luster.
Satin	A basic weave, characterized by long floats of yarn on the face of the fabric. The yarns are interlaced in such a manner that there is no definite, visible pattern of interlacing and, in this manner, a smooth and somewhat shiny surface effect is achieved. The shiny surface effect is further increased through the use of high luster filament fibers in yarns which also have a low amount of twist. A true satin weave fabric always has the warp yarns floating over filling yarns. Typical examples of satin weave fabrics include: slipper satin, crepe-back satin, faille satin, bridal satin, moleskin, and antique satin.
Saxony	Originally a high grade coating fabric made from Saxony merino wool raised in Germany.
Seersucker	A woven fabric which incorporates modification of tension control. In the production of seersucker, some of the warp yarns are held under controlled tension at all times during the weaving, while other warp yarns are in a relaxed state and tend to pucker when the filling yarns are placed. The result produces a puckered stripe effect in the fabric. Seersucker is traditionally made into summer sportswear such as shirts, trousers, and informal suits.
Sequinned	Fabric covered with sequins is available by the yard. Sequins are a shiny, usually metallic, decoration or spangle. Sequins are sewn to clothing, especially evening dresses because they shimmer and sparkle in the light. Sequins usually have a single, central hole for fastening to the garment or fabric. Sequins are also known as paillettes.
Serge	A very distinct twill (2 up/2 down) which shows on both sides of the fabric. On the face, the distinct diagonal runs from the lower left to the upper right – piece dyed. Has a smooth, hard finish that wears exceptionally well but will shine with use. The shine cannot be removed permanently. It is a good cloth in tailoring as it drapes and clings very well. Made in various weights. unfinished worsted and wool are not quite as clear on the surface. Used mainly for coats, suits and sportswear.

Shantung	A medium-weight, plain weave fabric, characterized by a ribbed effect, resulting from slubbed yarns used in the warp or filling direction. End-uses include dresses and suits.
Sharkskin	A hard-finished, low lustered, medium-weight fabric in a twill-weave construction. It is most commonly found in men's worsted suitings; however, it can also be found in a plain-weave construction of acetate, triacetate, and rayon for women's sportswear.
Sheer	The opposite of opaque. Sheer fabrics are usually made in an open weave to create fabrics with varying degrees of transparency. Batiste, organdy, and voile are examples of sheer fabrics.
Sheeting	Sheeting is a plain woven cotton cloth made from carded yarns that can be found in medium and heavy weights. Low thread count sheeting is called muslin, while high thread count sheeting with combed yarns is known as percale.
Sherpa	A heavy fabric with clumped pile resembling the fleece of a sheep. The name comes from the group of people who live near or on the Himalayan mountains. Used for outerwear trim and lining.
Shetland	Wool from Shetland sheep in Scotland. These sheep have a coarse outer coat and a very fine undercoat which gives added warmth. The best is the undergrowth. It is not shorn but pulled out by hand in the spring. Other wools sometimes called Shetland if they have a similar appearance. Shetland wools have a very soft hand and a shaggy finish of protruding fibers. It is very lightweight and warm. Much is made by hand and comes in distinctive soft coloring. Often the natural colors ranging from off-white, various grays to almost black and brown are used and not dyed. Real Shetland wools are expensive, high quality products. – In the same family group as homespun, tweed and cheviot. Used in coats, suits, and sportswear for both men and women. Fine Shetlands are made into fine shawls, underwear crochet, work and hosiery.
Shimmer	A lightweight fabric made of two different colored yarns. The fabric has an iridescent look and a crisp but not stiff hand. Shimmer is typically made of a rayon/polyester blend. Shimmer can also be made with a crushed finish which adds texture and brings out the shine in the fabric. Shimmer is most commonly used for apparel but can also be used to create sophisticated window treatments and pillows.
Slinky	A knit fabric. It drapes well, never wrinkles and washes beautifully. It's the perfect travel fabric with four-way stretch for ultimate comfort. Suitable for almost any wardrobe item.
Slipper Satin	Slipper satin is a tightly woven satin fabric, usually lighter in weight than duchesse satin, and used for many purposes including evening shoes or slippers.
Sparkle Organza	An organza woven fabric that uses a yarn, usually nylon with a high reflectance of light that gives the fabric a sparkled look.
Stretch	Rubber or man-made plastic fibers (such as spandex and anidex) that are naturally elastic or man-made fibers, highly twisted, heat-set, and untwisted to leave a strong crimp. Polyester has a certain degree of natural stretch and more can be given to the yarn in the processing or in the finishing of the fabric. Occasionally, polyester woven fabrics are described as stretch fabrics. Usually, stretch implies a degree of visible give in a fiber or fabric that stretches and then returns quickly to its original shape. Stretch fabrics are sometimes described as elastic.
Suede Cloth	A woven or knitted fabric of cotton, man-made fibers, wool, or blends, finished to resemble suede leather. It is used in sport coats, gloves, linings, and cleaning cloths.
Sueded	Sueded fabrics are brushed, sanded or chemically treated for extra softness. 'Suede' yarns are generally thick and plush.
Supplex®	Supplex® is a state-of-the-art nylon fabric. It was specially engineered by DuPont to provide the soft, supple touch of cotton with the strength, durability and performance advantages of nylon. It has high water and wind resistant properties, high abrasion and is tear resistant. Supplex® manages moisture and keeps its vibrant color, wash after wash. Clothes made of Supplex® will never fuzz or pill.
Surah	A light weight, lustrous twill weave constructed fabric with a silk-like hand. Surah is the fabric of ties, dresses, and furnishings. It is available in silk, polyester, and rayon.
T	
Taffeta	A lustrous, medium weight, plain weave fabric with a slight ribbed appearance in the filling (crosswise) direction. For formal wear, taffeta is a favorite choice. It provides a crisp hand, with lots of body. Silk taffeta gives the ultimate rustle, but other fibers are also good choices.
Tapestry	A heavy, often hand-woven, ribbed fabric, featuring an elaborate design depicting a historical or current pictorial display. The weft-faced fabric design is made by using colored filling yarns, only in areas where needed, that are worked back and forth over spun warp yarns, which are visible on the back. End-uses include wall hangings and upholstery.

Tartan	A pattern made of intersecting stripes. Each tartan pattern is associated with a certain specific family called a clan. Plaid, a term used for tartan, is actually the name of a shawl made of tartan fabric. The use of plaid has become so general that tartan is almost always limited to authentic clan designs. Some of the most common tartans follow, but there are many others.
Terry Cloth	A typical uncut pile weave fabric. This fabric is formed by using two sets of warp yarns. One set of warp yarns is under very little tension; when the filling yarns are packed into place, these loose yarns are pushed backward along with the filling yarns, and loops are formed. Typical uses include towels, robes, and apparel.
Terry Velour	A pile weave cotton fabric with an uncut pile on one side and a cut pile on the reverse side. Terry velour is valued for its soft, luxurious hand. Typical uses include towels, robes, and apparel.
Thermal	An adjective used to describe fabrics which are warmer for their weight than other fabrics. Thermal is usually limited to those fabrics woven in a honeycomb pattern leaving small spaces in which air can be trapped. Thermal fabrics are popular for underwear and blankets.
Thinsulate™	Thinsulate™ is a trademark of the 3M Corporation, for a type of synthetic fiber thermal insulation used in clothing. Thinsulate™ fibers are about 15 micrometres in diameter, which is thinner than the polyester fibers normally used in insulation for clothing such as gloves or winter jackets. The manufacturer claims that, for a given thickness of material, Thinsulate™ provides 1 to 1.5 times the insulation of duck down, while being much less water-absorbent and much more resistant to crushing. Thinsulate™ insulation works by trapping air molecules between you and the outside. The more air a material traps in a given space, the greater its insulating value. Because the microfibers in Thinsulate™ insulation are far finer than other fibers, they trap more air in less space, which naturally makes it a better insulator. Thinsulate™ is breathable, moisture resistant and machine washable.
Ticking	A broad term for extremely strong woven fabrics which are used as a covering for pillows, mattresses, and box springs, home-furnishings, and for work clothes and sports clothes. Ticking is a heavy, tightly woven carded cotton fabric usually in a pattern of alternately woven stripes in the warp, Jacquard or dobby designs, or printed patterns. It is usually twill but may be sateen weave. When ticking is used in clothing, striped ticking with narrow woven stripes is usually most popular. Red and white, black and white, and navy and white are the most popular ticking color combinations.
Tie-Dye	A form of resist dyeing. Items to be dyed are tied or knotted so that the folds of the fabric form barriers to the dye to create patterns or designs on the fabric.
Tissue Faille	Made from 100% micro fiber polyester, Tissue Faille (pronounced "file") is a lightweight fabric with a light faille weave, silky feel and a slight sheen. It has an excellent draping quality. Though lightweight, it is an extremely strong fabric.
Tissue Lamé	See Lamé
Tricot	A warp knit fabric in which the fabric is formed by interlooping adjacent parallel yarns. The warp beam holds thousands of yards of yarns in a parallel arrangement, and these yarns are fed into the knitting area simultaneously. Sufficient yarns to produce the final fabric width and length are on the beam. Tricot knits are frequently used in women's lingerie items such as slips, bras, panties, and nightgowns.
Tricotine	Tricotine weave has a double twill rib on the face of the cloth. Has a very clear finish. It drapes well, and tailors easily. Tricotine is medium in weight and usually made of wool and wool/rayon blends. Tricotine has exceptional wearing qualities. Very much like cavalry twill, but finer. In the same family as whipcords, coverts, and gabardines. Used mainly for Men's and women's suits and coats. It is also used for ski slacks in a stretch fabric
Trigger®	A durable heavy poplin made of blend of polyester and cotton. It is also considered a utility cloth and used for table cloths, chair covers, uniforms, and flags/banners.
Tulle	A lightweight, extremely fine, machine-made netting, usually with a hexagon shaped mesh effect. End-uses include dance costumes and veils.
Tussah	Silk fabric woven from silk made by wild, uncultivated silkworms. Tussah is naturally tan in color, cannot be bleached, and has a rougher texture than cultivated silk. Wild silkworms eat leaves other than mulberry leaves which cultivated silkworms eat exclusively. The difference in diet accounts for the different fiber and fabric characteristics. Tussah is also used to describe fabrics designed to imitate this kind of silk.
Tweed	A medium to heavy weight, fluffy, woolen, twill weave fabric containing colored slubbed yarns. Common end-uses include coats and suits.

FABRIC GLOSSARY

Twill	A basic weave in which the fabrics are constructed by interlacing warp and filling yarns in a progressive alternation which creates a diagonal effect on the face, or right side, of the fabric. In some twill weave fabrics, the diagonal effect may also be seen clearly on the back side of the fabric.
U	
Union Cloth	A traditional name for fabric made from two or more different fibers, such as a fabric woven with a wool worsted warp and a cotton filling. The term "union cloth" was used primarily when this fabric was used for underwear, perhaps because a union suit was another name for shoulder-to-ankle, one-piece underwear.
Ultrasuede®	Ultrasuede® is world's first ultra-microfiber. Ultrasuede® feels like natural suede, but it is resistant to stains and discoloration; it can be machine-washed; and because it is a non-woven fabric, it cannot pull or fray. Ultrasuede® also ages better than real suede, is stain resistant and is animal friendly. The fabric is multifunctional: it is used in fashion, interior decorating, automotive and other vehicle upholstery, and industrial applications, such as protective fabric for electronic equipment.
V	
Velour	A medium weight, closely woven fabric with a thick pile. It can be made using either a plain weave or a satin weave construction. It resembles velvet, but has a lower cut pile. End uses include apparel, upholstery, and drapes.
Velvet	A medium weight cut-pile constructed fabric in which the cut pile stands up very straight. It is woven using two sets of warp yarns; the extra set creates the pile. It is woven on a special loom that weaves two piece of velvet at the same time. The two pieces are then cut apart and the two lengths of fabric are wound on separate take-up rolls. Velvet, a luxurious fabric, is commonly made with a filament fiber for high luster and smooth hand. Velvet is a type of tufted fabric in which the cut threads are very evenly distributed, with a short dense pile, giving it its distinct feel. Velvet can be made from any fiber.
Velveteen	A cotton cut-pile weave fabric, utilizing extra fill yarn construction, with either a twill or a plain weave back. The fabric is woven with two sets of filling yarns; the extra set creates the pile.
Voile	A crisp, lightweight, plain weave cotton-like fabric, made with high twist yarns in a high yarn count construction. Similar in appearance to organdy and organza. Used in blouses dresses and curtains.
W	
Waffle	A fabric with a characteristic honeycomb weave. When made in cotton it is called waffle pique. It is used for coatings, draperies, dresses, and toweling.
Washed	Refers to fabrics that have been laundered before shipping. This may be done to reduce shrinkage, soften the hand, wash down the color or to give the fabric a used, laundered look.
Whipcord	A woven fabric with a very steep and compacted twill appearance on the face of the goods. End-uses for the fabric include dress woolens, worsteds, or wool blends, and many types of uniforms.
Worsted	A tightly woven fabric made by using only long staple, combed wool or wool-blend yarns. The fabric has a hard, smooth surface. Gabardine is an example of a worsted fabric. A common end use is men's tailored suits.
Worsterlon®	Worsterlon is a polyester flannel fabric that is washable and wrinkle free. It has the look and feel of wool without the maintenance and care. It is ideal for anyone allergic to wool. Proven in climates around the world, this fabric is worn by outdoor enthusiasts and travelers who demand durable clothing.

Notes

Notes

Notes

Notes

Notes

Notes

Made in the USA
Monee, IL
27 November 2021